CHRISTIAN WITNESS
IN CASCADIAN SOIL

CHRISTIAN WITNESS IN CASCADIAN SOIL

*Coworkers with God in the Land of Hiking,
Hipsters, and Hand-Crafted Lattes*

EDITED BY
Ross A. Lockhart

FOREWORD BY
Jason Byassee

CASCADE *Books* • Eugene, Oregon

CHRISTIAN WITNESS IN CASCADIAN SOIL
Coworkers with God in the Land of Hiking, Hipsters, and Hand-Crafted Lattes

Copyright © 2021 Wipf and Stock Publishers. All rights reserved. Except for brief quotations in critical publications or reviews, no part of this book may be reproduced in any manner without prior written permission from the publisher. Write: Permissions, Wipf and Stock Publishers, 199 W. 8th Ave., Suite 3, Eugene, OR 97401.

Cascade Books
An Imprint of Wipf and Stock Publishers
199 W. 8th Ave., Suite 3
Eugene, OR 97401

www.wipfandstock.com

PAPERBACK ISBN: 978-1-7252-6025-2
HARDCOVER ISBN: 978-1-7252-6024-5
EBOOK ISBN: 978-1-7252-6026-9

Cataloguing-in-Publication data:

Names: Lockhart, Ross A., editor. | Byassee, Jason, foreword.

Title: Christian witness in Cascadian soil : coworkers with God in the land of hiking, hipsters, and hand-crafted lattes / edited by Ross A. Lockhart ; foreword by Jason Byassee.

Description: Eugene, OR : Cascade Books, 2021 | Includes bibliographical references.

Identifiers: ISBN 978-1-7252-6025-2 (paperback) | ISBN 978-1-7252-6024-5 (hardcover) | ISBN 978-1-7252-6026-9 (ebook)

Subjects: LCSH: Missions—North America. | Christian leadership. | Twenty-first century. | Mission of the church—United States. | Christian leadership—United States. | Mission of the church—Canada. | Christian leadership—Canada. | Christianity—21st century.

Classification: BV2070 .C54 2021 (print) | BV2070 .C54 (ebook)

Manufactured in the U.S.A.   FEBRUARY 15, 2021

Scripture quotations marked NRSV are taken from the Holy Bible, New Revised Standard Version Bible, copyright 1989, Division of Christian Education of the National Council of the Churches of Christ in the United States of America. Used by permission. All rights reserved.

Scripture quotations marked (NIV) are taken from the Holy Bible, New International Version®, NIV®. Copyright © 1973, 1978, 1984, 2011 by Biblica, Inc.™ Used by permission of Zondervan. All rights reserved worldwide. www.zondervan.com The "NIV" and "New International Version" are trademarks registered in the United States Patent and Trademark Office by Biblica, Inc.™

Scripture quotations marked THE MESSAGE. Copyright © by Eugene H. Peterson 1993, 1994, 1995, 1996, 2000, 2001, 2002. Used by permission of Tyndale House Publishers, Inc.

For Stephen Farris,
Dean Emeritus of St. Andrew's Hall,
whose vision, grace, and good humor
helped created the conditions for
the Centre for Missional Leadership's
founding and early flourishing.

Contents

Foreword ix
JASON BYASSEE

Preface: Snow-Covered Palm Trees and Nurse Logs of Hope xiii

Acknowledgments xvii

Introduction: Hipster Haircuts and Neighborhood Exegesis:
The Delightful and Curious Aspects of Christian Witness in Cascadia xix

Tilling the Field
1. Seeking the Kingdom of God as a Church in a Secular Age 3
TIM DICKAU

2. Storytelling Praxis: Indigenous–Settler Relationships in Cascadia 13
DAVID WARKENTIN

3. Faith after Atheism: Christian Theology and Spiritual Formation
in a Landscape of Default Agnosticism 29
TODD WIEBE

Planting the Seeds
4. Exploring the Theological "Why" of Church Planting 41
DARRELL GUDER

5. A Sent Life Together:
A Reflection on Missional Community in the Lonely and Secularized
Area of Vancouver's Downtown Eastside 50

CONTENTS

STEPHEN BELL

6. Can Rocky Soil Be Tilled?
Growing a Church-Planting Ecosystem in Cascadia 62
ANDREA PERRETT

7. Arts Ministry Beyond the Sunday Worship Service:
How Can an Arts Ministry Be Missional in a Public Arena? 73
YOUNG TAE CHOI

Nurturing the Growth

8. Transformative Gardens within Cascadian Soil:
The Place and Shape of Friendship within New Faith Communities 89
ANNE-MARIE ELLITHORPE

9. Soldiers to Midwives:
Bearing Witness to the Triune God in Our Everyday Conversations 103
JENN RICHARDS

10. New Witnessing Communities in an Age of Decline 114
ANDREW STEPHENS-RENNIE

11. Ikea Christians in the School of Jesus:
Catechesis in Post-Christendom 128
ROSS LOCKHART

Awaiting the Harvest

12. Dying and Rising for Mission 145
RICHARD TOPPING

13. The Church God Is Planting in Cascadian Soil 158
CHRISTOPHER JAMES

14. Beloved Community as Missional Witness 169
JONATHAN WILSON

List of Contributors 181

Foreword

WHAT A JOY THIS set of essays is. A feast, a bonanza, a reason to say amen, hallelujah. You've heard and read and probably recited the dismal statistics. Church attendance is down to this. Money is down to that. We won't have denomination x in year 20-something. Sometimes these statistics are passed on with gloating, as though cheerleading the demise of a ghastly institution. Sometimes they are reported with sorrow, for the eclipse of a day that, for all its flaws, also had its glories. The response to these stats is itself a sort of liturgy: newspaper report, hand wringing, business as usual Sundays (just with fewer people and lighter plates). It's a dismal promenade.

Sometimes this liturgy of demise is interrupted. This set of essays is one such interruption. It originates from the northwest corner of North America, that mythical region of Cascadia (Oregon, Washington, and British Columbia), where the pot is penalty-free, the weather is broody and tempestuous, the tech is futuristic, the people are indifferent to one another, and no one's in church because they're all outside on Sundays (just ask the local political party, veterans' organization, bowling league, or parent-teacher council how they're doing with money and members—you'll find the same stats we got). Christendom has long since come and gone in the Pacific Northwest and British Columbia, if it was ever there to begin with (and there are good scholarly arguments that it never was). Other parts of North America were settled by Europeans for religious reasons: New England's Puritans, Maryland's Catholics, the Upper Midwest's Lutherans, California's Southern Baptists pushing west. Canada had some of each of these too. By the time Europeans pushed out as far as the northwest corner of the continent, whatever religious steam sent them across the Atlantic had dissipated. Folks were just less religious in general in the late 1800s than in the early 1600s. The first Europeans out this way came for extractive economies: timber and gold and fish—stuff to take away and sell elsewhere.

Foreword

We are still ruled by extractive economies, now tech and film and tyrannical real estate. The answer to the meaning of life, big-ticket questions out here have never been "Jesus," or "my church." It's been "my bank account," which one's neighbor had no right to inquire about.

Meanwhile, aboriginal folks in North America were funneled up this way by advancing Europeans. As it turns out, many longstanding ways of living among indigenous peoples are exactly those to which the rest of us should return in an age of eco-catastrophe. A way of life that respects creation and the Creator. A way of eating that respects the ground, the fish, the animals, and leaves God's teaming abundance for future generations. A sensitivity to the spiritual dimension of all of life, no separate "sphere" of the religious cordoned off from that which is not (it took Europeans to cook up something that destructive). There are also more recent arrivals still to these parts. Asian immigration is the present-day story. This is a different set of patterns than First Nations peoples, than European later arrivers. Often these newer Cascadians are quite a bit more Christian than the Europeans who've been here a while. There is a painful history of Asian–European interaction during the Second World War, of course; though most Asian-Americans and Canadians are not descended from Japanese internees, those scars are both deep and pan-Asian. Cascadians regard themselves as welcoming, but ask a Malaysian or Indian or Cantonese friend whether they find the culture so warm. Yet these folks are often interested in, or even worshipers of, Jesus (some statistics suggest they are more so once here than they were back in Asia). And often, wonder of wonders, indigenous peoples are the most interested in Jesus, despite the genocidal violence wreaked in his name by Europeans. Could it be that white Cascadians' irreligiosity is the exception, rather than the norm, in Cascadia?

That's Cascadia. And right here, in this most unpromising plot of ground, new ecclesial experiments are sprouting up. Do you not perceive them? They involve such delights as midwifery, as gardening, as friendship, as an old-and-new blend of monasticism, as witnessing to the resurrection of Jesus. These do not look like Christendom, with its imposing towers, built to shut the world out. They do not look like the great protests of the sixties, raining down opprobrium on precisely those same towers (until they inherit the keys to said towers, and become just as oppressive as the previous occupants). They certainly don't look like the gleaming glass and steel of Hong Kong–inspired high-rises—so secular they're almost religious again, as imposing as any gothic façade. No, these are small experiments in

Foreword

missional faithfulness. They involve a way of life our neighbors desperately need. One that suggests we are not reducible to our bank accounts. One that knows neighbors by name, and their kids by name, and their grilling preferences, and their dogs' names. One that treats them not like marks or projects or problems to be solved, but as human beings, with individual faces and stories and delights, mysteries rather than puzzles. One that worships Jesus while he brings a new city right here in the midst of the one we've ruined. If there is anything promising about the future of the church it is right here, writ small, in what would seem prima facie the most unpromising of places.

Jesus, preaching to a place not more promising than where we are now, said, simply, "The kingdom of God is here." All of his teaching and healing and exorcising and rejoicing and suffering are right here in our midst. His resurrection too. Want evidence? Look right here. Happy reading.

Jason Byassee
Vancouver School of Theology

Preface

Snow-Covered Palm Trees and Nurse Logs of Hope

It only snows a couple of times a year in Vancouver. Those of us who grew up "back East," as I did on the Canadian Prairies, moved to the West Coast to escape the cold and snow that is so much a part of life in the northern United States and the rest of Canada. In fact, one of the first things I did when we moved here was visit a local nursery and purchase a wee palm tree for our tiny back garden. Like planting a flag on the moon, it was my little horticultural statement of arrival in a new and strange land. A place where tropical plants thrive year-round, green grass grows cheerfully in January, and the first buds of spring are instantly uploaded to social media to "encourage" snow-bound relations back East. Now, don't get me wrong, we love the snow in Vancouver—as long as it stays up high in our beautiful North Shore mountains for skiing and leaves us alone down on the golf course by the Pacific Ocean.

Recently, however, we had one of those rare snow days where the schools were closed, and I looked out the back window as my beautiful palm tree was bent over like the hurting woman in Luke's Gospel,[1] begging for someone to shake the heavy snow off its tropical, leafy green branches. I live in North Vancouver halfway between the famous Capilano Suspension Bridge and the gondola to Grouse Mountain. Nearby, across from the Cleveland Dam, is a massive hill that turns into the perfect toboggan run on those rare snow days. I took my daughter up there to spend the afternoon sledding, laughing, and rolling in the snow.

There were many of us standing around on the hilltop: parents and grandparents pushing kids on sleds and delighting in their joy. I struck up

1. Luke 13:11.

a conversation with a dad beside me. He remarked on how lovely it was for the kids to have a day off school. I agreed and mentioned how nice it was to see the kids having a great time in the snow, the way I remembered growing up in Manitoba during long, cold winters. He mentioned that he was born and raised on the North Shore of Vancouver and never really experienced a full Canadian winter, unlike so many that have moved to the West Coast. Other pleasantries were exchanged as every few minutes our children would hustle back up the hill and ask us to hold their sled again as they prepared for another run. At one point the other dad said to me, "Hey, so what school does your daughter go to?" An innocent question. "Lions Gate Christian Academy," I replied not thinking much about it. The other man's body language changed, however, becoming frostier than the snow falling around us. "Oh," he said, taking a step back and looking puzzled. "So . . ." he stuttered, "you're a Christian?" The way he asked it made Christianity sound like a communicable disease. "Um, yeah, I'm a Christian," I replied with tempered zeal (like a good Presbyterian). He stood there quietly for a moment and continued, "I don't know any Christians. So, what *do* you guys really believe about climate change, anyways?" Lord, have mercy. I thought, here I am taking my daughter to the tobogganing hill and now I'm involved in some off the cuff apologetics.

"Well," I replied cautiously, "as Christians we believe God created everything in the universe, including the Earth, and that we are called to be good stewards of creation. As followers of Jesus, we believe in partnering with God in repairing the world and are happy to work with anyone, whether they believe in Jesus or not, to help take care of the planet." Not exactly sparkling evangelism, but it gave me time to continue the conversation and listen as he offered in return the various stereotypes about Christianity and the environment. You've probably heard it before, you know the usual conservative Christian media trope of "screw the planet since Jesus is going to return and rescue us from this place" routine.

My friend and colleague Jason Byassee rightly describes the Pacific Northwest as "rocky soil" for Christian witness, but in that moment with snowflakes swirling around, it felt more like hard, frozen land for sowing the gospel. By the end of the day, however, I knew more about my affable agnostic neighbor who grew up in this place without knowing any Christians by name. The neighbor shared with me stories from his work life as a paramedic, and the soul-crushing feeling of responding to endless overdoses in the city's on-going opioid crisis that left him feeling like life itself

Preface

was cheap and meaningless. A small window opened for us to find some overlapping consensus on the need for identity, purpose, and meaning in human life, even if we were coming at it from different directions. Like a Vancouver snow that only lasts a while before dissolving in the next day's rain, I felt like we were finding a common middle ground of engaged and compassionate humanity, as stereotypes began to melt away.

By the time my daughter and I packed up and headed home for hot chocolate, I reflected on what has become a normal Cascadian experience for me as a follower of Jesus. It's common to meet neighbors here with little to no working knowledge of Christianity, let alone experience of knowing Christians in the flesh. Here in the Pacific Northwest, you find a fascinating ecclesiastical and missional petri dish for those wanting to figure out what Christian witness will look like across a more secularized North America in the years to come. Whether rocky or frozen, the ground can at first look discouraging for Christian witness and the sowing of the good news in this corner of creation.

A week after the big snowstorm and life was back to normal in Vancouver. Snowbanks had yielded to green grass standing tall and snowflakes were replaced with the usual raindrops that bring us such comfort on the West Coast. I set off for a run in my neighborhood, and in the shadow of Grouse Mountain, I crossed the Cleveland Dam steps away from where we had tobogganed a few days earlier and disappeared into the rainforest known as Capilano Regional Park. I paused for a moment taking in the sight, sound, and scent of the massive Douglas fir and cedar trees around me, many of them hundreds of years old. I observed that two or three of these trees had fallen on their sides, due to old age or a windstorm, their enormous trunks rising above the ferns and other foliage on the ground. Despite their death, there were signs of new life, young trees growing up and out of the decaying tree trunks in a phenomenon called "nurse logs." On second thought, perhaps instead of saying "despite their death," I should say "because of their death" there was new life in something botanists call ecological facilitation. As the tree decomposes it becomes fertile space for seeds to take root amidst the soil, with moss and mushrooms springing up. Over a long period of time a new tree grows where the old one once "lay down its life." Of course, as you are about to read, our Pacific Northwest rainforests are not the only places where we witness life after death springing forth. The nurse logs of Western European Christendom, planted centuries ago in North America and now declining and decomposing, are

Preface

providing fertile soil for new forms of Christian witness in Cascadian soil. The resurrection faith of Christians in post-Christendom Cascadia is as fresh as mountain air, surprising as a nurse log sapling shooting forth, and as determined as a palm tree bent over with snow. Read on and see for yourself!

Acknowledgments

I AM GRATEFUL FOR all those who have helped in the development and flourishing of the Centre for Missional Leadership (CML) at St. Andrew's Hall over this past decade. I remember fondly participating in the early conversations developing this new vision for our college in my role as an adjunct professor and local congregational pastor. At that time, the board of management asked what the unique contribution of St. Andrew's Hall might be to the theological neighborhood at The University of British Columbia and across the wider Presbyterian Church in Canada. The board discerned, after consulting with leaders in church and academy across North America, that a focus on missional theology in our post-Christendom Cascadian[1] context was the next, most faithful step. With generous support from my fellow St. Andrew's Hall professors Stephen Farris and Richard Topping (who also serves as principal of the Vancouver School of Theology), I began work laying the foundations for what became the Centre for Missional Leadership. With the additional appointment of Darrell Guder as senior fellow in residence, upon his retirement from Princeton Theological Seminary, our work began in earnest.

I am grateful to all the congregational pastors, elders, and lay people who have participated in CML conferences, workshops, church-planting experiments, and congregational-equipping events offered from coast to coast across the country these past many years. The board's vision of embracing missional theology for the sake of a flourishing church in post-Christendom Canada has come to life in profound, humbling, and beautiful ways. Together, we are catching glimpses of shalom breaking forth as people understand and embrace their election as Christ's own to mean they are "saved to be sent" by the one who declared, "Peace be with you! As

---

1. A region consisting of Oregon, Washington State, and British Columbia, which have shared geographic, social, and cultural values in common.

Acknowledgments

the Father has sent me, I am sending you."[2] We have witnessed a renewed sense of Christian communities being equipped for mission and living fully into their mandate as the sent people of God, with an awareness of Father, Son, and Holy Spirit at work in their midst. Or as John's Gospel puts it, "The Word became flesh and blood, and moved into the neighborhood."[3] For all of these glimpses of glory, including those recorded in this pages ahead, I am grateful.

Of course, there are so many people involved in bringing a writing project like this to fruition. Working once again with the good people at Cascade Books has been a delight and pleasure. Thank you especially to Charlie Collier for his kind editorial work on this project and ensuring a smooth process from concept to final product. I am also grateful for my faculty colleagues (including Jason Byassee for his kind foreword) and the many friends in church and academy represented in this collection of essays. My last word of gratitude is reserved for my family. First, to my wife, Laura, whose enduring love and grace-filled kindness enables me to do all that I can in ministry. Secondly, to our children Emily, Jack, and Sadie who fill my life with laughter and teach me daily about discipleship (while often testing the limits of my sanctification), all the while keeping me well-grounded and humble! I am truly grateful for the blessing of family, friends, and colleagues in this good work of the gospel.

Ross A. Lockhart
St. Andrew's Hall, Vancouver

---

2. John 20: 21 (NIV).
3. John 1:14 (MSG).

Introduction

Hipster Haircuts and Neighborhood Exegesis: The Delightful and Curious Aspects of Christian Witness in Cascadia

For we are co-workers in God's service; you are God's field, God's building.

—1 CORINTHIANS 3:9

THE BELL ON THE door jingled softly as I walked into a local hipster barber shop and glanced around for a vacant seat. The employees and clientele all looked the same in the small, dimly lit room below street level, vibrating with indie folk music. The dress code was clear: skinny jeans, flannel shirts, and ironic facial hair. I felt immediately out of place. "Hey man," the one barber said, greeting me warmly, "welcome, we're so glad you're here. Take a seat. It won't be long, and we'll get you out of here feeling *and* looking better than ever. Let me grab you a craft beer while you wait." Instantly, I liked this place better than church. Even the best hospitality team doesn't sound like that on a Sunday morning! Sure enough, after a couple of minutes of sitting in the corner with my red solo cup, a young barber with a thick, long, pointy beard and waxed moustache offered me a seat in his barber's chair. With a snap of the barber cloth, and a quick sizing up of my head, he asked what kind of haircut I was looking for, and the usual process began. After a few minutes of small talk about the weather and the Vancouver Canucks hockey team, the inevitable question appeared. "So, what do you do?" asked the barber as he whirled around my head with sharp objects. I gave my usual answer that tends to confound people in Cascadia: "I'm

Introduction

a pastor," I replied. "Oh cool," said the barber, "so am I!" Well, I hadn't expected that response. I'm more used to people saying, "Oh, is that like a religious thing?" or "Um, I don't know what that means," or my personal favorite, "Is that a job in sales?" to which I replied, "Well, sort of." But a hipster pastor barber, that was new to me.

What followed was the most delightful half-an-hour conversation where I heard all about this barber's plans to plant a church in the neighborhood. He and his wife had moved nearby from a suburb of Vancouver and were starting a weekly gathering in their home. I asked the question, "So when your church grows large enough do you plan on giving up barbering?" He stopped. The noisy snapping of his barber scissors still echoing in my ear. He looked at me like a space alien, puzzled and temporarily unsure what to say. "Um, no, not at all," he stammered. "You see this work is the best thing I could ever ask for as a church planter. Giving haircuts is part of my neighborhood exegesis where God teaches me what he's up to in people's lives. Every day I mix with normal, ordinary people in this neighborhood. I listen to their stories, their hopes, their fears, and it feeds my missional response as a disciple of Jesus. I couldn't minister nearly as effectively if I didn't listen to what God was up to right here." He began snipping away again before continuing, "If I were *just a pastor*, I wouldn't have access to a quarter of the people I get to meet. This barber shop *is* my ministry."

That day the hipster barber taught me a lesson (as well as giving me a decent yet overpriced haircut). The apostle Paul tells the house church in 1 Corinthians 3:9 that "we are co-workers in God's service; you are God's field," but the hipster barber taught me to have a broader understanding of who God is enlisting in that work. Doing his neighborhood exegesis from behind a barber's chair, paying attention to the presence of Jesus, that church planter understood coworking with God to extend beyond "churchy people" to those in the community who were not yet Christian. They were coworkers in God's redemptive mission unfolding in empty cross and empty tomb and the sending of the Holy Spirit with much to teach us as followers of Jesus, just as we have much to share with them about the gospel. This kind of understanding of a missional God is critical for Christian witness in a post-Christendom landscape.

Five years ago, I founded the Centre for Missional Leadership at St. Andrew's Hall, the Presbyterian Church in Canada college at the University of British Columbia. Ever since the publication of *Missional Church: A Vision for the Sending of the Church in North America* in 1998, many of

Introduction

us as congregational pastors and academics had been reading, discussing, and exploring the key thinkers in the missional theology world. Indeed, I am personally grateful that while serving as a congregational pastor and adjunct professor at St. Andrew's Hall, I had Alan Roxburgh and his family worshiping in my congregation. Roxburgh was a participant in the Gospel and Our Culture Network project in the 1990s and a contributor to *Missional Church* that picked up on Lesslie Newbigin's work in the United Kingdom, applying a missionary's skill set to ministry in the secular West. As Newbigin asked, "What would be involved in a genuine missionary encounter between the gospel and the culture which is shared by the peoples of Europe and North America and their colonial and cultural offshoots, the growing company of educated leaders in all the cities of the world, the culture with which those of us who share in it usually describe as modern?"[4] Over regular sushi lunches on the North Shore of Vancouver, I picked Alan's brain on the missional conversation and what it meant to build, equip, and lead Christian communities in a post-Christendom cultural landscape, where confessing Jesus as Lord was increasingly met with puzzled looks or hostile stares.

Switching to a tenure track position at St. Andrew's Hall in 2014, the board of management encouraged me to explore how the college could help not only seminarians studying next door at our partner institution, the Vancouver School of Theology, but also church leaders in small and struggling congregations, who were overwhelmed with the pace of cultural change and felt ill-equipped to lead in these early decades of our secular age. Just as I am grateful to Alan Roxburgh for taking me deeper into the missional conversation, Darrell Guder's acceptance of the role as senior fellow in residence at the launch of the Centre for Missional Leadership was a tremendous blessing. Guder, editor of the *Missional Church* book project, had just retired as Henry Winters Luce Professor Emeritus of Missional Theology and Ecumenical Theology at Princeton Theological Seminary. Over these past six years, Darrell has not only given generously of his time and talent in helping to shape the Centre for Missional Leadership, but has also been an incredible mentor to me as a missiologist.

The desire to partner with the triune God in this curious cultural landscape has led us into so many fascinating friendships and networks. Indeed, the Centre for Missional Leadership is a humble yet earnest attempt to respond to the changing nature of Christian witness in a post-Christendom

---

4. Newbigin, 1984 Warfield Lectures, Princeton Theology Seminary.

Introduction

North American landscape. The Centre for Missional Leadership's vision is *flourishing Christian communities faithfully witnessing to God's mission*, while the mission of the Centre is to *equip missional leaders for Christ's church of tomorrow, today.*

In this work Darrell Guder has brought us back again and again to Jesus' imperative in Acts 1:8 to "be my witnesses" and to see our calling to help equip the church to be a witness (character), do witness (in service to the world in acts of mercy and justice), and say witness (the speech act of evangelism, a testimony to the hope that is within us, done so with gentleness and respect).[5] This is, of course, no small task and certainly for us an endeavor not once conceived of as being done in isolation. As a small college, in a small denomination, we have always imagined not only working with others of good intention and similar conviction, but we understand our work to be sanctified seasoning, a pinch of the salt of the earth, giving hope, adding flavor, and offering a foretaste of the One who is coming, and is present even now by the Holy Spirit.

What you hold in your hands is a good example of the conversations the Centre for Missional Leadership has convened over the last several years. In the pages ahead you will read rich and engaging theological reflections from leaders in the church and academy pushing us to a more thoughtful and effective Christian witness in a secular West that is increasingly unaware of the saving story of Jesus Christ that would have been taken for granted by our forebearers just a few decades earlier. Far from feeling discouraged, you'll find the friends of CML have stories, concepts, and actions to share in response to what the triune God is up to in our very midst. In the chapters ahead, you'll hear from some of the best thought-leaders we've come across in CML and I trust you'll set this book down more invigorated than you've felt in a long time, eager to participate in the healing of the nations that God is up to wherever this moment finds you.

The book is structured for reflection on what it means to plant, replant, and revitalize small but vibrant Christian witnessing communities in the soil of post-Christendom. We begin with "Tilling the Field," having Tim Dickau, David Warkentin, and Todd Wiebe bring decades of experience in church and academy to bear on paying (praying?) attention to the particular context we find ourselves in. How do the historical, theological, cultural, economic, and social realities of Cascadia impact the way we prepare the land for planting? Next we begin to "plant seeds" in this rocky

---

5. Guder, *Be My Witnesses*, 44.

Introduction

Cascadian soil with a theological reflection on church planting by Darrell Guder, followed by a trio of perspectives from Stephen Bell, Andrea Perrett, and Young Tae Choi—three of our recent St. Andrew's Hall graduates steeped in missional theology and active in church planting, arts ministries, and life in a hardscrabble downtown neighborhood.

Any experienced gardener will be quick to point out that once the soil is prepared and seeds planted, the important and delicate work really begins. How do you nurture growth when you are not fully in control? The next section of our work together attends to this nurture in partnership with the Holy Spirit. Ann-Marie Ellithorpe, Jenn Richards, Andrew Stephens-Rennie, and I attempt to describe what this nurturing might look like through theologies of friendship, evangelism, liberated imagination, and missional catechesis. Finally, with attention to the soil of this context, thoughtful planting of gospel seed, and nurturing the growth in difficult circumstances comes the eschatological anticipation of the harvest. In this last section, Richard Topping, Christopher James, and Jonathan Wilson reflect on Christian imagination for mission, the church God is re-placing and re-planning, as well as a vision of leaning into beloved community as missional witness.

Together, we explore Christian witness as coworkers with God in this spectacularly beautiful corner of God's creation. As you work your way through each chapter in this book, consider it an invitation for your own journey of growth and discovery. What might it mean for you to be active planting seeds of hope for the future, tilling soil, and caring for the space God has given to you, adding nutrients and water for growth and looking to the future God is bringing as together we await the harvest with hope? The landscape we will travel together is a curious one, especially for readers who live in parts of North America where Christendom lingers—like a recent flight from Atlanta I was on where everyone was talking about Jesus around me, from the passengers on either side reading Tim Keller and Adam Hamilton books, to the three rows behind happily chatting to others about Jesus as they left on a pilgrimage to Israel!

No, the Pacific Northwest has always been a different landscape of fickle faith and rugged individualism. Historians of religion in the region have noted that Christendom was never fully established here on the West Coast, with "Northwest secularity . . . [being] most evident in the region's strikingly low levels of involvement in, and attachment to, formal or organized religion."[6] Indeed, people move here from other places to escape commitments to social or religious institutions. A common late nineteenth-century expression said that "men left God behind when they crossed the Rocky Mountains into British Columbia."[7] Historically, with jobs and riches in the region provided by nature's bounty, "Many residents of Cascadia learned it may not have been a Supreme Being—but sheer hustle, luck and location, location, location (real estate boom)—that determined whether one fell by the economic wayside or joined the economic elite."[8]

But just as an unfair critique of Christendom makes it sound like God was absent from the West for fifteen hundred years or more, so too must we be careful not to perpetuate the heresy of deism by suggesting that a church without worldly power is evidence of an absence of the triune God. No, as you will see in this collection of essays, there is ample evidence of divine agency partnering with human agency in the Pacific Northwest offering hope today. Just like that hipster barber church planter, however, God is partnering with humans in unlikely ways and places, and not necessarily in the church. The church needs the world outside it, just as the barber needed his barbershop in order to learn what God was up to in the world. So, pull on those skinny jeans and grab a flannel shirt, put on your trendy hiking boots and grab an overpriced latte from the barista down the street. We have territory to cover together in the pages ahead, and as we've learned in missional theology, we're always playing catch up to what the Father, Son, and Holy Spirit are up to. Once again, God goes ahead of us into this post-Christendom landscape just like God did long ago with the people of Israel—a pillar of cloud by day and a pillar of fire by night. Our way maker God is on the move. Let's see what God is up to now!

Bibliography

Block, Tina. *Secular Northwest: Religion and Irreligion in Everyday Postwar Life.* Vancouver: University of British Columbia Press, 2016.
Guder, Darrell L. *Be My Witnesses: The Church's Mission, Message, and Messengers.* Grand Rapids: Eerdmans, 1985.
Marks, Lynne. *Infidels and the Damn Churches: Irreligion and Religion in Settler British Columbia.* Vancouver: University of British Columbia Press, 2017.

6. Block, *Secular Northwest*, 48.
7. Marks, *Infidels and the Damn Churches*, 5.
8. Todd, "Why Is British Columbia So Secular?"

Newbigin, Lesslie. "The Theory of Cross-Cultural Mission and the Ideology of Pluralism." 1984 Warfield Lectures, Princeton Theology Seminary. https://commons.ptsem.edu/id/04133.

Todd, Douglas. "Why Is British Columbia So Secular?" *The Vancouver Sun*, August 30, 2017.

TILLING THE FIELD

He that tilleth his land shall have plenty of bread:
but he that followeth after vain persons shall have poverty enough.

—PROVERBS 28:19 (KJV)

Work your garden—you'll end up with plenty of food;
play and party—you'll end up with an empty plate.

—PROVERBS 28:19 (MSG)

1

Seeking the Kingdom of God as a Church in a Secular Age

Tim Dickau

Painting a Picture of Our Secular Age

LIVING IN VANCOUVER, CANADA, for the past thirty-three years, I have witnessed a steady shift towards secularism and fragmented approaches to life.[1] While church attendance has decreased during those three decades,[2] the conditions of belief have also changed, as Charles Taylor has so well argued in his book *A Secular Age*.[3] Taylor describes how our "social imaginary" functions within an "immanent frame," a way of seeing and being in the world that excludes or ignores God's transforming activity.[4] In contrast to "subtraction theories of secularization"—the idea that with the

---

1. See Alasdair MacIntyre's description of our ideological fragmentation in *After Virtue*.

2. http://www.pewforum.org/2013/06/27/canadas-changing-religious-landscape/. The decline in Canada is from 41 percent church attendance in 1981 to 27 percent in 2011

3. Taylor, *A Secular Age*.

4. Taylor, *Secular Age*, 18. To say that our current form of secularism is susceptible to or reflective of pride is not to say that all secularism is a move towards pride. Taylor will argue otherwise, and I agree. However, I will lean towards the writers whom I discuss below such as Cavanaugh and Jennings, who believe that Taylor has underplayed the idolatrous nature of our allegiances within the immanent frame.

ascendancy of science and rationality, the church's authority recedes and religious narratives lose their power, resulting in an inevitable departure from belief in God—Taylor narrates a different story. He identifies intentional moves made within the Western world over the last five hundred years that would eventually locate meaning apart from God within this immanent frame. The locus of meaning would reside primarily in the arts and aesthetics (a development arising out of the Romantic period in part) and in the technological possibilities arising from the advances of science. What makes this secularism tougher to penetrate is that many of the moves towards the option of unbelief emerged initially within the life and theology of the church. Not only do many people live within this immanent frame, this secularism has been shaped or more often misshaped by forces of autonomy and individualism,[5] consumerism,[6] and economic inequality.[7] As William Cavanaugh argues, these powers have become our idols.[8] Our sites and objects of worship have migrated from the church and the triune God to the Market, the State, and the ever-present self.[9]

Willie Jennings offers a companionate story alongside Taylor's when he peruses that same time frame from the 1500s to the present and asks why our Christian imagination succumbed to colonial pathways that failed

---

5. On autonomy and individualism, see Taylor, *Sources of the Self*, and also Carkner, *The Great Escape from Nihilism*.

6. On consumerism, see especially Cavanaugh, *Being Consumed*.

7. On income inequality, see Bauman, *Collateral Damage*, and the now influential study by Picketty, *Capital in the Twenty-First Century*.

8. Cavanaugh, *Migrations of the Holy*.

9. In his essay entitled "Divine Excess: The God Who Comes After," Merold Westphal quotes Jean-Luc Marion, who argues that sites producing meaning within our world are fulfilling their intended good if they function as icons rather than idols. Marion believes that what distinguishes an icon from an idol is the "how" rather than the "what" of perception or use. In other words, a given text, person, or idea can function as either an idol or icon depending on the nature of the intentional acts directed towards it by the interpreter and user. It becomes an idol when the gaze of the interpreter or user is satisfied or fulfilled with what it sees, when it stops, freezes, settles, or comes to rest at its visible object. The same text, person, or idea becomes an icon when it is looked at differently, when the gaze does not stop. The iconic gaze believes that the object before it can lead to truth, but it does not believe that it gives the whole truth and nothing but the truth. See Merold Westphal, "Divine Excess: The God Who Comes After," in Caputo, *The Religious*, 258–76. *All this to say that the problem is not in attempting to find meaning in our immanent frame, whether in aesthetics or in the discoveries of science. The problem is in assuming that these immanent meanings exclude transcendent, larger meanings when in fact these transcendent meanings are crucial to rightly informing our perceptions of and actions towards these immanent sites of meaning.*

to direct us towards the social vision of fraternity and intimacy engendered in Jesus' mission.[10] Jennings tells a story of how this gaze of "whiteness" that emerged in the colonial age permeates so much of Western culture and academia, let alone our theology. For Jennings, whiteness is less a biological term and more an evaluative term that identifies people according to the color of the skin—and apart from their land or place—thereby organizing people into a column with white folks at the top and black folks at the bottom. Along with this diminishing of humanity was the concomitant treatment of land as property for our use or misuse (which in turn fuels so much of our commerce today). Jennings argues that this temptation towards racism makes us continually susceptible to displacing God's call to love our neighbor by developing relationships of mutual intimacy with instead a form of control and oppression. I believe that Jennings's story of the emergence of race as a corrupted organizing principle (along with the misuse of land) adds a key element to Taylor's thesis as to how and why the gospel has been distorted and undermined, thereby contesting belief in its goodness and in the God whose story it tells.

Giving In and Giving Up

In the face of these narratives that make unbelief a strong option and up against these misshaping forces, some churches have "*given up*." Daunted by these powers and the pervasive marketing and media machine that feeds them, I feel that temptation to give up myself at times. Other churches have been able to survive or even thrive by what I would call by and large "*giving in*" to these powerful misshaping forces. Across North America, we have ended up creating plenty of churches that ask little more than two hours on a Sunday and a small portion of a person's income in exchange for an entertaining style of worship that appeals to consumerist and autonomous impulses but fails to name these powers as idols or to call people to a sacrificial pursuit of and participation in God's kingdom of peace and justice. I offer this critique very aware that I also feel tempted to default to this response, to an easier, more comfortable way of being in a church that gives in to these forces.

---

10. Jennings, *Christian Imagination*.

Finding a Different Path through These Forces

The biblical vision of "laying down our lives" for the king and seeking first God's kingdom of restoration and reconciliation calls us to develop a very different kind of community, neither one that "gives up" or "gives in" to these forces. The starting point for this alternative response is this reality that Jesus has won a victory over these powers through truth and sacrificial love and is now redeeming these powers for the kingdom come and coming.

For the past thirty years, I have had the privilege of being a pastor as part of Grandview Church in East Vancouver, a church that has searched for this alternative path. In that time, we have sought to live into a vision of God's kingdom that counters these misshaping forces and bears witness to God's renewing action in Christ through the Spirit. The desire to bear witness to God's restoring and reconciling kingdom has led us down at least four trajectories towards fostering a diverse community, a more radical hospitality. Justice for the least and confession have both shaped our way of life personally and corporately.[11] Seeking the kingdom in this context has also led us to develop a number of initiatives and organizations, including a free community meal, housing, and support for refugee claimants, many community houses, and a social housing complex, social enterprises (including catering, pottery, and renovations business out of the church building), a policy-developing organization around issues of human trafficking and the sex trade, an initiative to help churches implement recommendations from the Truth and Reconciliation Commission, a support group for single moms, a social justice activist group, and an urban prayer and retreat space. All of these have grown organically out of the intersection of God's vision for the kingdom, the gifts and passions of our church folk, and the needs of our neighborhood and city. And while we are a church of only three hundred or so people with two congregations, we have and are developing a way of life in Christ and the power of the Spirit that continues to transform and sustain us and these initiatives.

The Importance of Theological Vision

That way of life has been shaped by a holistic theological vision. While at seminary, I had the privilege of taking two courses with N. T. Wright. His

---

11. See Dickau, *Plunging into the Kingdom Way*.

courses on the kingdom of God in the Gospels and how that kingdom vision was worked out in Paul's letter to the Romans grew my imagination for the kingdom of God. While I didn't know how that vision could be worked out in a secular, post-Christian neighborhood, I did come away with a vision of a church incarnated in a place seeking to participate in God's mission of making all things new. This hermeneutic that Wright articulated for working out the way of the kingdom—as Jesus to Israel, so the church to the world—became a lens through which to see how we could bear witness to the kingdom come in our neighborhood. In a North American culture where pragmatism and "building bigger churches" can become idols, I believe that having this broad and biblical theological vision of our participation in the mission of God is vital for renewing church life today.

Re-forming Community

The first ten years of this journey were about re-forming a community that had decided to quit but was willing to give it one last shot to see what could happen. When I first came to Grandview Church, people's experience of a shared life was self-admittedly very thin. Moving into the neighborhood (which made us three of only a handful of people who lived there), my wife, Mary, and I began a parent's group with our son, in part motivated by our desire to make some friends of our own age group to complement our friendships with the seniors in our church. We also made connections with refugee agencies and began connecting first with Latin American refugees and then folks from many parts of the world. These initial forays into relationships with our neighbors, especially the poor and vulnerable, had a boomerang effect of renewing and reforming our shared life as a church. To become a welcoming community involved plenty of grieving of the past, learning to trust and love one another, discussions and disagreements about how God was leading us, and movements towards hospitality with our neighbors and strangers.

This move towards a shared life was one of the key moves we made that led to renewal. For a good number of folks, this included living next door to each other or within the same household. Our own family "fell into" this way of shared living as we welcomed folks to live with us for a weekend or a week that morphed into a couple of years living together. Eventually we and other folks embraced this deeper shared life in a community as one of the ways in which we could form a community that was empowered to bear witness to God's kingdom. We now have over fifteen houses where people live together, as well as a new housing project that just opened that features a "shared living room" among every five suites as well as a floor of common space called the Co:Here Project.[12] Community living is not a magic bullet to church renewal or transformation but a deeper shared life is crucial to forming a community that resists the misshaping powers so that we might be transformed by Christ.[13]

Inhabiting a Neighborhood

That renewal is more likely if these communities inhabit a place. If we are to overcome the autonomy and fragmentation of contemporary life and contribute to the well-being of places in line with the kingdom's promise of restoration, and if we are to live into this vision of restoration that extends to public buildings, trees, sidewalks, as well as people, we need people who commit not only to each other but to a place—and learn to love it. Given that more than half of our church family lives within walking distance of the church, we have come to care about this neighborhood as our home. When you inhabit and embrace a place over the long haul, the shalom Jesus came to inaugurate—this culture in which humans flourish, relationships are restored, and creation moves towards completion—becomes more imaginable.

Shalom Takes Time

But it takes time. This phrase—"Shalom takes time"—comes from a book coauthored by Stanley Hauerwas and Jean Vanier.[14] Our experience has proven this to be true. As we have persisted in understanding our neighbors, power dynamics, and institutions in our neighborhood, we have been able to make some headway in addressing systemic issues of injustice. Take housing for example. Not only have we found creative and prophetic ways to bear witness to a different view of property and home by sharing houses,

---

12. For more information on the Co:Here Project: Home for Good see here: http://coherehousing.com

13. Hauerwas and Willimon's book *Resident Aliens* helped me understand at that time why we needed to be re-formed in community in Christ if we were going to live out a kingdom vision and be salt and light.

14. Hauerwas and Vanier, *Living Gently*, 201.

cars, tools, money, or by developing affordable housing over top of our church parking lot,[15] we have also participated in many forums, discussions with politicians, and campaigns such as "raise the rates" to increase social assistance, all in an effort to promote a shift in how we view housing from being a commodity to being a basic need for all. Pursuing the kingdom requires us to move beyond only personal and corporate responses to address these systemic issues of injustice and decay.[16] And this takes time, which is one reason we have called many folks to make commitments of stability instead of moving every five years as North Americans are prone to do.[17]

If we are to stay longer term in pursuit of this wider vision, we will also be confronted with our own idolatries. I once ventured out into unusual territory in sermon titles, which is daring for me, such as "You cannot watch movies three evenings a week and seek the kingdom of God." The point beyond the hyperbole was that seeking the kingdom in all these ways will confront our idolatry of entertainment and diversions. Instead, as we take up this costly way of the kingdom for the long haul, we will learn how much we need true solitude and empowering of the Spirit. In our own journey, the practices of confession and forgiveness—practices we foster in our weekly worship, in our pastoral meetings, and in inner healing prayer—have proven to be essential in our own conflicted relationships and in our own transformation. If we are to recover monastic practices of stability, a practice that I believe is a precursor for churches seeking to recover a kingdom vision, we will need to recover these basic formational practices of confession, repentance, and forgiveness along the way.

Indeed, a year ago I reached a stage of burnout from a failure to acknowledge my own limits. I was isolating and drinking more as a result. When I had a vehicle accident driving home one evening (in which thankfully no one was hurt), my burnout and increased drinking were exposed. My own burnout coincided with a broader fatigue of some of our other leaders who had been there for the long haul. While I have had

15. Go to http://salsburycs.ca for a description of the Co:Here Project from the perspective of a community housing society.

16. One of my pleas to preachers is to keep all three of these levels of transformation in view in our preaching. Too often we restrict preaching to personal or perhaps church transformation but don't get into how God wants to transform society. Preaching that also addresses the complex systemic issues of our day that will have a greater kingdom vision and impact.

17. See Putnam, *Bowling Alone* for evidence and statistics regarding our increasing transience and accompanying loss of social capital.

the opportunity to rest and recover this past year, others have dug in and shared a heavier burden. We have had to push a "reset" button this year as the church has made adjustments to address some of our weaknesses, such as a deficit of Sabbath and sabbaticals and the need to strengthen our core lay leadership.[18]

I tell this story in part to emphasize a few vital realities in seeking the kingdom of God. First, to reiterate, ours is not a story of "progress." As we take steps towards obedience, our own frailties and sin are brought into the light. While there are advances for the kingdom, there are also times of "regress." These can also become occasions that God can transform for good if we continue to be a repenting church. Secondly, we do not build the kingdom of God. To operate with this perspective is to concede to the immanent framework Taylor describes so well. Instead we build *for* the kingdom, always cognizant that the Spirit will test our work and refine it.[19] Thirdly, along the way, we have been coaxed and cajoled into fostering practices that open our eyes and hearts to the sacramental, incarnational agency of God in our secular age. For us, practices such as listening prayer, spiritual direction, and Lectio Divina have been vital in recovering a sacramental vision. Fostering a sacramental vision has been so integral to finding sustenance for the long journey of obedience.

Revamping our worship over the years in this direction has helped in this regard. In my time at the church, our corporate worship has shifted from a liturgy more typical of evangelical churches that includes corporate singing, announcements, and preaching to a liturgy more typical of the historic church. Our present liturgy includes a processional, call to worship, corporate singing, public confession, passing of the peace, Scripture readings (often dramatized), prayers of the people (usually by the congregation), preaching, Eucharist (each week), prayers, and sending. As James K. A. Smith argues in his book *Desiring the Kingdom*, these are commonly held practices within corporate worship across differing traditions of the church.[20] These practices not only have reshaped our desires, they have tutored us in discerning the movements of God in our lives and in the world. As we join in praise and thanksgiving for God's acts, as we humbly confess,

---

18. Since most of our lay leadership served on the initiatives we have developed for the neighborhood, our church council for example had become a leadership formation context rather than a group of elders. This year, the council has had to move towards the role of elders, a responsibility they have stepped into well.

19. See 1 Cor 1–3.

20. Smith, *Desiring the Kingdom*.

as we seek peace, as we listen God's story read and preached, as we lament and petition for God's kingdom to come, and as we lay down our lives as Christ has for us in the Eucharist, we catch glimpses of how and where the work of the Spirit is woven into our world.[21] And we have taken up these practices in worship in the context of traveling through the church year, we have begun to recover the "sacred time" connected to the Christian story versus the "homogenous empty time" characteristic of modernism.[22]

Holding Together That Which Has Been Torn Apart

In our continuing effort and struggle to live into a kingdom vision, one of the graces we have received is a holding together of elements of the mission of God that are often split apart. By seeking this vision over the long haul, we have been able to embrace both prayer and justice, personal and systemic transformation, holiness and prophetic witness, evangelism and formation, empowering leadership and relational accountability, and an emphasis on both our actions and the action of God.

Indeed, it is the recovering of our awareness of the agency and action of the God who is ushering in this alternative kingdom that has given us hope, courage, and creativity. The influx of people from many other countries and cultures has challenged the "immanent frame" and the accompanying idolatries that so many of us default to in the West. Together, we have found ways to resist these idols and to bear witness that the kingdom continues to take root today, even in secular Vancouver.

Bibliography

Bauman, Zygmunt. *Collateral Damage: Social Inequalities in a Global Age.* Cambridge: Polity, 2011.
Caputo, John, ed. *The Religious.* Malden, MA: Blackwell, 2002.
Carkner, Gordon. *The Great Escape from Nihilism: Rediscovering Our Passion in Late Modernity.* Rosshire, UK: InFocus, 2016.
Cavanaugh, William. *Being Consumed: Economics and Christian Desire.* Grand Rapids: Eerdmans, 2007.

---

21. See Williams, *Christ the Heart of Creation* for a brilliant historical argument for how God's action in the world does not compete for space with creation but is incarnational, thus following the model of Jesus as the second person of the Trinity.

22. See Taylor, *Secular Age*, 208–9.

———. *Migrations of the Holy: God, State, and the Political Meaning of the Church.* Grand Rapids: Eerdmans, 2010.

Dickau, Tim. *Plunging into the Kingdom Way: Practicing the Shared Strokes of Community, Hospitality, Justice, and Confession.* Eugene, OR: Cascade, 2010.

Hauerwas, Stanley, and Jean Vanier. *Living Gently in a World of Violence: The Prophetic Witness of Weakness.* Downers Grove: InterVarsity, 2018.

Hauerwas, Stanley, and William H. Willimon. *Resident Aliens: Life in the Christian Colony.* Nashville: Abingdon, 1989.

Jennings, Willie James. *The Christian Imagination: Theology and the Origins of Race.* New Haven: Yale University Press, 2011.

MacIntyre, Alasdair. *After Virtue: A Study in Moral Theory.* 3rd ed. Notre Dame: University of Notre Dame Press, 2007.

Picketty, Thomas. *Capital in the Twenty-First Century.* Boston: Harvard University Press, 2014.

Putnam, Robert. *Bowling Alone: The Collapse and Revival of American Community.* New York: Simon and Schuster, 2001.

Smith, James K. A. *Desiring the Kingdom: Worship, Worldview, and Cultural Formation.* Grand Rapids: Baker Academic, 2009.

Taylor, Charles. *A Secular Age.* Boston: Harvard University Press, 2007.

———. *Sources of the Self.* Boston: Harvard University Press, 1992.

Williams, Rowan. *Christ the Heart of Creation.* London: Bloomsbury, 2018.

2

Storytelling Praxis

Indigenous–Settler Relationships in Cascadia

David Warkentin

> The truth about stories is that that's all we are. . . .
> Want a different ethic? Tell a different story.
> —THOMAS KING[1]

Found within the story of Christ, our story intersects with God's story and we once again become humans in the way God always intended. As human beings, we all have a story to tell; but when we connect with God in Christ, our story becomes grand but our view of time still determines the story.
—RANDY WOODLEY[2]

Land Acknowledgment: I write these words as I sit at my desk in the traditional, ancestral, and unceded territory of the Stó:lō people, specifically the Matsqui and Sumas bands. As you read, join me in acknowledging the

---

1. King, *Truth about Stories*, 153, 164.
2. Woodley, *Shalom and the Community of Creation*, 140.

place you find yourself today and express gratitude for the hospitality of our Indigenous hosts and neighbors.

Witness Statement: I also write as a witness, not an authority on Indigenous perspectives. As a Settler-Christian,[3] I want to acknowledge that for many Indigenous people, my voice can remind them of past pain and suffering at the hands of religious leaders. Through listening to local Stó:lō elders in British Columbia's Fraser Valley, such as Ray Silver, Patti Victor, and Rena Point Bolton, I write as a witness to their stories and perspectives. For their example and willingness to teach me, I am grateful.

Cascadia's Indigenous–Settler Context

Living in Cascadia as a Settler-Christian who researches and educates on Cascadian culture, much of my work explores how people experience identity and belonging in this place. Notably, Cascadia is characterized by diversity.[4] While this diversity is a source of beauty, it is also the cause of considerable division. A quick scan of news headlines in recent years reveals political polarization, urban-suburban-rural community divisions, socioeconomic disparity, and ongoing racial tensions. Such conflicts disrupt the vision of Cascadia as a utopia, a culture of harmonious relationships between people and places.[5] Sadly, the dream of harmony can cloud the reality of deep division. This essay will focus on one specific Cascadian division: Indigenous–Settler relationships.

Pressing political, economic, and social developments often frame Indigenous–Settler relationships in Cascadia. From Indigenous governance, to pipelines and land development, to the incorporation of Indigenous cultural practices in education, there are complex issues in the *present* that have important implications for the *future* of Indigenous–Settler relationships in Cascadia. To move forward, however, requires attention to the *past*, a look

---

3. Here "Settler" refers to someone whose background is associated with the settlement of Turtle Island (modern day North America) via European colonization and subsequent immigration, including a recognition of the immense damage colonialism did to Indigenous peoples across this land. Furthermore, to identify as a "Settler-*Christian*" is to acknowledge Christianity's complicity in colonialism and to take responsibility to pursue reconciliation as a conviction of faith. See Dave Diewert, "White Christian Settlers, the Bible, and (De)colonization," in Heinrichs, *Buffalo Shout, Salmon Cry*, 127–37.

4. See Warkentin, "The Cascadian Self."

5. See Todd, *Cascadia*.

back at how Cascadia has arrived here.[6] Cascadia is a geopolitical region with a long history of unresolved Indigenous–Settler conflict, particularly in the significant injustices perpetrated by Settlers. In many areas of Cascadia, land was settled without treaties and reserve land was sold off without consultation. In Canada, Indigenous culture was eliminated through the atrocities of residential schools, what Canada's Truth and Reconciliation Commission summarized as nothing short of "cultural genocide."[7] Additionally, social and political issues, such as foster-care inconsistencies and a disproportionate number of Indigenous people in the criminal-justice system, reveal how systemic injustice has perpetuated problems for Indigenous people to this day.[8] Indigenous–Settler relationships in Cascadia are often determined by this history of injustice.

With this complex context in mind, this essay addresses Christian witness and formation in Cascadia by suggesting that a narrative identity framework rooted in a storytelling praxis can foster Indigenous–Settler relationships in Cascadia. In particular, this approach challenges Settler-Christians to take responsibility in fostering relationships with their Indigenous neighbors, both within the Christian community and the broader Cascadian culture. As long as Indigenous people are seen as "issues"—be those economic, political, or social—reconciliation will remain an arm's length away at best. As we will see, storytelling, by contrast, is fundamentally relational. How Cascadians tell our stories, then, will shape how we live together in this place.

Indigenous–Settler Stories

To better understand the role of storytelling in Cascadia's Indigenous-Settler relationships, I begin with two stories from early twentieth-century Cascadian history:

---

6. Pointing to the work of Elise Building, J. P. Lederach suggests that contextualized peacebuilding must incorporate a "200-year present" where any present engagement with conflict attends to how present relationships are shaped by the past, while also recognizing that relationships today in turn shape the future. See John Paul Lederach and America Ferrera, "The Ingredients of Social Courage."

7. *Honouring the Truth*, 1.

8. See Charles and Rah, *Unsettling Truths*.

Story #1: The Creation of Sumas Prairie

A growing population of Europeans was settling in British Columbia's Fraser Valley in the nineteenth and early twentieth century. With population growth came the need for land and agriculture to house and support the growth. The ingenuity of engineers and farmers, along with the political will of national and provincial leaders, led to the decision to drain and dike what was then known as Sumas Lake, a boggy stretch of water stretching up to twenty-five kilometers in length in the space between Sumas Mountain and Vedder Mountain. The place was seen as unusable land, a waste of space really.

The hard-working Settlers, many of whom were Dutch-Reformed and Mennonite Christians, applied their skills with diligence and experience in developing what is now known as the Sumas Prairie, a place of enormous economic wealth. Many people have benefited from the creation of Sumas Prairie in developing and sustaining a way of life for nearly one hundred years. For my own ancestors who were Mennonite Christians fleeing war-torn Europe, the opportunity to apply their agricultural prowess and exercise their values of financial stewardship was seen as nothing short of a blessing from God in this new land, a blessing of riches that continues to this day.

Story #2: The Loss of Sumas Lake

The Stó:lō people—"People of the River"—have always lived in relationship with the Fraser River and the surrounding wetlands. Salmon have been a source of sustenance for the Stó:lō people for thousands of years. Prior to population increase, Sumas Lake was a central hub for sustaining their way of life both in salmon production and for transportation. As the late Stó:lō Elder Ray Silver recounted, "The lake was our farm."[9]

When the Stó:lō people were not fishing, the lake was used for transport in hunting deer and waterfowl. This lake was part of the blessing from the Creator in sustaining life in the world. Several generations ago, however, Sumas Lake was lost and the Stó:lō people were forced into small, isolated areas, several of which no longer have access to the precious water source so essential to their way of life. For example, the Sumas Band reservation located in Kilgard at the base of Sumas Mountain once sat as lakefront

---

9. Silver, "Welcome."

property. With the loss of Sumas Lake, however, what was once a blessing became the curse of a lost way of life. The Stó:lō people are still dealing with the negative consequences of this reality to this day.

Which Story?

Making sense of these two contrasting stories surrounding one event in Cascadian history is complex. The first story makes a lot of sense from a Settler-Christian worldview, often influenced by a blending of economic pragmatism and theological justification. The land is for people to use for their benefit. And as some Bible translations describe the creation mandate in Genesis 1:28 (NIV), humans are to "rule" over the earth and "subdue" it. In draining Sumas Lake, a wild wetland was subdued. The land has served people and society for decades now. Any resulting hardship was the cost of socioeconomic progress.

The second story makes sense from an Indigenous perspective. For Indigenous people, social or economic progress is not linear but relational; more farmland and more money are not the goal. Draining Sumas Lake, therefore, does not equal harmony with the land and one another. In fact, it is quite the opposite. The lost connection to the river was not just the loss of a food source but a disconnection from a fundamental part of their identity. The "People of the River" lost their river.[10]

Cascadia is full of such contrasting stories between Indigenous and Settler peoples. And where trends of polarizing politics may tempt adversarial responses to these types of differing accounts—a politics of winners and losers—I want to suggest that a storytelling praxis rooted in a narrative identity can offer an alternative engagement to Indigenous–Settler relationships. Storytelling, as I explore below, is an essential Indigenous practice, but often absent in non-Indigenous conceptions of truth and identity. For Cascadia's Settler-Christians considering their "ministry of reconciliation,"[11] engaging narrative and storytelling can be a significant step towards acknowledging the different Cascadian histories. One must know one's neighbor in order to love them well.[12]

---

10. For a window into the impact of the draining of Sumas Lake on the Stó:lō people, see Point Bolton and Daily, *Xwelíqwiya*, and Cameron, *Openings*.

11. 2 Cor 5:11–20.

12. Matt 22:36–40.

One barrier to such engagement is the significant ignorance to the complex history of Indigenous people in Cascadia. It is often only the Settler perspective of history that gets told in schools, museums, community celebrations, and, dare I say, churches. Additionally, Settler-Christians often downplay their participation in many of the injustices against Cascadia's Indigenous people, unsure of how, or if they even want, to take responsibility.[13] To move towards relationship between Cascadia's Indigenous and Settler people, this history needs to be told, heard, and responded to. I want to suggest that Alasdair MacIntyre's work on narrative identity can serve to bridge the gap between Indigenous and Settler history in Cascadia.

Narrative Identity and Cascadia

In *Whose Justice? Which Rationality?*, Alasdair MacIntyre describes identity as a "socially embodied theory" that only finds coherence at the intersection of belief and practice.[14] To engage identity well, therefore, means recognizing and engaging the historical contingency of both one's own narrative identity and the rival narrative identities within one's context. To justify one's narrative identity means to understand its rootedness in time and place.[15] Engaging diverse narratives does not begin with an appeal to objective or universal truths to inspire agreement or unity. Thus, MacIntyre warns against "fictitious objectivity," an appeal to independent standards of rational justification to prove the validity of one's narrative identity without attending to the nuances of one's place or the complexities of the other narratives within that place.[16] In this sense, historical context is not "mere background" to truth.[17] Narrative identity, rather, is constituted by and within "a history neither distinct from, nor intelligible apart from, the history of certain forms of social and practical life."[18] For example, the diverse history of Cascadia requires attention to the particular aspects of

---

13. This sentiment is summarized by two common phrases I have heard when facilitating conversation with Settler-Christians on this topic: "We weren't there when the injustice took place" and "It wasn't that bad. Most people had good intentions."
14. MacIntyre, *Whose Justice? Which Rationality?*, 390.
15. MacIntyre, *Whose Justice? Which Rationality?*, 8.
16. MacIntyre, *Whose Justice? Which Rationality?*, 399.
17. MacIntyre, *Whose Justice? Which Rationality?*, 390.
18. MacIntyre, *Whose Justice? Which Rationality?*, 390.

this geopolitical place, both past and present, that shape conceptions of Cascadian culture today.

Engaging a narrative understanding of identity is a shift for non-Indigenous people who often prioritize disembodied truths and objective history. A narrative understanding of identity and culture, however, has always been fundamental for Indigenous identity. Indigenous people default to understand identity as a complex relationship with the people and places in the past, present, and future. Historical rootedness is found in the formational quality of oral history passed down by elders from generation to generation. Thomas King highlights how in Western approaches to truth, particularly in European versions of Christianity, this complexity of identity is often rejected. Western conceptions of truth, according to King, "are suspicious of complexities, distrustful of contradictions, fearful of enigmas."[19] On the contrary, an Indigenous approach to truth has the fundamental perspective, as Randy Woodley relates to Indigenous Christianity, that "true knowledge is not so much about facts as it is about gaining an understanding or a revelation from the Creator."[20] This step towards narrative identity can guide understanding of the various Indigenous and Settler histories in Cascadia.[21] In terms of Cascadia's Indigenous narrative identity, whether it is the Stó:lō Nation (BC), Duwamish Tribe (WA), Chinook Nation (OR/WA), or any one of the many other Indigenous groups throughout Cascadia, there is a long history of diverse Indigenous peoples residing here. Each group has a unique history of connection to their place along with a particular way of life. Yet often overshadowing their individual histories, Cascadia's Indigenous groups share a collective experience of displacement and suffering as the region was settled in recent centuries.

The trauma of this past and present history is significant in Cascadia Indigenous identity yet today. As Stó:lō elder Patti Victor explains from a Canadian perspective, "Intolerant and judgmental attitudes of the dominant Canadian culture live on, where cultural assimilation is still expected for Indigenous people."[22] Unfortunately, efforts at reconciliation are often developed and led by the dominant culture, leaving Indigenous people, as

---

19. King, *Truth about Stories*, 25.
20. Woodley, *Shalom*, 141.
21. The following paragraphs are adapted from my article "The Cascadian Self."
22. Victor, "Walking Together."

the "invisible minority."[23] Indigenous identity in Cascadia is a rich and diverse history marred by ongoing trauma and injustice.

Cascadia's original Settlers and the generations that have followed offer a very different picture of Cascadian narrative identity. The impulse to explore and settle in what was once seen as the edges of civilization is a prominent part of Cascadia's history. From Lewis and Clark's expeditions, to Hudson's Bay and the subsequent BC gold rush, to post-war urbanization, to more recent growth in modern technological innovation and development, visions of independence and prosperity have inspired countless people to repeatedly venture to Cascadia in the pursuit of opportunity. And while many came to Cascadia in pursuit of freedom, or adventure, or connection to family, many Settlers also found power, wealth, and property, including many of the religious groups that settled here. Much of this region's wealth and global influence comes from the Settler story that continues to carry influence in Cascadian culture.[24] In many ways, then, Cascadia's Settler identity is characterized by prosperity and growth.

These are the historical contingencies that MacIntyre exhorts modern society to acknowledge and which Indigenous people have known to be true all along. But broad-stroke historical accounts of Cascadia Indigenous and Settler identity risk impersonal historicizing that by itself does not address the question of Christian responsibility in responding to this history. Here is where a storytelling praxis is essential in moving engagement with history from ideas *about* historical truth to relationships *rooted in* historical truth. Indigenous author Tommy Orange expresses this necessity well: "All these stories that we haven't been telling all this time, that we haven't been listening to, are just part of what we need to heal."[25]

Storytelling Praxis

Storytelling is the practice of narrative identity. In practice, storytelling involves both sharing and listening to the embedded stories of others in a place, a practice MacIntyre suggests everyone can engage:

---

23. Woodley, "Ending the Reconciliation Paradigm." Woodley doesn't mince words: "White society needs us to not be able to help ourselves." For more extensive commentary, see Woodley's series "Cowboys and Indians."

24. See Gastil and Singer, *The Pacific Northwest*; Wrobel and Steiner, *Many Wests*.

25. Orange, *There There*, 112.

> Everyone has it in them to become a storyteller and everyone needs to learn how to become a good storyteller and both when and when not to tell a story. Everyone also needs to become a good listener to other people's stories, someone who can tell good storytelling from bad and who knows when to respond to a story and when to keep silent.[26]

Applied to Cascadia's Indigenous and Settler narrative identities, as illustrated in the above accounts of British Columbia's Fraser Valley, MacIntyre's emphasis on the practice of storytelling provides direction for engaging these diverse identities. Hearing how the Stó:lō people devastatingly lost their river is vital to understanding the historical contingency of Stó:lō identity today as the "People of the River." Likewise, hearing the story from the perspective of Settler groups, particularly religious Mennonite and Dutch Reformed groups, underscores the value these groups place on economic and social prosperity alongside committed religious devotion. In telling these stories, Cascadians are introduced to the contextual complexity of different narrative identities in relation to one shared history. Regarding the contested history of the Fraser Valley, for example, the practice of storytelling invites listeners to attend to local histories, which often generates empathy for alternative perspectives as a result.[27] Along these lines, Cascadia's Settler-Christians need to practice inviting their Indigenous neighbors to share their stories of life in this place and, in turn, listen well with an ear to understanding and empathy.

By itself, MacIntyre's philosophy serves as bridge for Settler-Christians to cross into relationship with Indigenous people. But once across this bridge, Settler-Christians cannot control the relationship as they have done so often in the past. Instead, as Settler-Christians engage relationships with Indigenous people, they need to go beyond listening to stories towards understanding Indigenous stories well.[28] In particular, Indigenous

26. MacIntyre and Dunn, "Alasdair MacIntyre on Education," 9.

27 See Senehi, "Constructive Storytelling." This connection of story and empathy has been particularly true of Settler-Christian Bible College students from Mennonite and Dutch Reformed backgrounds; hearing the devastation of Stó:lō life and culture brings a sobering reality to how these students process their own narrative history while also critiquing the narrow versions of the past in commonly told stories about British Columbia's Fraser Valley.

28. As Dave Diewert asserts, "White Christian settlers have a responsibility to engage in hard processes of truth telling and sustained practices of decolonization alongside our Indigenous sisters and brothers, to learn from them the insidious dynamics and devastating impacts of systemic racism that we cannot see, and to stand in solidarity with them

approaches to storytelling involve understanding the connection between truth, identity, and story, acknowledging the importance of oral history and tradition, and the practice of respectful listening.

First, understanding the connection between truth, identity, and story is fundamental in how storytelling functions within Indigenous communities. Unlike common Western perspectives that view stories as merely illustrative of greater truths, from an Indigenous perspective stories do not just illustrate the truth; stories are the truth.[29] Stories give a perspective on reality and form a way of being in the world that abstract ideas fail to fully capture. The truth of stories is not primarily about facts, but rather their formational nature. Myths and legends are not measured on historical accuracy but on the way in which they invite people to live. As Indigenous theologian Adrian Jacobs summarizes, "People restore their dignity by returning to their story."[30] Stories themselves, in this sense, are fundamental to shaping identity.

Second, oral history and tradition is a vital form for communicating and interpreting the formational truth of Indigenous stories. For non-Indigenous people, engagement must go beyond surface-level acknowledgment of oral history and tradition in Indigenous culture. Storytelling is not just a quaint cultural practice, or a primitive or lesser approach to history. Rather, oral tradition and history is a particular type of history integral to Indigenous identity and truth. Randy Woodley describes this essential approach to storytelling as a "primal power in the words of oral tradition."[31] With a history of commitment to the written word, particularly with the Bible, Settler-Christians need to restore a value in oral tradition, recognizing that even the Bible comes from a tradition of oral history sustaining the identity of God's people in the world.

Third, the practice of respectful listening allows the formational nature of storytelling to be heard and considered. While some non-Indigenous

---

in their struggle for justice and self-determination, regardless of the cost. Decolonization for white settlers will inevitably require a deepening understanding of past and present colonial violence, and a relentless refusal to reproduce that violence through consistent practices of solidarity" (Diewert, "White Christian Settlers," 136–37).

29. Woodley explains this difference: "Modern Americans seldom make time for story in our lives. We usually relegate story to children, even though science is now discovering that listening to stories has a healing effect on adults, including lowering one's blood pressure" (Woodley, *Shalom*, 137).

30. Adrian Jacobs, quoted in Woodley, *Shalom*, 143.

31. Woodley, *Shalom*, 140.

people may be eager to learn and engage Indigenous perspectives, often this eagerness risks imposing interaction that is hurried and disrespectful to the ways Indigenous storytelling is practiced. As a parent, I often tell my children that communication goes beyond what we say but requires attention to how we listen. Non-Indigenous people need this reminder. This is emphasized for Indigenous people in the pace of storytelling and in the role of elders. I have sometimes heard the phrase "Indian Time" in reference to the particular way Indigenous people view time, and often as a joke in settings where the timing of an event is late or unpredictable. It usually gets a good laugh. But besides perpetuating an assumption that Indigenous people have to justify themselves to Settler culture, when this concept is relegated to a passing joke, we miss just how important this Indigenous view of time is. As Randy Woodley critiques, "Modern notions of time have taken over American culture to our detriment."[32] To slow down and pace storytelling in a way that allows reflection is key to a deeper engagement that recognizes stories are not just ideas, but part of human identity. And Indigenous elders embody the wisdom of the stories they pass on to the next generation. Thus, to respect elders' contributions as wisdom keepers and storytellers is vital. For a Settler culture that often equates aging with decline and irrelevance, including within Christian communities, to listen to Indigenous stories with the respect of elders must be embraced and practiced. This practice can give Settler-Christians a window into the relational realities of the "great cloud of witnesses" (Heb 12:1) we are invited to honor and learn from. We do not just give homage to elders, we give our presence and attention, respectfully listening to stories that shape us.

Implications for Settler-Christians

With this understanding in mind, how can the many Christians who are part of Cascadia's Settler history engage a storytelling praxis? What does it look like to foster a culture of listening and relationship with Indigenous people, a commitment to embody the truths Christians profess? This essay

---

32. Woodley, *Shalom*, 137. He continues, "Time (Euro-western time) and 'efficiency' are the values that override everything else in our lives. These two short-sighted values, which are in most cases antithetical to shalom, enforce broad categorical assumptions via snap judgments, quick-fix solutions, and prejudice."

concludes with implications of a storytelling praxis for Settler-Christians in Cascadia.[33]

Engage Yourself

Grasping the concepts of this essay is an important step towards building Indigenous–Settler relationships, but if a person and/or group of people—i.e., Settler-Christians—are not prepared to engage vulnerably in this storytelling praxis, the likelihood of developing positive relationships is low. Key here is assessing one's openness to new perspectives. If Settler-Christians remain convinced that a Westernized approach to the gospel of Jesus, one that prioritizes abstract truths and hierarchical structures for community, Indigenous–Settler relationships will remain strained. A sense of Settler superiority will prevent the depth of engagement needed to engage the identity-forming nature of storytelling.[34] On the contrary, with a genuine openness to explore how Indigenous perspectives can enrich identity, including Christian identity, Settler-Christians should engage key perspectives within Indigenous worldviews. For example, this can include learning about the importance of land and identity or the nature of reconciliation as an ongoing journey. Settler-Christians need to receive the gift of these Indigenous perspectives as there is a wealth of wisdom we can learn from Indigenous people.[35]

Engage Place

From this openness to engage oneself, individually and corporately, Settler-Christians need to move beyond the ideas of Indigenous perspectives to

---

33. For a more in-depth overview of key areas of Indigenous-Settler engagement, see Mennonite Church Canada's trilogy responding to the Truth and Reconciliation Commission of Canada. The trilogy includes Heinrichs, *Wrongs to Rights: How Churches Can Engage the United Nations Declaration on the Rights of Indigenous Peoples*, Woelk and Heinrichs, *Yours, Mine, Ours: Unravelling the Doctrine of Discovery*, and Friesen and Heinrichs, *Quest for Respect: The Church and Indigenous Spirituality*.

34. Additionally, at a broader social level, such attitudes of Settler superiority only serve to perpetuate the ways systemic racism pervades North American society in repeated othering of Indigenous people. See Hogarth and Fletcher, *A Space for Race*.

35. For example, I've personally benefited from Randy Woodley's description of the Indigenous perspective of the "Harmony Way" as it has deepened my understanding of shalom in the vision for humanity we see in Scripture. See Woodley, *Shalom*, 20–22.

the places these ideas take root. Broadly, Cascadia has a diverse history of Indigenous peoples. There are many shared Cascadian Indigenous stories that Settler-Christians must learn; each local place has unique Indigenous people and culture, from larger urban centers like Portland, Seattle, and Vancouver, to suburban and rural communities like Chilliwack, Longview, and Salem. To be faithful in loving our literal neighbors, Settler-Christians need to learn the local stories of Indigenous people in our own communities.[36] Read local biographies and attend local Indigenous events without an agenda—just show up to listen. If you are a pastor or church leader, invite local Indigenous Christians to share their story in your church community. For churches or other groups, consider hosting or participating in community education sessions.[37] And during these experiences, Settler-Christians can practice respectful listening and presence with elders in engaging the oral history and traditions in contextual ways.

Engage Relationships

Displaying an openness to learn and engaging in local education are important steps, but a storytelling praxis also invites relationships with people in your place. Essential to reconciliation is the nature of the relationships in the process. Working as a Settler-Christian himself, John Paul Lederach regularly engages in peacebuilding with Indigenous people around the world, and he offers this challenge: "The moral imagination rises with the capacity to imagine ourselves in a relationship, the willingness to embrace complexity without reliance on dualistic polarity, the belief in the creative act, and acceptance of the inherent risk required to break violence and to venture on unknown paths that build constructive change."[38] Here, Settler-

---

36. For example, the website www.native-land.ca is a good place to start as the website gives direction to local Indigenous groups' websites and contact information. This can be a helpful resource to foster knowledge about and connection with local Indigenous groups in one's own area.

37. For example, the Kairos Blanket exercise is an excellent experiential learning session that highlights the impact of colonialism in North America (https://www.kairosblanketexercise.org/). Additionally, there are several documentary films on Indigenous–Settler relationships (e.g. *Reserve 107*, www.reserve107thefilm.com).

38. Lederach, *The Moral Imagination*, 29. Lederach recognizes the vulnerability of this suggestion in this poignant poem: "Reach out to those you fear / Touch the heart of complexity / Imagine beyond what is seen / Risk vulnerability one step at a time" (*The Moral Imagination*, 177).

Christians need to be attentive to and repent of the past injustice against Indigenous people so as not to repeat the mistakes of the past. Too often Indigenous people, including Indigenous Christians, are treated as outsiders, viewed with suspicion or as special projects. Andrew Victor, Stó:lō chief and Christian pastor, recently offered this pointed rebuke to Settler-Christians: "I don't have to be someone's Samaritan."[39] Settler-Christians need to understand what it is like for Indigenous people to repeatedly be treated like Samaritans, like outsiders. Instead, without an agenda, talk to your Indigenous friends, neighbors, or coworkers. Listen to their stories of life in your place. Sit with the discomfort of the difficulties they have faced and refuse the impulse to fix the problem yourself.

This storytelling praxis will require recognition of the historical rootedness of identity in Cascadia. There are complex ways in which Cascadia's many narrative identities are formed in this place which includes both Indigenous and Settler groups. For Settler-Christians, this recognition will necessitate listening and engaging Indigenous stories in a way that stretches self-understanding, deepens engagement with our local places, and, most importantly, is rooted in relationships with the Indigenous people around us. Cascadia will no doubt continue as a culturally diverse region. And as socioeconomic and political developments adapt to this reality, my hope is that a storytelling praxis can lead to Indigenous–Settler relationships that contribute together to the peace of Cascadia.[40]

Bibliography

Cameron, Laura. *Openings: A Meditation on History, Method, and Sumas Lake.* Montreal: McGill-Queen's University Press, 1997.
Charles, Mark, and Soong-Chan Rah. *Unsettling Truths: The Ongoing, Dehumanizing Legacy of the Doctrine of Discovery.* Downers Grove: InterVarsity, 2019.
Diewert, Dave. "White Christian Settlers, the Bible, and (De)colonization." In *Buffalo Shout, Salmon Cry: Conversations on Creation, Land Justice, and Life Together*, edited by Steve Heinrichs, 127–37. Kitchener, ON: Herald, 2013.
Friesen, Jeff, and Steve Heinrichs, eds. *Quest for Respect: The Church and Indigenous Spirituality.* Winnipeg: Mennonite Church Canada, 2016.

---

39. Victor, "Unceded: Land Acknowledgement." Victor elaborated this point by explaining how Christians often have a high view of Scripture but we don't have a high view of cultures. Needed, therefore, is deeper consideration for how different cultures may carry the faith through the generations.

40. Jer 29:7.

Gastil, Raymond, and Barnett Singer. *The Pacific Northwest: Growth of a Regional Identity*. Jefferson, NC: McFarland, 2010.

Heinrichs, Steve, ed. *Buffalo Shout, Salmon Cry: Conversations on Creation, Land Justice, and Life Together*. Kitchener, ON: Herald, 2013.

———, ed. *Wrongs to Rights: How Churches Can Engage the United Nations Declaration on the Rights of Indigenous Peoples*. Winnipeg: Mennonite Church Canada, 2016.

Hogarth, Kathy, and Wendy L. Fletcher. *A Space for Race: Decoding Racism, Multiculturalism, and Post-Colonialism in the Quest for Belonging in Canada and Beyond*. New York: Oxford University Press, 2018.

Honouring the Truth, Reconciling for the Future: Summary of the Final Report of the Truth and Reconciliation Commission of Canada. Canada: The Truth and Reconciliation Commission of Canada, 2015. http://www.trc.ca/assets/pdf/Honouring_the_Truth_Reconciling_for_the_Future_July_23_2015.pdf.

King, Thomas. *The Truth about Stories: A Native Narrative*. Toronto: House of Anansi, 2003.

Lederach, John Paul. *The Moral Imagination: The Art and Soul of Building Peace*. New York: Oxford University Press, 2005.

Lederach, John Paul, and America Ferrera. "The Ingredients of Social Courage." *On Being with Krista Tippett*, October 24, 2019. Podcast, MP3 audio, 51:34. https://onbeing.org/programs/america-ferrera-john-paul-lederach-how-change-happens-in-generational-time-jun2018/.

MacIntyre, Alasdair. *Whose Justice? Which Rationality?* Notre Dame: University of Notre Dame Press, 1988.

MacIntyre, Alasdair, and Joseph Dunne. "Alasdair MacIntyre on Education: In Dialogue with Joseph Dunne." *Journal of Philosophy of Education* 36 (2002) 1–19.

Orange, Tommy. *There There*. New York: Knopf, 2018.

Point Bolton, Rena, and Richard Daily. *Xwelíqwiya: The Life of a Stó:lo Matriarch*. Athabasca: Athabasca University Press, 2013.

Senehi, Jessica. "Constructive Storytelling: A Peace Process." *Peace and Conflict Studies* 9.2 (2002) article 3. https://nsuworks.nova.edu/pcs/vol9/iss2/3.

Silver, Ray. "Welcome." Opening Address at Journey of Reconciliation Conference, Columbia Bible College, Abbotsford, BC, April 2016.

Todd, Douglas. *Cascadia: The Elusive Utopia; Exploring the Spirit of the Pacific Northwest*. Vancouver: Ronsdale, 2008.

Victor, Andrew. "Unceded: Land Acknowledgement." Lecture, Trinity Western University, Langley, BC, December 3, 2019.

Victor, Patti. "Walking Together." Interviewed by David Warkentin. *Christ & Cascadia*, December 20, 2016. http://www.journal.christandcascadia.com/2016/12/20/walking-together/.

Warkentin, David. "The Cascadian Self." *Christ & Cascadia*, November 5, 2018. http://www.journal.christandcascadia.com/2018/11/05/the-cascadian-self/.

Woelk, Cheryl, and Steve Heinrichs, eds. *Yours, Mine, Ours: Unravelling the Doctrine of Discovery*. Winnipeg: Mennonite Church Canada, 2016.

Woodley, Randy. "Cowboys and Indians: Dismantling the Western, Settler-Colonial Worldview (Part 1)." *Red Letter Christians*, April 2019. https://www.redletterchristians.org/cowboys-and-indians-dismantling-the-western-settler-colonial-worldview-part-i/.

———. "Ending the Reconciliation Paradigm." Lecture, Inhabit Conference, Seattle, April 2019.

———. *Shalom and the Community of Creation*. Grand Rapids: Eerdmans, 2012.

Wrobel, David M., and Michael C. Steiner. *Many Wests: Place, Culture, and Regional Identity*. Lawrence: University Press of Kansas, 1997.

3

Faith after Atheism

Christian Theology and Spiritual Formation in a Landscape of Default Agnosticism

Todd Wiebe

> Ravia of Basra was seen running through the streets of the town carrying a pot of fire in one hand and a bucket of water in the other. When asked what she was doing, she said, "I want to put out the fires of hell and burn down the rewards of paradise."
> She prayed, "O Lord, if I worship You for of Fear of Hell,
> then burn me in Hell;
> if I worship You for the rewards of Paradise,
> then exclude me from Paradise;
> but if I worship You for Yourself alone,
> then deny me not your Eternal Beauty."[1]

To talk about Christian mission is to talk about the mission of Jesus Christ. Mission, as David Bosch echoing Karl Barth has reminded us, is an attribute of God before it is a task of the church. "In attempting to flesh out the Missio Dei concept, the following could be said: In the new image mission is not primarily an activity of the church, but an attribute of God.

---

1. Barnstone and Barnstone, *Book of Woman Poets*, 90. Taylor, *Holy Envy*.

God is a missionary God."[2] As Jesus said, "If you have seen me, you have seen the Father"[3] and "I am the fulfillment of the law."[4] When reflecting on Cascadia, what might missional faith look like in a landscape of agnosticism by default?

We have often been reminded, in Christian scholarship and practice, that Christian faith without witness is not Christian faith at all. However, we have also pushed past the idea that we should seek to simply change the other person. It is true that evangelism and witness have in some expressions provided historical examples of triumphalism, domination, and ignorance. For these reasons, and some others, we have the sense that many people in Cascadia are not at all interested in hearing about what we call the gospel.

Cascadia is among the least churched regions in the Western world. If one were to focus on areas within the region making up British Columbia, Washington, and Oregon, looking for the most "secular" of all, that focus would move towards Vancouver and then to places like The University of British Columbia, or to places like my community, North Vancouver. On Easter Sunday the community newspaper in my neighborhood ran an article outlining a study that on the North Shore the rate of church attendance is 3 percent.[5] The article mentioned, as well, that though very few people attend church, most still do not profess absolute disbelief in God. People are not, then, closed off to the transcendent; rather, people lead lives defined as secular. Our neighbors are mostly or entirely secular. But so are we. The idea that our neighbors are secular while we are religious is not a helpful or accurate description. Those of us who do attend church regularly are secular, too. Most people would maintain that in fact we live in a secular culture. Even those who participate consistently in religious services or practices navigate mostly well in this secular environment and are thus just about as secular as their neighbors. The point of saying this is not condemnation but rather to point out our solidarity instead of some artificial separation between the religiously observant and the majority in our culture. Instead, if we are to consider our neighbors, who do not believe what we believe in matters of faith, such consideration could most helpfully start with a more thoughtful definition of secularity.

2. Bosch, *Transforming Mission*, 382 (Kindle loc. 9484).
3. John 14:9 (ESV).
4. Matt 5:17.
5. Canseco, "Most B.C. Residents Believe in God."

The book *Leaving Christianity*, based on an extensive study of church attendance in Canada, points out that the high-water mark for participation in church was in the year 1971.[6] Since then attendance has gone pretty much downhill. Interpretations of the study posit that it may not be the case that a large swath of religious people became non-religious, but rather that going to church was the societal expectation. Once that expectation was removed, however, with guilt and obligation no longer effective, large numbers of people decided to simply stop attending. The authors also point out the idea that conservative churches grow while more liberal churches fade is a myth. All denominations saw decline in the time covered in the study. There may be something noteworthy in the idea, however, that conservative churches grow or hold steady while liberal churches do not. While all denominations faced decline, the conservative expressions held out a little longer before the decline became evident. This may be because of the identity that comes with conservatism. Conservative expressions of faith or politics or views on sports and culture tend to starkly express what is believed and who is in or out, good or bad. This clarity can offer a sense of identity. In turn, this identity can break down once people start challenging the orthodoxy by asking questions, but a defined identity, even if that identity is ultimately faulty, can help people through the day. Defined identity can tell us what to think about social problems or about people who are unlike us or about the most intractable problems facing our world. Here is where a hint of how we might approach matters of witness and evangelism begins to appear. The questions to be considered are around matters of identity and secularity. How do we define ourselves in the world in which we live, and if we have not given up on being open to the transcendent, what might it mean to be secular and yet to have faith?

Canadian philosopher Charles Taylor has looked exhaustively at what "secular" means. In his book *A Secular Age*, Taylor asks how the Western world became a secular world. For Taylor there are no "straight line stories." That is, there was not simply an awakening that moved people to throw off the vestiges of religion. Instead, Taylor describes how movements within faith and religion contributed to what we now call secularism. Taylor says that he intends to ask one question: "Why was it virtually impossible to not believe in God in 1500 in the West, when by 2000 non-belief was very easy, indeed assumed?" Taylor outlines three "construals"—three ways of seeing the world that were broken down and largely abandoned in the

---

6. Clarke and Macdonald, *Leaving Christianity*, 5

five-hundred-year span on which he focuses. Firstly, he says, events in the natural world were explained by belief in God.[7] Storms and skies and times; weather and clouds were explained by God and by God's blessing or judgment. Secondly, the rituals of society were ordered by a shared concept of God.[8] The calendar and the seasons were marked by religious order. In the years between then and now, that ordering shifted from being religious to being civic, and now it is shifting again to being about the school calendar and events of sport or popular culture.

Thirdly, people lived in an enchanted world.[9] Objects were thought in and of themselves to have spiritual meaning and power. This was a power that could be exerted into the world and even over people. Taylor argues that the Christian church was largely responsible for disenchanting the world. For example, the idea that a chair or a mask or any other object projects meaning and power was seen to be pagan, not Christian. So, the church worked to break this idea down. People were reminded that God, not that mask or that painting, has power. It is a long road from then to where we are now, but Taylor says this process of disenchantment was largely a project of religion and the Christian church in particular.

There has been some pushback to Taylor on this. Perhaps even our secular neighbors see the world as more enchanted than we sometimes think. Whatever the case, Taylor uses the idea of disenchantment to discuss the concept of the self. How do people view themselves? How do we make sense of who we are in the world? For Taylor, as the three construals mentioned above broke down, people began to have different ideas of the self. He says that before the secular age the self was seen as "porous," that is, open to influence by the enchanted world. In the move to secularity, however, the self slowly became seen as "buffered," that is mostly or entirely closed. Meaning was not projected from the world to the self, but rather the self, particularly the mind, decided and determined how to make sense of the world.

The age of secularity, Taylor argues, affects not only non-faith, but faith as well. So, if we are to talk about "connecting with our secular neighbors" we must accept that we do so as people who do not believe as people did five hundred years ago or more. We must face the question of the desire to go back in time to this earlier stage rather than lean into the new reality before us and around us. For example, I have yet to meet someone,

---

7. Taylor, *Secular Age*, 25.
8. Taylor, *Secular Age*, 25
9. Taylor, *Secular Age,* 26.

no matter how religious they are, who answers positively to the question, "Would you prefer to live in the year 1500?" And yet, if more people believed in God back then, and if presumably believing in God makes things better, wouldn't it be preferable to live then instead of now?

So, how do we connect with our secular neighbors? There are clearly some major shifts happening in the Christian church currently, including new forms of Christian community and church plants. It may be the case that most new initiatives are basically new forms of similar theology. In starting a new work there are certainly questions of culture and practice. How can we do things differently? How will this work look? There should also be questions of faith. How are we going to design things differently because we believe differently than we did years ago? What are the fundamental theological shifts that dictate how we will structure and carry out this work? For me, the difference is hope. Christian faith has often been presented as a rescue mission from infernal flame and terror. I think that we do better to understand that God, in Christ, is making all things new. Ours is a story of hope, and when seen as such, it alters the way in which we speak or share faith with neighbors and friends who have been defined as secular.

The infernal-rescue-mission theological approach has been accompanied, in evangelical circles, by a particular model of evangelism. That model is defined by the descriptor "attractional." We live and work among many people who have no religious narrative at all. Church and Christian faith have not been part of their cultural memory. Therefore, in this context one of the first things that ought to change is our allegiance to attractional models of church.

A community of reflection and photography has arisen around abandoned shopping malls. Not all of these malls are old, but they have fallen into economic collapse due to the changing retail landscape. They are often referred to as "ghost malls."[10] If there is one word to describe malls, as we have known them, it is "attractional." Many now carry an apocalyptic look. Retail is decidedly not dead, but many malls are.

The first enclosed mall in Canada was here in Cascadia. It was Park Royal in West Vancouver, opened in 1950. For decades it remained relatively unchanged. There were certainly some additions and major expansions and new stores are part of the attraction of a mall, but things mostly stayed the same. The devotion to the attractional model was unchallenged

---

10. Lawless, "America's Creepiest Abandoned Malls."

and the shoppers kept coming—until recently. Park Royal, like many other retail shopping centers, was impacted by the change in consumer habits driven largely by the Internet. People could now purchase most things that they wanted without leaving home.

In the last few years Park Royal did something akin to what many churches have done as they have faced societal shift and potential decline. Park Royal doubled down. What was built to replace the old mall is now a "Lifestyle Centre." The attractional ante was raised with spas and pubs, anchor "lifestyle" stores. When I say that churches have done the same, I mean that many of the churches that are considered successful or thriving have managed to find attractional ways to continue to draw a crowd with promises of events for every age and seamless almost slick running of everything from parking to video presentation. I used to say, in years of pastoral work in churches, that even for smaller churches, people wanted to be sure that the church had every program they wanted or needed, for whenever they chose to show up. But I don't think that malls are coming back, just as bank branches are not coming back. So, what about churches? How do we connect with our secular neighbors if the attractional model is in its death throes?

If we have been living in a secular age for generations, then much of the openness to faith, to the Christian gospel, will come after atheism (or a form thereof). We must face the truth that most of our neighbors do not experience a "God shaped hole" in their lives. This it to say that they may struggle with questions of existence and meaning, but the truth is for most that they have been able to establish positive moral living, love for family and community, and some sense of obligation beyond themselves just fine without Christian faith.

John Flett points out that as the influence of the church began to wane in Europe, "a corrosive secularism and nascent paganism grew within Christendom's ruins."[11] Religious leaders looked for a "point of contact" with society, a means by which to anchor the religious message, even in a world becoming more secular. The point of contact that was largely agreed upon was guilt.[12] Suffice it to say that it is easy to see how such a point of contact led to conversion and sanctification being understood as personal, based in the individual and largely about moral reform.

This faith within a moralism frame was bolstered by the centrality of belief—that is, the idea that it is first and foremost what we believe that

---

11. Flett, *Witness of God*, Kindle loc. 98.
12. Flett, *Witness of God*, Kindle loc. 100.

determines our eternal destiny. In Christian history this has not always been the case, but in post-Reformation Christendom belief has been the deciding factor. In the evangelical church of my upbringing, this is what it meant to "pray the prayer." You were to declare first of all your own sinfulness, your own deserving of punishment. Then you were to declare your faith, belief, and acceptance of Jesus. This then would "save" you.

In a secular age, perhaps belief is not what is going to be the most beneficial frame for mission—at least, not individual, personal belief that is focused on moral reform. James Carse, formerly of Yale University, argues that there is major difference between belief and enquiry. Carse mentions that a compendium of Christian belief in the world called *Creeds and Confessions of Faith in the Christian Church* runs five volumes in length. His point is that belief might not be what matters most. Belief is a stance. Evangelicals and other Christians have loved to think that faith is largely about taking stands, but as Jason Byassee, professor at Vancouver School of Theology, has said, "I hope that Christians have something better than a stance."[13]

Enquiry moves us out into the neighborhood. Instead of promoting attractional models of church that are based on bringing people from the world into the church, enquiry means that we look to establish gatherings, ministries, and events that present Christian understanding and the implications of a hopeful gospel in the world itself. We have a model of encouraging enquiry in Jesus himself. He rarely pressed for decision but rather asked questions. These questions still resonate in our world today if we ask them well and translate them culturally.

- "Why do you see the speck in your neighbor's eye and not the log in your own?"[14]
- "Can any of you by worrying, add a single hour to your span of life?"[15]

Or a devastating question in our world today,

- "For who is greater, the one who is at the table or the one who serves?"[16]

Locally I have participated in some gatherings and events that have sought to work according to such a model. Another minister and I from different

13. Byassee, "Christianity in the American South."
14. Matt 7:3–5.
15. Luke 12:25.
16. Luke 22:27.

denominations partner up to run events that we call "Tasting Room Theology." We book out local craft breweries or tea shops, everything from gyms to olive oil stores. We bring in twenty to fifty people who hear from the owner and learn about the business. In turn, the locally owned company gets some new customers and visibility. We then have a speaker on a topic of cultural and theological concern. These have included "Scotch, Chocolate, and Death"; "Faith and Mental Health"; "To Hell with Hell?"; "Coffee with the Damned"; "Is Church Dangerous?" (with three former pastors talking about faith); and an upcoming event at a local high-end fitness center on "The Quantified Life."

A second series of gatherings that we have run is a partnership with a local psychology practice. This is called the "North Shore Stress and Anxiety Clinic." Doctors from the clinic come to the church to give a talk on a topic such as "Understanding Obsessive Compulsive Disorder" or "Post-Traumatic Stress Disorder" or "Depression in Teenagers," "General Anxiety Disorder," and so on. The gathering is mostly of people from the community, and the two sponsoring churches simply welcome and present why this presentation lines up with our Christian faith and hope, and why we welcome such events in our church buildings. Along the same lines, we have organized community symposiums. A well-attended recent event was called "Caring for Aging Parents." The intent was to help the community practically, emotionally, and spiritually, but we also outlined at the event why it was at a church and what Christian hope means in the context of caring for someone who is dying. What better place to outline a hopeful eschatology than among those considering the end of things as they see it?

Locally we are also learning from the ministry and example of Barry Jung. Barry helps run and organize many "neighboring" events and activities.[17] His concept is built upon the model of mission into the neighborhood and on the important idea that God is with our neighbors as well as with us. Barry has taught many of us a lot about connecting with secular neighbors. He points out that one of the very first things that has to be dropped is the sense that a neighbor is a project. There are theological underpinnings to neighborhood ministry, first among them being that the gospel is hope and good news for all.

As we consider how to connect with our secular neighbors there are certainly theological understandings and shifts required. We so often live faith as if theology is fixed. While we can remain grateful for the past, we

17. See Jung, "Art of Neighbouring."

are not imprisoned by it. Nostalgia is fleeting as a virtue. Nostalgia is a powerful feeling, but it is not mission. No matter what we feel about Christian mission in the years ahead, it must be forward looking; there is simply no other option. Christian mission can never be described by the contention that "things used to be better." Bertrand Russell said that nostalgia is "homesickness for a place that never existed."[18] Nostalgia is powerful not only in the church, but in the world. Secular people speak out regularly to keep the local bowling alley the same, even though they may never go there anymore. While few actually visit bowling alleys, the community still objects to seeing them demolished to make way for the new condo development. True Christian mission will see that we have something so much better to offer the world than nostalgia, beginning with hope. Connecting with our secular neighbors must be hopeful. The Christian ought to be the most hopeful person in the room. This again is because of an important piece of theological understanding. Christians must see that in the end, it is not our future or fate or eternal destiny that matters most. Rather, it is the future of Jesus Christ. And his future is established and secure.

Finally, a practical note to consider in connecting with secular neighbors is the manner in which we as Christians relate to other religions. William Cavanaugh in *The Myth of Religious Violence* speaks of the people who truly kill a religious movement. He says that such deaths are caused by those he calls the "true believers." What he means is that to grow and reach out, religions must be open to the other. They must welcome the stranger. He presents this as key in the Abrahamic covenant. Therefore, in relation to those who believe differently than our own Christian communities, we ought to take up some advice from Krister Stendahl, who had among his rules of engagement of other faiths:

1. When trying to understand another religion, ask adherents of that religion, not enemies.

2. Do not compare your best with their worst.[19]

If we are to connect with our secular neighbors, there are no doubt mostly practical aspects to this call. We have to engage; we have to invite and

---

18. Quoted by Peter Nosco at a Tasting Room Theology Event, April 2019, attributed to Bertrand Russell.

19. Krister Stendahl (formerly of Harvard Divinity School, bishop of Stockholm), in a 1985 press conference on the occasion of opposition to the planned construction of a temple for the LDS Church; quoted in Taylor, *Holy Envy*, 65.

connect and listen. Barry Jung points out that the most important aspect of growth in a growing neighboring ministry he has seen is the ability to *receive* from our neighbors. This demonstrates a trust in the other and a trust in God.

In closing, I turn to Karl Barth, who was known as the "cheerful theologian." He warned against transferring an anxious Christianity onto our understanding of Jesus.[20] Christianity that sees itself as an infernal rescue mission will be by nature anxious. Christianity that sees itself as first fruits of the renewal of all things will be hopeful. "The Christian hopes in order to show thereby that there is good cause and ground for all men [sic] and the whole world to hope with him."[21] In the end, our call is a call of hope. If we long for another age, one that is past, and never actually existed, we will fail to hear the call of Christ for mission today.

Bibliography

Barnstone, Aliki, and Willis Barnstone, eds. *A Book of Woman Poets from Antiquity to Now*. Rev. ed. New York: Schocken, 1992.

Barth, Karl. *Church Dogmatics*. London: T. & T. Clark, 2004.

Bosch, David. *Transforming Mission: Paradigm Shifts in Theology of Mission*. 20th anniversary ed. Kindle ed. Maryknoll, NY: Orbis, 2011.

Byassee, Jason. "Christianity in the American South: Is This What We Believe?" Presentation at a Tasting Room Theology Event at Sons of Vancouver Distillery, 2016.

Canseco, Mario. "Most B.C. Residents Believe in God, but Few Attend Church Regularly: Survey." *North Shore News*, April 18, 2019.

Clarke, Brian, and Stuart Macdonald. *Leaving Christianity: Changing Allegiances in Canada Since 1945*. Montreal: McGill-Queen's University Press, 2017.

Flett, John. *The Witness of God: The Trinity, Missio Dei, Karl Barth, and the Nature of Christian Community*. Kindle ed. Grand Rapids: Eerdmans, 2010.

Jung, Barry. "The Art of Neighbouring (Neighbourhood Small Grants Available Until April 9)." Church for Vancouver, March 22, 2018. https://churchforvancouver.ca/the-art-of-neighbouring-neighbourhood-small-grants-available-until-april-9/.

Lawless, Seph. "A Haunting Look Inside America's Creepiest Abandoned Malls." *Huffington Post*, https://sephlawless.com/inside-creepiest-abandoned-malls/.

Taylor, Barbara Brown. *Holy Envy: Finding God in the Faith of Others*. New York: HarperCollins, 2019.

Taylor, Charles. *A Secular Age*. Cambridge: Harvard University Press, 2007.

---

20. Barth, *Church Dogmatics*, IV.3.1:239.
21. Barth, *Church Dogmatics*, IV.3.2:933.

PLANTING THE SEEDS

"But now I will not deal with the remnant of this people as I did in the past," declares the Lord Almighty. "The seed will grow well, the vine will yield its fruit, the ground will produce its crops, and the heavens will drop their dew. I will give all these things as an inheritance to the remnant of this people."

—ZECHARIAH 8:11-12 (NIV)

"But things have changed. I'm taking the side of my core of surviving people:
Sowing and harvesting will resume,
Vines will grow grapes,
Gardens will flourish,
Dew and rain will make everything green.
My core survivors will get everything they need—and more."

—ZECHARIAH 8:11-12 (MSG)

4

Exploring the Theological "Why" of Church Planting

Darrell Guder

Mission after Christendom

IN A GERMAN DISCUSSION of the large issues of church, church planting, and church experimentation in Western Christendom, we might find ourselves talking about the institutional church in terms of the provision of *Flächendeckende Dienste*. It's a very Germanic term for the church's activity of ensuring that the entire territory is supplied with religious resources: it means "providing ministries that cover the territory." The geography of European Christendom is divided up into parishes, each of which has at its center a distinctive building with a spire or tower that contains bells. Everyone lives within hearing range of those bells, and all the basic rhythms of life are governed by their tolling. They mark the major thresholds of life: birth, vocation, marriage, parenting, and death. The layout of those distinctive buildings with spires and bells and cemeteries is arranged in such a way that everyone can receive the benefits of Christian identity within walking distance. That access brings with it the assurance that one will receive eternal salvation when the final chapter closes—everyone can receive the benefits of Christian faith by living by the church's rules. We call this vast and complex cultural system Christendom.

It is a continuing challenge to understand and analyze the story of Christendom in order to grasp its impact and its importance, even as it is going through radical change. Part of that analysis is to grapple with the theological problems that we inherit from this Christendom legacy. For decades, I have sought to interpret these problems with the term "reductionism." I have claimed that Western Christendom, over time, has profoundly reduced the gospel to personal savedness. In doing that, it has reduced the church's purpose and function to the management of savedness. The result is a theology of the church that is inwardly focused, that centers upon the benefits of the gospel for the member and the ways that the member gains access to those benefits. The result is reductionistic because its grasp of the gospel and of the church is too small, too uni-dimensional, too vertical at the cost of the horizontal. The gospel is still heard and encountered, and God is still at work in the church's proclamation. But that is due to God's all-embracing grace and not the merit of either the institutional church or the compliant believer. I stress to my students that we can only address these themes fairly if we do so dialectically, recognizing the profound tensions that inhere in the legacy of Christendom. We must be cautious about oversimplifying the complex history of Christendom. God has not been absent through all the generations of priests celebrating masses and monks copying manuscripts . . . and missionaries evangelizing the Scots and the Picts!

A Complex Legacy

One outcome of this reductionism is the gradual disappearance of "mission" as a central theme of Western Christian theology. The missional focus of apostolicity as it is encountered in the New Testament record largely dissipates in the spread of Christianity to become an all-embracing cultural and political reality. The Constantinian establishment of Christianity and its institutions results in the comprehensive claim that Europe is rightly called "The Holy Roman Empire." In that empire, the church does its theological reflection with ecclesiologies that never mention or account for mission. Everything is Christian from the soil on which we are born to the soil in which we are buried. Like our calendars, every aspect of society can be described with the genitival definition of ownership: Domini, "of the Lord."

To be sure, mission continues as an activity of the church, especially on its boundaries to the still pagan tribes not yet evangelized. By the twelfth century, the Christianization of Europe from the Atlantic across to the

Russian Pacific coast was largely finished. Mission was a local activity and not a central definition of the church's purpose and action. Apostolicity was no longer the emphasis upon the continuation of the early church's sending and witnessing "to the ends of the earth," but was the guarantor of the genealogical purity of lineage traced back to the original twelve. Church planting was not an issue, because the bells were now heard everywhere in Christendom.

The modern missionary movement reintroduced "evangelization" and "church planting" into the vocabulary of Christendom. From William Carey's epochal "Inquiry" onward, we have heard the Great Commission at the end of Matthew as a direct challenge to the present-day church, after explaining it away for centuries as applying only to the pre-Constantinian world replaced by Christendom. With the rapid decline of Western Christian denominational cultures, church planting has become an electrifying theme and option. Our sister communities in the majority world outside Western Christendom are rapidly expanding, founding churches with energy and enthusiasm all across Africa, Southern and Eastern Asia, Latin America, and the South Pacific. And we are in this particular corner of North America exploring Christian witness in Cascadian soil. But we are no longer asking how to produce a religious system that will blanket the territory with access to Christian ministries. Many are asking whether church planting in the West should happen at all. Shouldn't we, after the blunders of Christendom, accept the judgment of history and give up expansionistic and triumphalistic distortions of Christianity? I will argue that there is a compelling theological "why" to the endeavor of church planting in our post-Christendom context that strongly affirms the ongoing validity of the mandate of the apostolic mission: planting witnessing communities.

But there are certainly ways of going about church planting in our context that are theologically hard to validate. There are many ways in which the Christendom legacy continues to haunt the scene with visions of cultural conquest and the reclamation of the hegemony of institutional Christianity. The prosperity gospel as developed in and exported by American proponents to much of the non-Christendom world is a highly questionable distortion of the apostolic mission mandate. In response to that aberration and other similar remnants of Christendom in the West, our undertaking must start with contrition, repentance, and humble modesty. There is no "Christian culture" that needs to be restored to power. This is why the thoughtful engagement with Christendom and its impact is so urgent: we need to be discerning about the temptations to distort the apostolic mission mandate, which we have done for centuries. As Christendom disappears into the sunset, we can hear the biblical mandate anew and discover what Christian witness today must look like if it is to be the responsible continuation of the apostolic mission. The challenge is summarized by Paul when he writes to the Philippians, "Only let your manner of life be worthy of the gospel of Christ" (Phil 1:27).

Biblical Formation for Mission

With this reference to Paul, we confront the biblical message as it relates to church planting. The skeptic, whether a critic or a proponent of Christendom, might argue that there is no "biblical message that relates to church planting." There are very good reasons to proceed with caution. But it may be regarded as an outcome of the missional church initiative of the last twenty years that the early Christian movement was, in fact, centrally and pervasively focused upon the mission mandate with which Acts begins: "You shall be my witnesses in Jerusalem, and in all Judea and Samaria and to the ends of the earth." For that purpose, the apostolic mission, starting at Pentecost, focused upon the formation of witnessing communities. The apostolic proclamation moved from the invitation of the gospel to "become fishers of people," to the formation of communities whose life and action both drew people to Christ and sent them out as his witnesses. The theological "why" for church planting is grounded then on the apostolic mission as its first generation. The apostolic invitation is thus followed by apostolic formation. Evangelization with invitation leads to catechesis, the outcome of which is baptized communities of intentional witnesses.

The "why" for church planting is then firmly rooted in the missionary mandate of the first-century Christian movement. This is an exegetical foundation for the theological unfolding of the identity and practice of a truly missional community. The New Testament documents largely focus upon that catechesis of witnessing communities. It is in the Gospel accounts of discipleship and the epistolary continuation of apostolic formation for mission that the Christian movement is shaped for its calling. This fundamental insight is supported by the rapidly expanding exploration of what has come to be called "missional hermeneutics," interpreting Scripture as the source and guide for the continuing formation for missional witness. And the continuation of that witness was the purpose of the founding of all the communities documented in the New Testament. It is yet another aspect of the reductionist impoverishment of Christendom's theological legacy that this missiocentric purposefulness of the biblical record gradually faded from the scene. Now we find ourselves in an exciting chapter of investigation and discovery as biblical scholars engage in rigorous biblical research, asking some version of this basic question: "How did this text continue the formation of faithfully witnessing communities then, and how does it do so today?" As the process of biblical exploration and community experimentation progresses, more dimensions of missional formation will emerge. We can, for instance, expect the distinctive emphases of missional formation in the Four Gospels to become more radically formative as we grasp the significance of the narratives of discipleship as they lead to our apostolate. With the disciples, the members of the Spirit-empowered community discover that their vocation to follow Jesus as his disciples is leading inexorably to their vocation as apostles, whose task is "to be with him and to be sent out to preach and have authority to cast out demons" (Mark 3:14–15).

The community formation which the New Testament attests is empowered by the presence and action of God's Spirit. It is the work of the Spirit to enable the hearing of the gospel to become the confession of this good news. The formation of communities of new believers is thus not an act of human entrepreneurship but a surprising initiative in which God's Spirit draws followers to Jesus and thus to each other as his witnesses in particular locations. The patterns of response and community formation are innumerable, but they always draw the new believer to the confession, "Jesus Christ is Lord." That confession bonds the respondent to others who share that experience, and out of that divinely enabled formation the missional church in particular places emerges and commences its spiritual journey. Church planting is, in that process, an outcome of God's initiation, ensuring that the apostolic mission continues its way towards "the ends of the earth" and "the drawing near of the kingdom" (Acts 1:8; Mark 1:15).

Missional Communities and Missional Leadership

As the theological "why" for church planting is further explored and tested, there is growing awareness that the Spirit appears to work in a twofold way to generate witnessing communities. The awakening and empowering of response to the gospel invitation is often accompanied by persons with particular giftedness for articulating the apostolic mandate in a specific context. As groups of witnesses coalesce and become identifiable communities, there is often an apostolic role that the Spirit uses to articulate the mission and elicit affirmative responses. The emergence of such missional communities is always mysterious and not reducible to pat cause and effect explanations. There is a profound modesty in the emerging community of witnesses, an awareness of God's agency, and a sense of delight with the surprises that God's Spirit reveals. The "apostolic interpreter" of God's call helps an emerging community sense "what God is doing." The result in such processes of community formation is a growing conviction of the priority of this new thing the Spirit is doing. What may have started as a living-room Bible study begins to take form as a called community, and with time, there is a strong sense that yet another expression of a new church is coming to fruition. The processes of discernment are diverse, but the outcome is a growing joy about this new thing God is doing. It cannot be organized, but with time such communities will find that their disciplined work with Scripture is leading them to take concrete steps together to define themselves and articulate their sense of their calling. They may discover, as have innumerable Catholic communities over time, that God has given them a particular "charism" of the gospel that becomes their lens for reading how the Spirit is working in their midst.

The formation of a new church is not so much planned as received and discovered. The key concept that will always define a missionally alert new church is witness. This basic New Testament term (the root is *martus*, martyr) aptly captures the core reality of the missional new church: the witness is a person whose life provides evidence of the gospel that God's Spirit uses for its purposes. Such persons drawn into community present their witness (*marturia*) before a watching world. Thus, their life corporately and individually is a process of witnessing (*marturein*) that the Spirit uses to draw others into the service of Christ. The missional centrality of witness in its many dimensions has been profoundly captured by Karl Barth in his exposition of the basic theology of the community of faith and service (this discussion is based upon Barth's discussion of "the vocation of man," and especially "the Christian as witness"[1]).

Barth develops his missional ecclesiology with a threefold movement that draws the basic convictions of the gospel into a theology of the church that is profoundly missiocentric. The Spirit gathers the community

---

1. K. Barth, *Church Dogmatics*, IV.3.2, 2nd half: para. 71, esp. 4.

of respondents to the good news of justification; as a gathered community they experience the presence of God's Spirit equipping them for his service, that is, their sanctification, and out of that redeeming good news their understanding of themselves as witnesses defines their vocation. For all followers of Jesus that vocation is witness: this is the undergirding understanding of the missional church. It is highly significant that justification and sanctification lead into and generate vocation as the overarching reality that defines Christian life and action. With the focus upon vocation, the reductionisms of Christendom are, in effect, challenged and overcome.

Discipleship for Apostolate

The theology of "why" supporting the planting of new churches includes the reinterpretation of "apostolate" and "apostolic." This immediately calls for rethinking of our interpretation of the seminal passage in Ephesians 4:11: "And his gift was that some should be apostles, some prophets, some evangelists, some pastors and teachers, for the equipment of the saints for the work of [service], for building up the body of Christ" (Eph 4:11–12). If Markus Barth is correctly guiding our interpretation of this basic ecclesiological biblical text with his suggestion that the five roles—apostle, prophet, evangelist, pastor-teacher—should be interpreted as the ways in which the word of God works in the community to equip the saints for the work of service, then the apostolic role equips the saints by focusing the community on God's mission and its calling to be and to do the witness to that mission.[2] The apostolic role in church planting is the Spirit-empowered articulation of God's mission and its translation into the particular context of the emerging missional community.

I am suggesting that, for fundamental missional reasons, apostolicity is more than descent or genealogy. The earliest Christian mission understood itself as apostolic not merely as a pedigree, but as its continuation of the primitive apostolic mission. I have contended that the purpose of the apostolic mission was the planting and nurture of witnessing communities: mission is the goal and action of the gathered community in a particular place. For the formation and action of the witnessing community, apostolicity is the sense of call and the provision of gifts for the planting of new missional congregations in obedience to God's mandate. Apostolicity is not an activity that "covers the territory" and facilitates access to the benefits of

---

2. M. Barth, *Ephesians 4–6*, 478–81.

Christian faith. Apostolic mission is not the preservation of an institutional legacy—say, the Presbyterian or Wesleyan presence. It is not a defense against the secularization of culture. Nor does it serve as the custodian of the artistic and architectural legacy of the institutional church in all its variety. It does not serve to reclaim the hegemony of Christianity in Western cultures, nor does it compete with other forms of Western religiosity. The basic "why" of church planting is the continuation and expansion of the apostolic mission as inspired and empowered by the triune God. Church planting is the consequence of the work of the Spirit in calling and forming witnesses and drawing them together for the practice of mission in a concrete context. There is no established pattern for the gathering of such communities. There is an infinite variety of ways in which people experience the gathering work of the Spirit and begin a communal journey of faith. At this point, the apostolicity and the catholicity of the church work together theologically in the service of the *missio Dei*.

Missional Witness: Being, Doing, and Saying Good News

As the experiments in church planting continue and expand, we see evidences of both the vocation of missional communities and of missional leaders. That evidence may take the form of the translation of the gospel into pre- and post-Christian contexts. It may be seen in the discovery of God's preparatory work in unexpected contexts. It may entail our recognizing how the continuation of the apostolic mission is happening now in the forming of witnessing communities shaped by Scripture and empowered by the Spirit. It may be witnessed to in missional communities for whom their vocation is becoming a transforming reality that focuses their lives on the service of Christ. They are discovering their utter dependence on prayer for their continuing formation. Their communities are forsaking old patterns of power manipulation as they learn to wait for the Lord and act out of a divinely given sense of consensus. And as they wait and learn, they risk experimental creativity serving their outward witness in the world. This is a journey to be celebrated as it arises out of God's faithfulness now and in the coming fullness of the reign of God.

God is the initiator and enabler of this missional journey. God's faithfulness will be made known within the community by the mutual recognition of calling and gifts to serve God's mission and not just our spiritual needs. The community will be characterized by its modesty about its journey, giving the glory to God and not to us. Its candor about its human weakness will be an essential part of its witness as it lives out of forgiveness. In every dimension of its life, its priority will be God's mission, defining its identity and its actions. As it grows and explores, it will recognize and appropriate the spiritual legacy of mission as a historical witness that guides, enriches, and challenges us today (neo-monasticism!). Its experimentation with the forms of gathering, equipping, and sending will enable it to address the challenges of our difficult mission fields in Western contexts. In this understanding of the "why" of church planting, mission will no longer be one of the strands of churchly activity but rather the basic definition of the church's nature, purpose, and action. Its goal will not be to cover the territory with religious practices and services, but to be, do, and say Christ's witness "in Jerusalem, Judea, Samaria, and to the ends of the earth."

Bibliography

Barth, Karl. *Church Dogmatics*. Edited by Thomas F. Torrance and Geoffrey W. Bromiley, translated by Geoffrey W. Bromiley. Edinburgh: T. & T. Clark, 1962.

Barth, Markus. *Ephesians 4–6*. Anchor Bible 34A. New York: Doubleday, 1974.

5

A Sent Life Together

A Reflection on Missional Community in the Lonely and Secularized Area of Vancouver's Downtown Eastside

Stephen Bell

As Christendom in Canada began to crumble sometime after the First World War (1914–18), people in Vancouver really didn't seem to notice. It was probably because many of Christendom's rights and privileges never existed here in the first place.[1] And while the rest of the church in Canada continued to face disestablishment, losing the lion's share of their special privileges, British Columbians were already out surfing, "leaving God behind" back in the nineteenth century.[2] If you're reading this book and you grew up in a different time or in a different area other than present Cascadia, you need to know that even "cultural Christianity" isn't here anymore. Younger people don't say "I may not be *religious*, but I am *spiritual*" like their Gen-Xer parents do. Now they announce, proudly, that they are neither religious nor spiritual.

Let me give you an example of what I mean by that: there was a time when the members of our missional/incarnational community were

1. Marks, *Infidels and the Damn Churches*, 7.
2. Marks, *Infidels and the Damn Churches*, 7.

cleaning the blood off of a teenaged sex worker after she had a "bad date" in Vancouver's Downtown Eastside (DTES); and when we started talking to her about what our community was all about (and what we were even doing there to begin with), she told us that she "had no idea that Jesus was a part of Christianity." Think about that for a moment. This was a seventeen-year-old girl who was born here, who went to school a few blocks away from here, and who had probably worked down here for most of her post-pubescent life, and still she had no idea who Jesus was, what he did, or what the Holy Spirit continues to do. Of course she didn't run to the church with her problems. She didn't even know that Jesus had a second name to his title that made up the first six letters of our religion. And why would she? She's so far out of the Christendom loop that she's lapping the rest of the world. Younger people like her weren't taught Christianity at school. They didn't grow up going to Friday night youth groups, nor as kids did they ever drink powdered orange juice out of giant coolers in musty basements, coloring in pictures of Noah and his family stepping off of an ark. They didn't have Christian parents, nor did they in their formative years ever wonder where Jesus was in the midst of their suffering. And that's what's happening to the rest of Canada now. It's called post-Christendom.

So, here are some things to ask yourself and your congregation: in this time and place of Cascadian secularization, how would you talk to this teenage girl about the reconciling blood of Christ as he calls both her and the community of God into a greater well-being *together*? How do you have witnessing dialogue with people who are from a part of a city that is already entrenched in brokenness? How do you show who Christ is and what his community can do when the major social justice missions of the day are no longer spearheaded by the church?

For us, it began with putting things in perspective as to the reality of what was going on here, mainly done through an "exegesis of the community." Through our exegetical work, we learned that the government spends about a million dollars a day combating the problems in our eight-block area.[3] To put that into perspective, if our local presbytery sold everything they had (churches, land, everything) and put it all into helping the people here, we wouldn't have enough money to last a year. But along with our financial problem, we also have a problem with the HIV/Hep-C rate, which matches that of Botswana.[4] These things are difficult to handle when you're

3. McMartin, "High Cost of Misery."
4. See "Dan Rather Reports."

homelessly entrenched, perhaps also being forced into the area through the Correctional Service of Canada, which uses the "DTES" as a proverbial dumping ground for many of Canada's high-risk offenders on parole. It's also where those from the old mental health hospital were let off the bus one day when Riverview closed down. Adding even more fuel to this proverbial fire, we saw in our ongoing community exegesis that alcoholism and drug use in the area remained rampant; but as stated by Judy Graves, a legendary advocate for the homeless in Vancouver, "Alcoholism doesn't start with alcohol. It starts with a broken heart and a broken world."[5] There are words of wisdom there. And if you look closely at Judy's words, you'll hear the call to Christian mission, for a church without the broken is actually a *broken church*.[6]

But you don't have to stay in the DTES to see broken people. Loneliness runs rampant through the entire city of Vancouver. It's now such a problem that our major news outlets are doing interviews with local residents that state, "I was raised in Ottawa and in France, and Vancouver is, without a doubt, a city with no soul. People are polite and friendly, but that's as far as it goes. There is no depth whatsoever." Another stated, "I haven't made a new friend in Vancouver since university and I graduated nearly a decade ago. My few friends moved away, and I really haven't had a friend here for the past six or so years."[7]

The people of this place are indeed marked by the apprehension of organized spirituality, but although we are obsessed with things like justice, beauty, and healthy globalization, we are also a people who have a profound sense of emptiness.[8] But in this problem, the church can provide a solution. A community built for the glory of God and the repair of the community can and will bring fulfillment to the lives of broken, lonely people (both here and sent) in such a time and place as this.

Some years back, one of the original starters of our community was sent to a tent city aptly named "Oppenheimer Park." She put down a picnic blanket and called to the locals of the area as they walked by, asking, "Hey, do you want to be my friend?" And it worked. People sat down and began to talk. That's how lonely people are here—but that's also how quickly our community began to form around what God continues to do in the area.

5. White, *Fully Human*, 88.
6. Stetzer, "Connecting to a Post-Christendom World."
7. Baluja and Wilson, "You're Not Alone."
8. Lockhart, "Evangelism in Cascadia."

We finally knew an answer to the question: money is not what will eventually help the addiction, disease, and brokenness of the area—but a community grounded in the *missio Dei* for everyone could.

So, our "primitive salvationism" form of praxis came to Vancouver's Downtown Eastside in the form of a missionally sent incarnational movement, living in an old dentist office one block from Main and Hastings. Led initially by a commissioned husband and wife team, the goal was to follow the early missional markings of an incarnational community and then later, a hybrid of the New-Monastic movement. This sent witness was not going to happen by simply bringing bagged lunches to the area and then going home to our safe neighborhoods in different parts of the city when we were done for the day. It would happen through having "a sent life together" in the area. Together, and only together, did we believe that our mission would be able to live up to its vision of seeing the area rebuilt, restored, and renewed as per the ongoing prophecy found in Isaiah 61:4, which states, "They [the community of God in the local area along with others] will rebuild the ancient ruins [of a broken-down neighborhood but also ourselves] long since devastated [in Canada's poorest postal code]." But how the culturally postmodern/post-Christendom church should operate in its "sent" theology and praxis through the connection of gospel, church, and culture in order to graft the lonely into the family of God can be more than a little tricky. So, in case any of these terms are new to you, this is what I mean:

"New monastics are living intentional, disciplined lives in response to a critique of the culture . . . but the nature of that critique, and more importantly their understanding of the gospel, leads them more deeply into the culture and into mission in the midst of the world, not into a geographical isolation and purist withdrawal from the world."[9] As for the definition of what a "sent" missional church should look like, as stated by Darrell Guder, "This risen Lord now sends his disciples into the world to carry out the Mission of God that was the purpose and content of his life, death, and resurrection. The mission of the Christian church is defined by the entire event of the life, teaching, proclamation, and passion of Jesus."[10]

For us, these two theological definitions were to be carried out into a commission praxis by having Christians from all over the world relocate to

---

9. Wilson, *Living Faithfully*, Kindle loc. 104.
10. Guder, *Continuing Conversion*, Kindle locs. 629–31.

the margins[11] of the Downtown Eastside and to live in witness, to the best of our ability, in an incarnational way with themselves and with those in the area, not only giving a critique of the culture that it called into question,[12] but through growing deeper and wider as a *sent* community of God in *missio Dei*. As stated by my presbytery colleague Brian Fraser, this could not be done through an evangelical *monologue* (as many imagine evangelical witness happening), but through evangelical *dialogue*: through research and conversation with local residents, and then joining in on the repair, restoration, and renewal in an area full of disorientation and disrepair,[13] being attentive to the space around us and to the work God is doing in our very own neighborhood.[14]

As stated above, we got to know the area in question through the exegesis of the community,[15] but also through living in the community. Housing was attained at 219 Main Street not only for the missional church to live in but for the wider community as well: for those in the area who desperately needed both housing *and* the benefit of hospitality to the stranger.[16] As stated by Tim Dickau, another local Christian leader in East Vancouver, "It's hard to imagine living out the Kingdom of God if you don't inhabit the place."[17] Those sent to the community took jobs that most would have seen as "below them" in order to get to know the people in the area. One of our students even worked as the Front Desk Manager at the Empress Hotel, a place thought of by many to be one of the most dilapidated single-room-occupancy-unit living-spaces in the area. Through these actions, "God was sending His transforming Spirit into the area so that all could be transformed."[18] It must be stated again that this was not "us helping them," but a dialogue of everyone uplifting everyone—changing each other for the better. Bosch and Duckworth both speak to this in their books *Transforming Mission* and *Wide Welcome*, depicting how old-timers and newcomers

---

11. Andersen, "12 Marks of New Monasticism," 2.
12. Newbigin, *Foolishness to the Greeks*, 4.
13. Blenkinsopp, *Isaiah 56–66*, 77.
14. Smith and Pattison, *Slow Church*, 16.
15. Smith, "Urban Ministry," 12–15.
16. Andersen, "12 Marks of New Monasticism," 2.
17. Dickau, "Missional Theology."
18. Dickau, "Missional Theology."

in the church need to work with one another not only to survive but to flourish with others[19] as we are transformed together.[20]

The vision for those living in the old dental office "community house" was to carry out the purpose and content of the Christ event in the modern/local setting, diving deeper as a church community but also in its sent-ness. After the fact, local missiologist Ross Hastings had an idea taken from John 20:19–23, a pericope that he calls "the Greatest Commission" (in critique of what we have come to know as "the Great Commission" found in Matthew 28):

> . . . because [this commission] is the deepest and the widest. It is wide in that it connects theologically with the fullness of God's mission in terms of creation and redemption. The presence of Jesus as the risen One imparting shalom to his people and through them to the world evokes the notion of the new creation and the reconciliation of all things. It is the commission above all, however, because it connects the mission of the church deep into the eternal purpose of the Godhead. The sentness of the church is connected to the sentness of the Son by the Father, a sending planned in eternity past within the covenanting councils of God. Mission is expressed as flowing from within the very life of the Trinity.[21]

So that's what we were all trying to do. We began to worship regularly in a homeless shelter in front of Blood Alley, using its attic space (a former meth lab) for our offices and a prayer space. We invited those from work who began to trust us by working with us and seeing how we were living. Many community members started part-time jobs alongside those who were living with us while living out the proclamation of the gospel translated for the local area in the local area. Those living around us (and those we worked with) started to become interested in the lives we were living and how we were meeting some of the needs in the community through what people in the area thought were needs, not just what we thought were needs. After a time, they decided to check out our cell groups, our worship times, our accountability groups, and our apartment where we were sharing our lives together. But please note that there was no church building; just an old dentist office and a shelter we had to be out of by 9:30 p.m. so those who were at our events could also have a place to sleep at night. Seeing an opportunity

---

19. Bosch, *Transforming Mission*, 375.
20. Duckworth, *Wide Welcome*, Kindle loc. 70.
21. Hastings, *Missional God, Missional Church*, Kindle locs. 267–72.

here, I started to work in the shelter so as to have a better connection with those in the program and work as a liaison between both worlds, and so I could help many people in our community obtain jobs in the shelter (who had at least one year clean of substance abuse) that held to a living wage according to the area.

We began to see new options to put the lonely into families: at night, the homeless would stand in line out in front of the shelter just to talk to each other, even though it was the middle of summer and there was no competition for shelter space there. Again, notice not just the loneliness here but the attempt to connect with others in any way possible. We started a coffeehouse in the shelter where people in the community could drink coffee, play games, watch movies, and talk with those who lived around them. Out of this, a coffeehouse community was formed, where a cell group began to grow, and the gospel was witnessed from Scripture. The cell started to get so big that multiplication had to happen. People living in the single room occupancy units in the area started to ask if they could move into our community. The regular answer was, "You already have." As stated by Jean Vanier,

> In years to come, we are going to need many small communities which will welcome lost and lonely people, offering them a new form of family and a sense of belonging. In the past, Christians who wanted to follow Jesus opened hospitals and schools. Now that there are many of these, Christians must commit themselves to these new communities of welcome, to live with people who have no other family and to show them that they are loved and can grow to greater freedom and that they, in turn, can love and give life to others.[22]

After twenty-three people were living in the one location (filled also with post-gap-year students and locals from the area), and with most to all of them now living intentional/disciplined lives, additional housing was created. These different housing families also consisted of the addicted, former sex workers and those who were coming back to church after years of absence. Yet, somehow, the vast majority of us were now trying to be committed to missional/incarnational living. While the culture in the area was

---

22. Vanier, *Community and Growth*, 283. In light of recent revelations about Jean Vanier and the sexual abuse allegations toward women, Vanier now becomes problematic in a similar way to quoting from John Howard Yoder. Nevertheless, I am trying to draw here upon the principle of his teaching, without in any way trying to minimize his unethical and devastating personal behavior.

content with letting addicts, sex workers, and "part-time" Christian youth continue in their lifestyles (which is easy when you don't know them or what happens to them on a daily basis), our community responded with a critique: we are all called to a deeper life in Christ, helping each other repair our personal and communal brokenness. We all had to turn away from the idols present in our lives. In short, this was not only a call to "the others" but a call for all who lived in the house who wished to live transparent lives found in a deep calling of repentance.[23] After coming together and listening as a group, we quickly learned that any of our present actions would only lead to a form of isolation and "otherness," a lack of horizontal/communal connection. We asked for their forgiveness and, together, we all repented to God for the wrong we had done. David Bosch talked about that. He said that the mission of the Christian community involves the reversal of all the evil consequences of sin and that it doesn't just have a "vertical" dimension, but a dimension for those we are with as well.[24]

But getting a group of people who all smelled differently into a house as they did life together had to begin with trust, and that trust needed to be born from a place of reconciliation within that horizontal dimension as well. There were people in the house who knew that they had fears of living with "the other" in both directions. In short, the merging communities (now supposed to be one) feared what the other group might do to them. This unreconciled thought proverbially permeated the air in both directions. Sessions of intentional reconciliation simply had to be scheduled to get the community off the ground. To quote Lois Barrett, "As a process of concern, involvement, and reconciliation, the practice of binding and loosing involves truth-finding and community building. Thus, the communal practice of recognising and dealing constructively with differences and dissension develops skills and offers a model for dealing with conflict in other social relationships and contexts."[25]

Time was spent listening to the stories of people who lived in (or visited) the communal house. These testimonials were given during our house-worship times, given by everyone, intentionally done week after week—and every week it looked different. There were stories given from people who were detoxing on the couches of friends, waiting to get into treatment. Others were teenagers in gap-year programs who came from well-to-do

---

23. Dickau, "Handout for Post-Modern Theology Class," 2.
24. Bosch, *Transforming Mission*, 153.
25. Guder, *Missional Church*, 168.

European families. There were others in their mid-twenties who had lived in Mount Pleasant their entire lives, who grew up in Vancouver but were still brand new to this part of town. Some grew up in abuse, while others had only heard of it in theory. When it came to addressing reconciliation and repentance concerning how each group felt about one another, truth was found and community was built: and peace slowly but surely became the norm. This was not simply a peace due to a lack of conflict, but a peace from the sharing of lives in the context of church from the "new humanity":

> The telos of Christian mission is thus human beings becoming humans fully alive. However, this equally asserts the ecclesial nature of the new humanity. God's mission was to be carried out by the church as a signal of the new humanity, the church as the sign and servant of the kingdom of God, for the re-creation of the cosmos.[26]

Such thinking is echoed by Bryan Stone when he states that one of the best ways for a Christian community to do well is through daily formation that looks at the entirety of our lives, and how our lives work in relation to one another.[27] Comedian Chris Rock said it better: you have to learn to love more than the center-goodness of a person, you have to learn to love the crust of them—even the little annoying crumbs that fall into the bottom of the toaster.[28] Examples of this love over our time together were staggering. People learned not only how to love the crusts of one another, but the more detail they were able to depict concerning their lives, the more there was for us to love.

The congregation changed. The gospel was seen in new ways. Relationships were rebuilt, families were brought back together, some struggling with addictions won their battles, and people who never worked a day in their lives started their employment careers at local eateries, shelters, and even commercial kitchen appliance stores. The love of those sent into the community continued to grow until ultimate signs of life were born. People from different parts of life were married in a prophetic ceremony in Blood Alley. Friends from different social structures went to movies together, and those with money gladly paid for the tickets of those with less. Eventually, a common purse idea was even suggested so that money for communal activity was not given, but shared, used by whoever needed it at the time. People who had never been to a church service in their lives were submitting to

---

26. Hastings, *Missional God, Missional Church*, Kindle loc. 308.
27. Stone, *Evangelism after Christendom*, 46.
28. Rock, *Bigger & Blacker*.

Christ's body, the church,[29] joining in on accountability groups and communal worship in the most peculiar of places: everywhere.

After many years, some people in the community went on to attend Carey Theological College, Regent College, Tyndale Seminary, and St. Andrew's Hall. Some even became ordained themselves and are now running their own communities. Many went on to take semester classes offered by our community and were later deployed all over the world. But perhaps one of the most fascinating outcomes was a program run by one of the women in the church who was willing, for the price of a proverbial song, to take care of the children of all those who were starting new jobs and new lives between 8 a.m. and 6 p.m.

Gap-year students were living in the Empress and Balmoral hotels at Main and Hastings, starting cell groups with healthy attendance, while helping to clean its halls. Why? Because they volunteered to be sent here. They paid tuition to be here. The worshiping community was able to multiply quickly due to their welcoming of lost and lonely people, listening to their needs, and listening to God's plan. Together, they were representing an outliving of Christ and his work by taking the lonely and putting them into families.[30] The appeal of this was that it showed the action of God who sent Christ, who sent the Spirit to all of us to help restore creation in our area. The communities saw a need to see the Spirit's action in the world and experience that transformation and join in with what was happening.

What perhaps was more important was that the original leaders who started all of this were gone in the first few years. The rest was done by regular, non-ordained people from all over the world (including the local area) who wished to be part of a sent incarnational witness of the gospel. The people who stayed after the founding leaders left "were not superstars . . . they were normal people inspired by the Holy Spirit . . . who [wished to] mix mercy and justice in order to change conditions and circumstances by introducing love and peace, living out redeemed lives of marginalised people around the world."[31]

As I draw my reflections to a close, I note that some of the older community leaders went on to other projects, but they still live in the community and are not planning on leaving the area anytime soon. What has been wonderful to see is the number of people who are still a part of being

---

29. Andersen, "12 Marks of New Monasticism," 2.
30. Ps 68:6.
31. Campbell and Court, *Be a Hero*, 42.

"sent to the area where God is already working." This author is still living in a community house at Hastings and Dunlevy (where a guy living beside us just had his apartment burn down from a meth fire he accidentally started last month) and is completing his master of divinity at St. Andrew's Hall and the Vancouver School of Theology in order to be ordained with the Presbyterian Church in Canada. Another started his own church over on Main Street. And still another is living over on Powell Street, heavily involved in peacemaking after the recent multiple shootings around Oppenheimer Park. He set up a prayer tent in the middle of it, while befriending some of the hardest people in the neighborhood. And where is he currently finding God in his story? He's back at the same place a picnic blanket was put down seventeen years ago, where members of the congregation asked people if they wanted to be our friends.

Bibliography

Andersen, Josh. "The 12 Marks of New Monasticism." *Sojourners Magazine* (Jan 2007) 1–3.

Baluja, Tamara, and Jennifer Wilson. "You're Not Alone: Vancouverites Share Their Stories of Loneliness." CBC News: British Columbia. Last modified November 20, 2018. https://www.cbc.ca/news/canada/british-columbia/you-re-not-alone-vancouverites-share-their-stories-of-loneliness-1.4913290.

Blenkinsopp, Joseph. *Isaiah 56–66: A New Translation with Introduction and Commentary.* New York: Doubleday, 2003.

Bosch, David J. *Transforming Mission: Paradigm Shifts in Theology of Mission.* 20th anniversary ed. Maryknoll, NY: Orbis, 2011.

Campbell, Wesley, and Stephen Court. *Be a Hero: The Battle for Mercy and Social Justice.* Shippensburg, PA: Destiny Image, 2004.

"Dan Rather Reports—A Safe Place to Shoot Up." YouTube, theratherreports, November 27, 2011. https://www.youtube.com/watch?v=rbxmXja0b9s.

Dickau, Tim. "Handout for Post-Modern Theology Class." Vancouver School of Theology, October 4, 2018.

———. "Missional Theology: The Importance of Parish." Lecture, Vancouver School of Theology, Vancouver, BC, November 15, 2018.

Duckworth, Jessicah. *Wide Welcome: How the Unsettling Presence of Newcomers Can Save the Church.* Minneapolis: Fortress, 2013.

Guder, Darrell. *The Continuing Conversion of the Church.* Kindle ed. Grand Rapids: Eerdmans, 2000.

———. *Missional Church: A Vision for the Sending of the Church in North America.* Grand Rapids: Eerdmans, 1998.

Hastings, Ross. *Missional God, Missional Church: Hope for Re-evangelizing the West.* Kindle ed. Downers Grove: InterVarsity Academic, 2012.

Lockhart, Ross. "Evangelism in Cascadia." Lecture, Vancouver School of Theology, Vancouver, BC, March 8, 2018.

Lupick, Travis. "Is Vancouver's Downtown Eastside Still the 'Poorest Postal Code' in Canada?" *The Georgia Straight*, April 8, 2019. https://www.straight.com/news/1225081/vancouvers-downtown-eastside-still-poorest-postal-code-canada.

Marks, Lynne. *Infidels and the Damn Churches: Irreligion and Religion in Settler British Columbia*. Vancouver: University of British Columbia Press, 2017.

McMartin, Pete. "The High Cost of Misery in Vancouver's Downtown Eastside." *Vancouver Sun*, May 5, 2016, Featured. http://www.vancouversun.com/health/pete+mcmartin+high+cost+misery+vancouver+downtown+eastside/11632586/story.html.

Newbigin, Lesslie. *Foolishness to the Greeks: The Gospel and Western Culture*. Grand Rapids: Eerdmans, 1986.

Rock, Chris. *Bigger & Blacker*. Comedy Special. Harlem: HBO, July 10, 1999.

Smith, C. Christopher, and John Pattison. *Slow Church: Cultivating Community in the Patient Way of Jesus*. Downers Grove: InterVarsity, 2014.

Smith, Glenn. "Urban Ministry: How to Exegete a Neighbourhood." https://churchforvancouver.ca/urban-ministry-how-to-exegete-a-neighbourhood/.

Stetzer, Edward. "Connecting to a Post-Christendom World: A Word to Leaders." *Christianity Today*, February 8, 2017. https://www.christianitytoday.com/edstetzer/2017/february/connecting-to-post-christian-world-word-to-leaders.html.

Stone, Bryan P. *Evangelism after Christendom: The Theology and Practice of Christian Witness*. Grand Rapids: Brazos, 2007.

Vanier, Jean. *Community and Growth*. 2nd ed. New York: Paulist, 1989.

White, Aaron. *Fully Human*. Grand Rapids: Baker, 2020.

Wilson, Jonathan R. *Living Faithfully in a Fragmented World: From "After Virtue" to a New Monasticism*. Kindle ed. Cambridge: Lutterworth, 2010.

6

Can Rocky Soil Be Tilled?
Growing a Church-Planting Ecosystem in Cascadia

Andrea Perrett

> Some fell on rocky places, where it did not have much soil. It sprang up quickly, because the soil was shallow. But when the sun came up, the plants were scorched, and they withered because they had no root.
>
> —MARK 4:5–6

THERE ARE MANY PASSAGES in Scripture that can be inspirational for leaders taking part in the incredibly difficult work of starting new churches. Luke 10:2 encourages the church that "the harvest is plentiful, but the labourers are few." Jerimiah 29 comforts those carried into foreign lands to settle and put down roots in their new communities. While these passages can be inspirational to church planters, the verses that seem to make church planters come alive are the ones that acknowledge the challenges and frequent failures experienced by folks starting new churches. In my own experience, rather than joyfully focusing on the fruits of the harvest, church planters would rather spend hours discussing the soil conditions for where they have been called to plant.

Gone are the days of the post-war North American church planting strategy of "build it and they will come," where new church buildings in developing suburbs were filled to capacity with young families on Sunday mornings. While there are some exceptions, the experience of church planters in the Pacific Northwest is more about working with less than ideal soil conditions. I have found myself in more than one conversation with church planters musing whether the soil that we have been called to plant in is rocky or thorny, debating whether church starts are being scorched by the sun, withering away with no roots, or if they are being choked out by thorns and yielding no grain. On our darker days, we might even lament that it feels like we are planting on the path, where the birds immediately eat up all the seed.

Like the sower in the parable, church planters scatter seeds far and wide, not knowing if the initiatives will take root and flourish. When failures build up, it is hard not to take a step back and wonder about the efficiency and efficacy of the planting strategy. Should the sower keep doing the same thing over and over again, praying for a different result? Do we keep sowing the seed broadly, or do we focus our efforts? Or can we spend time working the field, tilling the soil so that the rocky and thorny soil becomes fertile? By examining the recent experience of Presbyterian efforts to establish a church planting network in this Cascadian soil, this chapter will attempt to answer the question: "Can rocky soil be tilled?"

The experience of the church here in the Greater Vancouver area is distinct from the narrative of the Prairies, central Canada, or the Maritimes. This populated swath of land, the Lower Mainland, stretches from the shoreline of the Sunshine Coast in the west, up the Fraser Valley to the Cascade mountains in the east. With vast mountain ranges separating the region from the rest of Canada, this region was not swept up in the western expansion narrative and churches never got the same foothold that was established on the Prairies. While spirituality in general is embraced, affiliation with established religious organizations is low. This highly secular region has been deemed a window into the future for other Canadian cities,[1] giving a glimpse of what is to come as Christendom is dismantled across the nation. For the denominations which were established in Canada by Northern European immigrants, and who historically benefitted from close political and social ties, this changing landscape has been difficult and the soil in which these churches inhabit seems rockier than ever.

Another social reality that is amplified on the West Coast is the elevated presence of loneliness and isolation. While it was a long-held stereotype

---

1. Byassee, "Vancouver's Stony Soil," 27.

that Vancouver was unfriendly, in 2012 the "Community and Connections" report from the Vancouver Foundation demonstrated that it was actually difficult to make friends in Vancouver.[2] In 2017 the latest report from the Vancouver Foundation showed that while isolation is not getting worse, people are still craving deeper social connections.[3] One quarter of residents spend more time alone than they would like, and one in seven people are often or always lonely.[4] However, even with the desire for deeper community, it is still difficult to gather people in the region. Initiatives that take off in other areas of the country don't seem to take root on the West Coast in the same way. There is also the so-called "BC Bail Culture" where people cancel plans at the last minute. This non-committal attitude is so prevalent that organizations plan on people not showing up to events, even if tickets have been pre-purchased.[5]

It is prudent to note that the soil conditions across the Lower Mainland are not uniform. There are pockets of this region where there are still glimpses of Christendom. In and around the Abbotsford area, the Canadian equivalent of mega churches have taken root, consistent mostly of evangelical churches. Additionally, many Roman Catholic churches are thriving across the region. St. Mary's Joyce Street on the east side of Vancouver has Sunday attendance of seven thousand parishioners and at St. Andrew Kim in Surrey six thousand people worship each week primarily Filipino and Korean immigrants.[6] Clearly, there is some good soil in certain areas.

While it is important to discuss the soil conditions, another thing that makes church planting difficult in this area is that the metaphorical sowers have fallen out of practice of planting churches. In recent decades the collective denominational church planting muscles have atrophied, for example, in the Presbyterian Church in Canada. The older model of New Church Development included buying a piece of land in a growing suburban area, constructing a building, calling a charismatic leader, and sending a launch team from an established congregation to start a new church. This used to be a vibrant and effective church planting method and was how most of the current congregations in the Lower Mainland were started. However, as time passed and congregations switched to maintenance and

2. Vancouver Foundation, "Connections and Engagement Report," 7.
3. Vancouver Foundation, "Isolation and Loneliness," 1.
4. Vancouver Foundation, "Isolation and Loneliness," 3.
5. Lawrence, "The Infamous BC Bail."
6. Byassee, "Cracks in Secularism."

survival modes, church planting became a historical task. In the experience of the Presbytery of Westminster, the regional body that covers the same geographical area of the Lower Mainland, the last spurt of Presbyterian church planting occurred in the 1970s. As the expanding population crept up into the Fraser Valley, the Presbyterian churches followed. While there were a couple of attempts at church plants in the past two decades, a coffee shop church and a contemporary worship service church, they are no longer around, and church planting fell off of the presbytery's agenda.

However, in the last five years or so, as the missional theology discussions have increased, there has been a shift towards rediscovering church planting. An example of this shift is when the Centre for Missional Leadership (CML) at St. Andrew's Hall had its foray into replanting a church. As the missional hub at the Presbyterian theological college, the CML was created to enable Christian communities to flourish and equip leaders for God's mission in our changing context. One of the early initiatives of the CML was to learn and practice a missional approach to revitalizing and restarting churches. In 2016, stemming from the desire to provide students with hands-on missional experience rather than just teaching about missional theology, the CML began a missional experiment; a dinner church replant in a nearby congregation. Stepping just off of the University of British Columbia campus, the CML experimented in the neighborhood of West Point Grey and landed in the aptly named West Point Grey Presbyterian Church.

West Point Grey Presbyterian Church's narrative is similar to the experience of many mainline congregations. Early in the 1900s, the church was planted in the newly incorporated Municipality of Point Grey. Still considered part of "the bush," and a bumpy journey on the single-track trolley from the City of Vancouver,[7] West Point Grey Presbyterian Church started worshiping in a school gym in 1912 with thirty-two members on the communion roll.[8] The building where the West Point Grey congregation worshiped after that was built in 1927, with the typical hodgepodge additions for Christian education and offices being completed in 1949.[9] By all accounts the congregation flourished during the mid-century, with the Sunday school swelling, Scottish cultural groups thriving, and mission projects booming. When the neighborhood makeup shifted in the 1980s and

---

7. West Point Grey United Church, "A Journey of Faith," 3.
8. West Point Grey Presbyterian Church, "Golden Jubilee," 5.
9. West Point Grey, "Golden Jubilee," 8.

1990s, West Point Grey found a niche with multicultural ministry, creating space for Japanese, Korean, and Chinese worshipers. However, with the new century, there were new challenges. There was dwindling attendance, declining membership, and an aging building with increasing demands for maintenance. In 2013, with the retirement of their full-time minister, they were faced with the reality that there were not funds to continue on in the same way. While there was a strong desire to continue to be a congregation and worship in the beautiful building, the viability of the congregation was bleak.

Under these conditions, a seminary searching for a place to give students practical experience in church planting, and a congregation in search for a new way forward, a church replant was born. The arrangement was simple: the West Point Grey congregation would donate their basement space on Sunday evenings to the replant group, but for the first year, the congregation would be separate and not attend the replant. In a new wineskins sort of way, this arrangement would give the new community time to establish its own patterns and find its own identity. In turn, the Centre for Missional Leadership would finance the replant and provide the personnel to lead the initiative. The mutual hope was that this replant would be the start of something new within the walls of West Point Grey, which could eventually grow into a new entity.

After a rushed summer of planning, in the fall of 2016, St. Andy's Community Table was born. This dinner church was led by a staff member, a faculty member, and two student leaders from St. Andrew's Hall. As one of the student leaders, I can personally attest to the work that was put into developing, growing, and nurturing St. Andy's Community Table. We had set out to not just be another worship service; the intention was to have a low barrier for entry, but high expectations for commitment. This meant that while all participants were made to feel welcome, they were also expected to engage with others on a deeper level. Also, we were purposely not just looking at metrics of attendance but looking for stories of transformation within those who attended.

With a focus on food, faith, and friends, the group met every Sunday evening in the basement of West Point Grey gathered around a home-cooked meal. On the center of each table, there were mason jars, spray-painted metallic gold and filled with questions to discuss over the meal. After the meal and discussion, the whole group reconvened for singing, led by the participants who had brought their guitars that evening. There was a rotating list of preachers, local ministers, seminary students, and lay preachers, who were encouraged to give their best seven-minute sermon or "sermonette for Christianettes." After a final praise song, the group cleaned up the space and was sent out into the world for the coming week.

However, after two years, it came time for the experiment to wrap up. Having a rent-free space, with fun music, good food, and a child-friendly atmosphere did not directly translate into a sustainable, thriving community. There never was any integration with the West Point Grey congregation, which during the same time frame wrapped up its own lifecycle, ceasing to worship together as a community. Other things that stacked up against the continuation of St. Andy's included the struggle for the leadership to meaningfully connect with the surrounding community and the low turn-out of new Christians. While there were many good things about the experience of St. Andy's, after two years this replant experiment of the CML wrapped up. In the darker moments, it really did feel like rocky soil, where something had sprung up but had no roots and withered away.

As so often happens, however, it is in these darker moments of despair where the Holy Spirit makes a move. The same month that the dinner church wrapped up, an opportunity for addressing the Cascadian soil conditions popped up in our own backyard. Appropriately, the story of Cyclical Cascadia, a church planting ecosystem, begins with a meeting in the rose garden at the University of British Columbia.

In May 2018, while on a lunch break from a conference at St. Andrew's Hall, representatives from the Centre for Missional Leadership and the Northwest Coast Presbytery of the Presbyterian Church (USA) had a meeting in the garden about Cyclical, an American church-planting network. In recent years, given their geographical proximity, there had been growing cooperation between the Presbyterians on either side of the forty-ninth parallel. The Northwest Coast Presbytery covers churches in northern Washington state, as well as in Alaska, and the Presbytery of Westminster is nestled in the geographical gap in between.

During this rose garden meeting, Ross Lockhart, the director of the Centre for Missional Leadership, and Corey Schlosser-Hall, the executive presbyter for North West Coast Presbytery in the Presbyterian Church (USA), along with myself were discussing how Cyclical INC had been on the radar of both organizations. Northwest Coast Presbytery was in the final stages of launching their network, funding had been approved, and a director was being hired, all while the CML was struggling to figure out how, in its small capacity, it could launch a full network. Based on this situation, there was a decision to make the most of geographical proximity and to partner together to become one network, Cyclical Cascadia. Working across two different countries, two different denominations, and a three-hour drive between Vancouver and Seattle, a local church-planting network was established. Each organization would gather participants to join the network and would provide a director, with Assistant Director of Cyclical Cascadia added to my own work profile. After a midsummer visit to Los Angeles, the birthplace of Cyclical INC, for orientation and training, the network was set to launch in October 2018.

Cyclical INC is a church planting network that grew out of the Presbytery of San Fernando in California. After his experience of planting Northland Village Church in Pasadena, Nicholas Warnes founded Cyclical LA in 2015 as a network to help local church planters work towards sustainability. As Cyclical LA grew, other regions from Southern California became interested, the network multiplied, and Cyclical INC was created. By 2019 there were fifteen local networks growing in three different countries.

The structure of Cyclical is designed to help bridge the gap between ideas and sustainability and promote the natural and historical lifecycle of starting new churches. This is primarily done through equipping leaders in the three stages: discerners, starters, and churches. Discerners are those individuals discerning a call to start a new church, while starters are the ones who have done the work of discernment and have started a new church. Finally, churches are challenged to start new churches themselves with their own gifts and resources. The most visible part of this supporting is done through monthly gatherings, where around a table with good food, leaders are encouraged and equipped through mutual learning with their peers.

The book *Starting Missional Churches*, which was edited by Mark Lau Branson and Nicholas Warnes, describes the approach to starting new churches that Cyclical INC embodies and promotes within its networks.[10] Branson and Warnes identify four preconceived notions of church planting in North America: suburban sprawl, protestant splitting, expert strategies, and charismatic figures.[11] This highlights the misinformation that many people hold about church planting—that churches are to be planted in the suburbs, as neighborhoods expanded, that they begin because of a split of congregations, where one side leaves to start a better church. It is also

---

10. Branson and Warnes, *Starting Missional Churches*.
11. Branson and Warnes, *Starting Missional Churches*, 14–23.

assumed that churches can only be planted by experts who have developed strategies, and that they need to be led by a charismatic figure, who is most likely tall, white, and male.

However, Warnes and Branson show that over the last fifty years church planters are not necessarily fitting the preconceived notions of how to plant churches. Four missional priorities which lead to sustainability are identified for starting churches.[12] First, there is a high priority on discerning God's initiatives—listening to what is already going on in the communities and discerning where God is active. The second priority is treating neighbors as subjects; rather than assuming what neighbors need and treating them like objects that need saving, approach neighbors as mutual subjects, approaching the same God together. Third, there is a priority on boundary crossing; church plants engage those who are different and include multiple generations, ethnicities, and socioeconomic differences. Finally, the fourth priority is on plural leadership; have a complement of leaders with diverse gifts, character traits, and practices.

The work of Cyclical networks is to create an ecosystem where these priorities can be elevated and leaders can be equipped for the changing context. One of the ways that Cyclical INC promotes these priorities is by shifting the metaphor from a plant to a garden. Rather than putting all of the metaphorical chips on just one new plant, Cyclical tries to create the ecosystem of a garden where many plants can sprout and reproduce overtime. Given this, it is expected that not all the individuals who join a discerners group will end up starting a new church. Also, within this garden, not all of the new churches that are started will be the equivalent of giant, towering oak trees. There might be several new churches that resemble vines and brush. All of these expressions are necessary and contribute to the health of the ecosystem.

Another shift that has occurred within Cyclical is changing the church planting conversation from *location, location, location* to *leadership, leadership, leadership*, ensuring that you find the right leader for the specific context is more important than finding the perfect suburban parcel of land. Additionally, there is no one single type of person who is a church planter, and the assessments and coaching aspects of Cyclical focus more on leadership, ministry, and entrepreneurial characteristics.

Cyclical Cascadia sprouted up in October 2019 when nine individuals from Canada drove down to Bothell, a suburb north of Seattle, to meet

---

12. Branson and Warnes, *Starting Missional Churches*, 36–42.

seven others for the first discerners dinner. A meal was shared at a local pub, along with a presentation and encouragement from Brandon Bailey, who had planted Tidelands Church in northern Washington in 2012. The participants at the meeting were diverse, in all aspects of the word. There were women and men, millennials and boomers. Some participants were lay people, and some were clergy, already in established churches. Individuals there came from four different continents and represented a variety of ethnicities. Some participants were undergrad students, one was a PhD candidate, and a few had sworn to never go back to school. The folks who gathered were also at all different stages of discernment—some were just thinking about starting something new, while others had already started to gather people for worship. Overall the evening was a chance to share a meal around a table and hear what other people were dreaming, visioning, and planning. It was a moment for the participants to take a step back from their busy lives and listen to where God was calling them.

Now, this is not a perfect story; how could it be when the theme of this paper is rocky soil? While the dinners have continued monthly since October and new faces have continued to join the group, there have been some challenges of developing a network across an international border. After six months of late-night drives to Bothell, the trip south was becoming increasingly wearisome, and some individuals, especially students on international visas, were not able to easily cross the border. Additionally, in a surprising twist, the Cyclical director for the Northwest Coast left his position after four months. This was not the end of the network, however. Due to the strong partnership we have been able to keep going while they search for a new director. With additional support from Cyclical INC, the network has continued to adapt to the local context. While there will still be cooperation between Washington and British Columbia, in September 2019 we separated into two networks and Cyclical Vancouver took up residence north of the border.

The launch of Cyclical Cascadia is certainly not the end of the story, this is just a taste of what it requires to take root and grow. During the time that the local Presbyterian church has been developing a church planting network, there is also a national Cyclical network being developed in Canada. This national network, Cyclical PCC, will complement and amplify the support that is available at a local level. Additionally, this shift towards church planting is not limited to Presbyterian circles: in the past few years, our mainline sister denominations such as the United Church of Canada and the Anglican Church of Canada have also moved towards church planting.

Looking back over these past few years of struggling with church planting in rocky soil, it has been amazing and humbling to see God's guiding hand throughout this process. It is clear that we are not alone in this work, and it is also clear that we are not in charge of the plan; the "Master Gardener" has been leading this initiative the whole time. As much as I still like to complain about the soil conditions here in Cascadia, I have come to understand that our work is not so much about tilling the soil but learning how to respond to different soil conditions. Like the sower in the parable, we do not get to choose where we scatter the seeds and are not called to only scatter seeds on the good soil. We are called to share the gospel, even in the rocky corners of our communities. While we still should be good stewards of our money and time; ultimately, we are not the ones to say if it was worth planting in rocky soil or not. As we are reminded in Mark 4, "The kingdom of God is as someone would scatter seed on the ground, and would sleep and rise night and day, and the seed would sprout and grow, he does not know how."[13] Even though the dinner church replant only lasted two years, for those two years St. Andy's Community Table shared a glimpse of the kingdom of God.

The ecosystem analogy for church planting is very helpful in understanding soil conditions. Having diversity in the garden is what helps different types of life to grow and thrive, even under rocky soil conditions. A multi-tiered network, like Cyclical, works to help the entire system adapt to changing conditions. In the work of Cyclical Cascadia, it is not just the individual planters being equipped, but also the local congregations and the regional and national judicatory bodies.

Ultimately, it seems that the tilling of the soil is up to the Master Gardener. Church planting is difficult work, but the Holy Spirit is already out in the garden, tilling the soil, preparing the people and places where we are being called to plant. Our work, as the laborers in the field, is about following the lead of the Holy Spirit. Our work is more about equipping leaders to be better prepared to work in rocky soil, or thorny soil, or on the garden path. Our work is to develop leaders to be more resilient and better able to respond quickly to changing conditions. Our work is to develop leaders who are able to listen to where the Spirit is leading them and respond with the next most faithful step as sowers of the seed.

13. Mark 4:27–28.

Bibliography

Branson, Mark Lau, and Nicholas Warnes. *Starting Missional Churches: Life with God in the Neighborhood*. Downers Grove: InterVarsity, 2014.

Byassee, Jason. "Cracks in Secularism: Thriving Churches in Vancouver." *The Other Journal*, June 7, 2012. https://theotherjournal.com/2017/06/07/cracks-secularism-thriving-churches-vancouver/.

———. "Vancouver's Stony Soil." *The Christian Century*, December 28, 2015. https://www.christiancentury.org/article/2015-12/vancouver-s-stony-soil.

Lawrence, Grant. "The Infamous BC Bail." *Vancouver Courier*, March 10, 2015. https://www.vancourier.com/news/the-infamous-bc-bail-1.1788168.

Vancouver Foundation. "Connections and Engagement Report." July 2012. https://www.vancouverfoundation.ca/about-us/publications/connections-and-engagement-reports/connections-engagement-report-2012.

———. "Isolation and Loneliness in Metro Vancouver." 2017. https://www.vancouverfoundation.ca/sites/default/files/documents/Connect%20%26%20Engage%20Mini-Reports.pdf.

West Point Grey Presbyterian Church. "Golden Jubilee 1912–1962." Congregational newsletter, 1962.

West Point Grey United Church. "A Journey of Faith." Congregational newsletter, 1986.

7

Arts Ministry beyond the Sunday Worship Service

How Can an Arts Ministry Be Missional in the Public Arena?

Young Tae Choi

In 2005, I was leading a Christian art club called *Choi-Ye-Ha*[1] at Korea National University of Arts. About twenty students from the department of visual arts regularly gathered in an empty classroom or the school garden to share a time of devotion in the early morning before classes began. Often, we met again after school to study translated works on Christianity and the arts—which were hard to come by in Korean—such as Brand and Chaplin's *Art and Soul*.[2] Guest speakers helped us quench our thirst to learn how to view the arts and culture from a Christian perspective. We fearlessly put our understanding of the Christian faith and art into practice by exhibiting group shows expressing a Christian worldview in various media in campus galleries. It was not long before the size of the group doubled. Forty students from different arts departments were participating in our gathering, and *Choi-Ye-Ha* went public via a popular Christian magazine

1. *Choi-Ye-Ha* is the abbreviation for "Choi-go-eui Ye-sul-ga-i-sin Ha-na-nim," which means, "God Is the Best Artist."

2. Brand and Chaplin, *Art and Soul*.

called *Sena*. I was so proud of our little club, seeing how we had come to play a valuable role in preserving the Christian identity from fading away in the most avantgarde school in South Korea.

Some years later, however, I faced a big challenge in leading the club. It became clear that, being influenced by anti-Christian teaching in their university courses, group members were dividing into two extremes. Not surprisingly, the Christian content in their work was not seen as acceptable in the secular classroom, while, in the church, their pastors considered the art world to be a dangerous and harmful realm to the Christian life, failing to see the enormous capacity in creative callings. As a result, some students who were particularly devout renounced their own creative gifts to go to seminary or pursue other forms of vocational service in Christian organizations. On the other hand, other students, who strongly desired to become influential artists in the mainstream, began to compromise their Christian faith with cultural trends. By doing so, they ended up forsaking the community life of the club as well as the local churches they attended. They no longer wanted to be identified as confessing Christians in the university. Both decisions, in one direction or the other, appeared to me entirely dualistic. At that moment, I realized that there was a great need to build understanding and trust between the Korean church and the arts.

This lesson, gained from leading that small group fifteen years ago, still remains in my heart to this day. In the Greater Vancouver area, where I have been residing for the past decade, local Protestant churches tend to value Christian artists to the extent that they are useful for local church activities, although the appreciation of creative callings in the church is rapidly and continuously increasing.[3] Nevertheless, there is rarely theological room to support artists in living out their creative vocations in a faith-filled way when compared to the theology of liturgy for corporate worship. In my observation, Christian artists struggle with confusion about the nature of their calling unless we acknowledge its missional aspects. Given this challenge, it is urgent that we equip artists to be faithful stewards, serving

---

3. Noland, *Heart of the Artist*, 30. Noland also affirms, "I believe we are on the verge of a golden era for the arts in church. I believe we are entering an era in church history when God is calling thousands of artists to use their gifts for Him as He never has before." In Greater Vancouver, several churches are worth visiting to look at how to animate corporate worship services with the arts, including: Tenth Alliance Church, Grandview Calvary Baptist Church, Artisan Church, Christ Church Cathedral Anglican Church, Westside Church, Brentwood Presbyterian Church Jazz Evensong, and Christian Life Assembly.

with excellence in their professional field of art.[4] To this end, we should develop arts ministry, that is, a specialized ministry for artists. This inventive form of ministry enables us to maximize the vocation of artists in the world.[5] Our central question, then, should be, "How can arts ministry be missional? How can it equip artists to be missional witnesses to the gospel of the kingdom of God in the public arena, beyond Sunday worship?" As a practitioner, I will briefly respond to this question here: arts ministry is missional by pastoring artists, promoting artistic gifts, and producing art.[6]

First, arts ministry is missional by equipping Christian artists to be *faithful* to the triune God in their art. As I mentioned earlier, in pursuit of secular success, Christian students and professionals in the field of art oftentimes are tempted to compromise holiness, the norm of the Christian life, with the postmodern worldview. Regrettably, the church tends to ignore the missional role of the arts beyond worship music, while, on the other hand, religious colors or Christian themes in the arts are not warmly welcomed in the secular art world. That is to say, Christian artists are seen as strangers in both territories. For this reason, many Christian artists are desperate to find a mentor who understands their struggles and can guide them to employ their God-given creative abilities in line with genuine Christian faith. To meet this need, the art minister, above all, shepherds each artist to live authentically as an "in-Christ" person characterized by an intimate relationship with Christ, as a lover of Christ, in all aspects of

---

4. Anderson, *The Faithful Artist*, 1–10. Anderson describes three major obstacles he as a visual artist has faced in the church: (1) the absence of a mentor, (2) the ignorance of the church about visual arts, and (3) religious tradition opposed to the art world. I think his observations reflect the near-universal experience of Christian artists internationally.

5. An arts ministry as I define it is a ministry that is to serve the church and the culture for the glory of God and the enjoyment of him through Christ Jesus by the power of the Holy Spirit, just as all other ministries do. But it does so distinctively by pastoring artists, promoting their artistic gifts, and producing art, as I will present in this chapter. Arts ministry cultivates redemptive images, sounds, spaces, and stories that contribute to the animated transformation of the church and culture. This ministry, as a creative response to the cultural (Gen 1:27–28) and missional (Matt 28:16–20) mandates, aims to bring shalom to the world.

6. Joshua Banner, "The Practitioner: Nurturing Artists in the Local Church," in Taylor, *For the Beauty of the Church*, 123–144. I am indebted to Banner for his phrases, "pastoring, promoting and producing," from his essay "The Practitioner." I found that those roles of arts ministry are holistic in nurturing Christian artists mainly in a local church setting, as he argues. As you will see in this paper, I extend their meanings and roles into my context *missiologically*.

life, including artmaking.[7] Artists are thus enabled to honor the Lord of art with their artistic productions and performances, and, indeed, with their entire journeys.[8]

In the Poieo Centre of Arts Ministry, where I serve as an art minister, I give pastoral care to my team members and several young artists who have joined our mentoring program.[9] I meet regularly with each of them for an hour a month, offline or online, depending on their geographical proximity. Basically, I check in about two matters—how their lives are going and how their creative projects and work are going. As I try to listen carefully and prayerfully to what is happening in their hearts, thoughts, and lives, I also share my life with them, even vulnerable and painful things from my past, as transparently as possible, acknowledging that I am like them a sheep who needs the Shepherd. Sometimes our conversations deal with particular techniques in the arts, but far more often, we talk honestly about the real and tough questions we face in our journeys of life: marriages in trouble, addictions, even the interpretation of difficult biblical texts. This reminds me of the simple fact that these artists are, as human beings, no different from members of other professions in terms of their human nature. Here, I play a pastoral role in reorienting their life focus to Christ, who navigates for them by speaking of who God is and how God is at work within their lives from day to day. Personally, I love this pastoral responsibility, as it truly deepens our relationships in Christ.

One day, a famous Christian artist opened up to me about his struggle with an addiction to pornography. His mind was so preoccupied by lust that he could not stop watching it. I saw him wrestling with this habitual sin every day. His ongoing struggle seemed familiar to me. As I shared with him my own previous experience of fighting against a particular besetting sin, I spoke about John Owen's *Overcoming Sin and Temptation*.[10] I gently invited him to take a closer look at the reality of sin and its power. He was then able to identify the damaged place inside himself where he needed daily application of the grace of God. Admitting his enslavement to strong

---

7. See Sven Soderlund, "Paul: The Christian as an 'In-Christ' Person," in Houston and Zimmerman, *Sources of the Christian Self*, 114–15. What does it mean to be a Christian? Soderlund contends that those who are *in Christ* are Christians, according to the apostle Paul. The Christian imitates the life of Christ in following him in word and deed.

8. Joshua Banner, "The Practitioner: Nurturing Artists in the Local Church," in Taylor, *For the Beauty of the Church*, 141.

9. See Poieo Centre of Arts Ministry, www.poieocentre.com.

10. Owen, *Overcoming Sin and Temptation*.

sexual desire, he began to try to reorient his desire toward Christian freedom—freedom from sin. I asked him to be watchful in prayer against any tempting situation that the devil could use to attack his point of weakness again, exhorting him not to renounce the good fight for godly character. Of course, it was not easy for him to overcome sexual temptation all at once. He has been keeping up his spiritual fight, asking the Holy Spirit for sanctification and healing of his brokenness. This artist told me one day how thankful he was to walk his spiritual journey so closely with someone else, as he had been doing with me. Not only he, but many Christian artists are broken by sin and temptation in one way or another. Given this reality, pastoring artists to live in faithfulness is a lifelong process in building up a Christ-centered life rather than a self-centered one of pursuing "art for art's sake" that "indulge[s] all the cravings of the sinful heart of unredeemed man."[11]

Secondly, arts ministry is missional by fostering artists' artistic gifts holistically such that they may be able to become faithful *artisans*. Jesus' life of complete integrity between words and deeds reveals who he is—the Son of God who brings the kingdom of God into the world. Interestingly, the way that Jesus teaches the disciples about his kingdom has three aspects—theoretical, archetypal, and practical. Jesus first proclaims what the kingdom of heaven looks like (theory). He then exemplifies the kingdom, actually showing his disciples what it looks like in himself (archetype). Lastly, Jesus gives them his authority to do the same (practice). Mark 6:6–13, as an example, demonstrates this pattern as follows: Jesus taught and healed the sick throughout villages (vv. 5–6), He gave the disciples authority over unclean spirits, including specific instructions (vv. 7–11), and they preached about repentance, drove out many demons, and healed the sick (vv. 12–13). This example clearly shows us how Jesus effectually trained the disciples to become powerful followers manifesting the reality of his kingdom.

Following the same pattern, arts ministry can support artists to make art for the kingdom of God in three modes. First, *theoretical*: seminars, conferences, and study groups on theology and the arts can equip the artists with a theological framework for the arts so that they may be able to use

---

11. Rookmaaker, *Creative Gift*, 118. This book is a collection of Rookmaaker's essays on the arts. It is worth reading his appendix, "Letter to a Christian Artist," because, even though the letter was written about five decades ago, in 1966, it carefully addresses widespread misunderstandings about Christian visual artists and issues, such as creative freedom in artmaking, in a way that is still relevant to today's artists.

their creative abilities and lives in ways that reflect the perspective, attitudes, and values of the kingdom of God. Second, *archetypical*: art ministers ought to exemplify what it is to be faithful artists. To mentor artists responsibly, these pastors must not only live out godly disciplines, but also possess theological acumen for the arts, develop their own creative potential, and grow in awareness of how the church community works.[12] Third, *practical*: art workshops, through actual artmaking in the community, set up a crucial platform in which young artists can discover their artistic talents, discern their own strengths and weaknesses, and gain access to diverse venues to show their work to wider audiences, both within and beyond the church.[13]

This practice can easily be initiated from a local church setting. For example, I helped Richmond Presbyterian Church design their advent worship service last year. One design element was a weekly children's art workshop that reflected four advent themes—hope, peace, joy, and love. The senior minister, Rev. Victor Kim, explained each theme to Sunday school leaders in advance, using simple symbols so that the leaders could digest the meanings of the themes and prepare to guide the children to express the subjects (theory). Two members of the church, visual artists, assisted the kids, showing them how to use the provided art supplies (archetype). The children who were too young to make a work of art by themselves took part in a collage collaboration using the shapes of the given symbols. The older children chose their materials and freely expressed their thoughts related to the topics (practice). The children had enough time and opportunity to digest the abstract themes by making tangible pieces of art with their hands over the four weeks.

The completed works of art were displayed in the church hall one week ahead of each theme of the season. As the church space gradually filled with the children's colorful paintings and sculptures, advent themes were displayed visually. Rev. Kim invited the child artists to the front of the sanctuary, and they shared the intentions of their pieces during the children's message time. The whole congregation was so impressed by their imaginations and the unique styles expressed in their artwork. Rev. Kim said to the congregation, "We'd better skip the preaching today. This work is like a sermon!" One Sunday, a mother told me she had never seen her son stay in his chair for a full two hours before, focusing on just one thing,

---

12. Bauer, *Arts Ministry*, 280–83.

13. Joshua Banner, "The Practitioner: Nurturing Artists in the Local Church," in Taylor, *For the Beauty of the Church*, 131–35.

painting. We were glad to see the boy's incredible concentration and artistic gift for painting. This little project not only helped both the children and the adult congregation to meditate on the Advent themes in fresh and engaging ways, it also enhanced the worship service, bonded younger and older generations under the roof of a traditional Canadian Presbyterian church, animated the liturgy of the church calendar with a fresh form of expression, and uncovered the children's artistic talents.

Lastly, arts ministry is missional by producing life-transforming artwork in the culture. Generally, there are four approaches to missional artmaking. First is *creation*: natural art reveals God's beauty and goodness toward his creation. This is because the artistic enterprise begins with God's good creation (Gen 1:25). All visible and invisible elements of beauty—such as order, shape, color, space, time, tone, sound, harmony, rhythm, and function—are good indeed. Our innate capability to sense beauty was designed by the triune God, as we see when the Lord expresses an aesthetic appreciation for his creation, "good (*tov*)!" seven times.[14] When the author of Genesis uses the term *tov*, it does not mean eternal prettiness. In Hebrew, *tov* covers aesthetic beauty, ethical goodness, and functional appropriateness, which is a holistic view.[15] Thus, it is right to see that art is counted among the natural gifts and that art has a value in itself.[16] A landscape piece, a still life, a National Geographic documentary film, bodily dance, and music, expressing the beauty of God's marvelous creation, should all be considered meaningful as providing "testimonies of the divine goodness."[17]

Among contemporary North American Christian visual artists, Makoto Fujimura is one of the most well-known for expressing the beauty of God.[18] His work has been shown in churches, galleries, and museums around the world, including at the Museum of Contemporary Art in Tokyo. His painting style originates from a traditional Japanese painting technique called *nihonga*. *Nihonga* is a water-based medium of brush on paper. Its natural colors are derived from natural ingredients, such as minerals, shells, corals, and even stones. For instance, the medium of Fujimura's series "The Tears of Christ" is mineral pigments on Belgium linen. As a limited edition of prints, the images were touched by Fujimura's hand with real gold and

---

14. Gen 1:4, 10, 12, 18, 21, 25, 31.
15. J. Gordon, "טוֹב," in VanGemeren, *Dictionary of Old Testament Theology*, 346–47.
16. Schaeffer, *Art and the Bible*, 33; Calvin, *Institutes*, 273.
17. Calvin, *Genesis*, 219.
18. See https://www.makotofujimura.com/works/.

platinum. The organic colors of the works have power to lead viewers to experience the beauty of the Creator in praise and awe, especially when appreciating them in person. Such natural art bearing witness to the splendor of God can provide us with a glimpse of God's transcendent hospitality and his redemptive grace that created, sustains, and will renew the creation wholly on the day of his second coming.[19] Natural art has an unlimited function as a channel through which we can anticipate a hopeful reality, the new heaven and new earth to come.

The next approach to missional artmaking is *evangelism*: Christian artists can evangelize nonbelievers via authentic evangelistic arts.[20] The Bible affirms that the proclamation of the good news of Jesus Christ arises naturally from believers' love for God and appreciation of all that God has done for them (Isa 52:7; Mark 1:1). Jesus commands his disciples to preach the gospel according to the missional mandate (Matt 28:16–20). In this respect, it is appropriate for Christian artists to share the gospel of Christ with viewers by means of their artistic specialty. The form of evangelistic arts can vary greatly, affecting those impacted in such a way that coming to faith is a gradual process toward Christlikeness through diverse channels.[21] Evangelistic arts generally describe figures or scenes of the biblical story or personal testimonies so as to plainly communicate the message of God's unimaginable salvation in Christ to nonbelievers, especially those who do not possess the Bible in their own language.

Two years ago, I happened to meet a Bible translator in Kona, Hawaii. His English name is Solomon. He came to Kona from a tiny isolated island, the name of which I do not even remember. He worked as a translator for a Christian organization, the *Jesus* Film Project.[22] He was involved in making minority-language subtitles for the *Jesus* film, which depicts the life of Jesus from the Gospels. He told me that through the *Jesus* film his team had

---

19. Begbie, *Redeeming Transcendence in the Arts*, 184. Begbie in his writing recalls that from an illuminating conversation with a Vancouver-based painter he began to explore God's gracious transcendence of the created world.

20. See Campbell, *Outreach and the Artist*. Campbell in his book discusses threefold arts evangelism in detail—evangelism *with* the arts (which has huge capability for outreach), *through* the arts (which looks into life's big questions with nonbelievers in engaging ways), and *to* the arts (which builds accessible networks that reach out to unreached artist groups). In this section of my paper, I emphasize evangelism *with* and *through* the arts.

21. Bowen, *Evangelism for "Normal" People*, 83–86.

22. https://www.jesusfilm.org/.

shared the gospel with a great number of ethnolinguistic minority people who had never heard about Jesus. In amazement, the team had witnessed the sick being healed as they watched scenes of Jesus healing the sick in the film and demons being cast out of possessed people during the scene in which Jesus casts demons out of the possessed. After the movie screening, most people in this minority group repented of their sins and decided to follow Jesus Christ as their own savior. Solomon's testimony bears witness that God employs such films to convert culturally and spiritually isolated persons to become his own children by the power of the Holy Spirit. Evangelistic art is art that witnesses to the reality of the triune God and helps viewers to encounter our Savior, Christ Jesus.

The third approach to missional artmaking is *reconciliation*: Christian artists can bridge the gap between conflicting sides in a hostile culture. The New Testament presents reconciliation as characteristic of God's salvific work. God, through his Son, Christ Jesus, reconciles his whole creation to himself, breaking down barriers of hostility and estrangement (Col 1:21; Rom 8:19). At the right time, God the Father will bring unity to all things in heaven and on earth under Christ (Eph 1:9–10). Given this vision of restoration in Christ, reconciling artwork aims to bring down spiritual, generational, cultural, denominational, ethnic, theological, creational, and professional barriers we face in society and even in the church today. Christian artists, as a reconciled and reconciling community, are invited to participate in Christ's ongoing reconciling ministry, just as the apostle Paul exhorts the Corinthian church to become "ambassadors of reconciliation" in the Roman culture (2 Cor 5:20).

The group show "A Reconciling Hope" was held in January 2017 at Lookout Gallery in Vancouver.[23] This show was designed to picture what Christian hope looks like amidst the brokenness and crises in our violent world. Multi-ethnic Christian artists from different denominational backgrounds gathered to present diverse art pieces based on Colossians 1:21. Some pictured personal wounds; others, social and cultural brokenness. I joined this project by designing one conceptual art project with twenty participants. The title of my group work was "Ash on Fire." I collected twenty drawings in which participants had put images of their own relational brokenness on paper, and then I burnt them to ash for a lamp. I displayed this piece of work with an artist's note as part of the exhibit in the gallery.

---

23. See "A Reconciling Hope," https://www.lookoutgallery.ca/exhibitions/2017/a-reconciling-hope.

Here is the note that I wrote accompanying the display:

> This work is not merely an art piece, but a liturgy exploring our personal brokenness. None of us wants to show our wounds of brokenness to strangers. In most cases, the brokenness we experience is so painful that we tend to hide it from others. With this in mind, I sought to hide our brokenness from this exhibition's viewers by burning all the pieces of our work and expressing our private brokenness through ash. This is the secret debris which remains in our hearts after experiencing various broken relationships.
>
> However, most of us wish that our wounds would be healed completely. For healing, we often turn to different kinds of human treatments, such as counselling. But we soon realize that these treatments do not last forever. We may one day have a nightmare in which the shadow of the memory haunts our souls, where we resign ourselves to fate and give up any hope of a happy ending. Thus, the question, "Is there hope for such a broken life?" is one which we will inevitably raise.
>
> Nevertheless, as Christians we put our hope in Christ who is bringing the final broken chapters of human history to their end, even while our lives seem irredeemable and look like hopeless ash. I pray that through this communal work our focus will shift (even just a little) from the past to the future; from our brokenness to the hope of the reconciling power of Christ, as from ash to the fire of God. This shift is the purpose behind my contribution to this project.
>
> Let us anticipate the day of full reconciliation in the new heaven and earth to come. This cooperative working process was like a collage which drew from the twenty fragmented pieces and resulted in a display of the hope that comes from faith in the reconciling work of Christ Jesus.

The fourth and final approach to missional artmaking is the *prophetic voice*: prophetic art proclaims visionary messages addressed to an unjust society. The Scriptures state that God created the world in justice and expects his creatures to treat one another fairly. Sin brings injustice into the world, which causes human justice to fall short of God's standards, as we witness daily in the news. Nonetheless, God requires justice to be evident in the lives of his people, who are granted the status of being righteous in God's sight through justification (Mic 6:8; Matt 5:17; Rom 13:10). Reflecting a God who is righteous, prophetic artists have ethical sensitivity, ethical imagination, and the will for justice in particular contexts.[24] Prophetic art demands of viewers "moral, economic, and religious integrity" in communities in which they are involved, thereby calling for the renewal of a society.[25]

At the eleventh Annual Missions Fest Vancouver Film Festival, we, the film festival committee, decided with unanimous approval to screen director Brian Ivie's documentary *Emanuel* (2019) as the opening film.[26] The film is a cinematically well-made movie addressing a contemporary social issue from a Christian perspective. As a prophetic film, *Emanuel* deals with the Charleston shooting case that killed nine members of Emanuel African Methodist Episcopal Church. A young white supremacist, Dylan Roof, shoots at them during a prayer service, and two days later the families of the victims offer words of forgiveness to the killer in federal court. Through interviews with survivors and families of victims, the film inspects the history of racism in the Charleston area and, in the end, invites viewers to reflect on how they relate to justice in such a situation of terror and what it might mean to surrender to God's vision of restoration in a culture of racism. *Emanuel* speaks with a compelling prophetic voice, interpreting the ongoing racist culture in North America in our time, and, at the same time, interpreting the Christian faith for such a time through the examples of the families who respond with Christian justice in light of the cross— embracing the murderer into the selfless love of Christ.[27] It is heartrending to watch, yet Ivie's film illuminates the possibility of change, linked to his personal yearning for a transformation of white society.[28] In such ways, prophetic art boldly displays the righteousness of God in the midst of a biased and threatening society.

Thus far, I have concisely dealt with the three missional roles of arts ministry that holistically shape Christian artists into innovative missionaries. As we have seen above, this creative ministry can foster a vibrant missional community serving Christ's artists, his church, and his world, since the ministry is able to pastor artists to become faithful stewards of their

---

24. Bauer, *Arts Ministry*, 144–49.
25. Davis, *Biblical Prophecy*, 7.
26. Ivie, *Emanuel*.
27. Davis, *Biblical Prophecy*, 3. The biblical prophets "interpreted the faith for their time and, equally, they interpreted the times for the faithful." So do prophetic artists in their time as well.
28. Brueggemann, *The Prophetic Imagination*, 9.

covenant relationship with the triune God and their creative callings, to nurture their artistic gifts theoretically, archetypically, and practically, and to empower their redemptive imaginations and creative abilities to engage the culture through the common language of the arts, thereby bringing shalom into the broken world. Arts ministry not only presents an exciting vision of deepening the affinity between artists and their aesthetic vocation, but also functions as an alternative source of healing to the church and the artistic community, advancing ever-increasing understanding and trust between them to the glory of God. May the Lord breathe life into dry artists, dry churches, and dry cultures through the mouth of arts ministries filled with the Spirit, such that these dry bones may come to life.

Bibliography

Anderson, Cameron J. *The Faithful Artist: A Vision for Evangelicalism and the Arts.* Downers Grove: InterVarsity, 2016.

Bauer, Michael J. *Arts Ministry: Nurturing the Creative Life of God's People.* Grand Rapids: Eerdmans, 2013.

Begbie, Jeremy. *Redeeming Transcendence in the Arts: Bearing Witness to the Triune God.* Grand Rapids: Eerdmans, 2018.

Bowen, John P. *Evangelism for "Normal" People: Good News for Those Looking for a Fresh Approach.* Minneapolis: Augsburg Fortress, 2002.

Brand, Hilary, and Adrienne Chaplin. *Art and Soul: Signposts for Christians in the Arts.* 2nd ed. Carlisle, UK: Piquant, 2001.

Brueggemann, Walter. *The Prophetic Imagination.* 2nd ed. Minneapolis: Fortress, 2001.

Calvin, John. *Genesis.* Translated and Edited by John King. London: Banner of Truth Trust, 1965.

———. *Institutes of the Christian Religion.* Translated by Ford Lewis Battles, edited by John T. McNeill. Philadelphia: Westminster, 1960.

Campbell, Constantine R. *Outreach and the Artist: Sharing the Gospel with the Arts.* Grand Rapids: Zondervan, 2013.

Davis, Ellen F. *Biblical Prophecy: Perspectives for Christian Theology, Discipleship, and Ministry.* Louisville: Westminster John Knox, 2014.

Dyrness, William A. *Visual Faith: Art, Theology, and Worship in Dialogue.* Grand Rapids: Baker, 2001.

Houston, J. M., and Jens Zimmerman, eds. *Sources of the Christian Self: A Cultural History of Christian Identity.* Grand Rapids: Eerdmans, 2018.

Ivie, Brian, dir. *Emanuel.* Documentary, 1 hr 30 min. JuVee Productions, Arbella Studios, Fiction Pictures, 2019.

Noland, Rory. *The Heart of the Artist: A Character-Building Guide for You and Your Ministry Team.* Grand Rapids: Zondervan, 1999.

Owen, John. *Overcoming Sin and Temptation.* Edited by Kelly M. Kapic and Justin Taylor. Wheaton: Crossway, 2015.

Rookmaaker, H. R. *The Creative Gift: Essays on Art and the Christian Life*. Westchester: Cornerstone, 1981.

Schaeffer, Francis A. *Art and the Bible: Two Essays*. L'Abri Pamphlets. Downers Grove: InterVarsity, 1973.

Taylor, W. David, ed. *For the Beauty of the Church: Casting a Vision for the Arts*. Grand Rapids: Baker, 2010.

VanGemeren, Willem, ed. *New International Dictionary of Old Testament Theology and Exegesis*. Vol. 2. Grand Rapids: Zondervan, 1997.

NURTURING THE GROWTH

I planted, Apollos watered, but God gave the growth. So neither the one who plants nor the one who waters is anything, but only God who gives the growth.

—1 CORINTHIANS 3:6–7 (NRSV)

I planted the seed, Apollos watered the plants, but God made you grow. It's not the one who plants or the one who waters who is at the center of this process but God, who makes things grow.

—1 CORINTHIANS 3:6–7 (MSG)

8

Transformative Gardens within Cascadian Soil

The Place and Shape of Friendship within New Faith Communities

ANNE-MARIE ELLITHORPE

I ADVOCATE FOR NEW faith communities to be conceived of as multigenerational "gardens of friends," characterized by relationships of mutuality and inter-dependence.[1] I draw this metaphor from Brian McGuire's book *Friendship and Community*. McGuire notes that, within the twelfth century, a synthesis of classical and theological insights contributed towards the monastery becoming a "garden of friends whose very existence provoked and transformed the world of which monastic community formed an integral part."[2] I assert that new faith communities have the potential to become "gardens of friendship" with their own transformative impact within the radically different context of Cascadian soil, that is, within the "unique coastal bioregion that defines the Pacific Northwest of the United States and Canada."[3] To this end, however, the social and theological imagination

---

1. I use the language of faith communities as being inclusive not only of new worshiping communities, but also of new communities that may primarily be at a pre-worship stage.

2. McGuire, *Friendship and Community*, 427.

3. Cascadia incorporates "all of or parts of southern Alaska, British Columbia,

of community gardeners needs to be captured by a vision of friendship that includes personal, civic, and divine dimensions of friendship.[4]

Yet while friendship has been celebrated within the Christian tradition, friendship has also been neglected, ignored, or simply regarded with suspicion. Thus, my focus within this paper is on the relevance of friendship in relationship to the planting and nurturing of new faith communities within Cascadia, and on the shape of friendship relevant to such planting and nurturing.[5]

I consider the relevance of friendship, broadly construed, in light of the relational nature of God and human beings, and the sacramental nature of friendship. I then consider the shape of friendship relevant to such planting and nurturing, acknowledging that the friendship inherent to the planting of new faith communities may differ somewhat from contemporary cultural norms of friendship. Finally, in the light of these assertions regarding the place and shape of friendship, I provide further suggestions for local community gardeners seeking to nurture new faith communities within Cascadian soil.

Friendship's Relevance

Despite the devaluing of friendship within aspects of the Christian tradition, friendship has been recognized as essential to the fostering of new faith communities within Cascadian contexts. This is evident in *Church Planting in Post-Christian Soil: Theology and Practice*, by Christopher James. James notes that no amount of marketing within post-Christian contexts is going to draw people from the general public to "show up on Sunday."[6] Rather, the proactive building of genuinely mutual friendships is recognized as the "most basic and essential practice for ecclesial vitality"

Washington, Oregon, Idaho, Montana, and Northern California" and is defined through the watersheds of the Fraser and Columbia rivers. See https://www.cascadianow.org/.

4. Drawing on but going beyond Aristotle's advocacy for civic friendship, Sibyl Schwarzenbach identifies the ideal of civic friendship as including all activities "which citizens reciprocally perform for each other for no other reason than the construction and maintenance of a flourishing set of civic relationships and their social union as a whole" (Schwarzenbach, "Fraternity, Solidarity, and Civic Friendship," 12).

5. I draw on a variety of sources, including Aelred of Rievaulx's *De spiritali amicitia*, Christopher James's *Church Planting*, and my PhD dissertation, "Towards a Practical Theology of Friendship."

6. James, *Church Planting*, 227.

in such contexts.[7] Church planters are encouraged by James to proactively build friendships of *genuine* mutuality with workmates, neighbors, and the like and to "welcome them into a community of friends, some of whom are seeking to pattern their lives in the way of Jesus."[8] But on what basis is this valuing of friendship to be grounded?

I am convinced that authentic friendship is integral to the fostering of new faith communities. Yet, like the practice of hospitality, friendship's importance is not primarily as a "relational recruitment strategy."[9] (Indeed, when friendship is treated in such utilitarian ways, we may question whether it is it indeed authentic friendship). Rather, friendship is integral to the fostering of new faith communities because friendship is integral to creation, to God, and to relationship with God. Human beings are image bearers of a relational God.[10]

Similar themes are expressed in the twelfth century writing of the monastic abbot, Aelred of Rievaulx, whose imagination has clearly been captivated by a theological vision of friendship. I weave a number of insights from his work into these reflections, whilst also acknowledging that the monastic context of twelfth-century Britain within which Aelred sought to foster friendships contributes to some of his understandings being too narrow for our context. For example, Aelred asserts that friendship is "nothing other than agreement in all things divine and human with benevolence and charity."[11] While mutuality in good-will and love remain integral to friendship, this focus on agreement in all things appears to be too narrow for our current contexts, characterized as they are by a significant degree of diversity (and, at times, polarization).

Aelred recognizes that the mutuality of friendship is integral to creation. Indeed, friendship is recognized as being part of the cosmic order.[12]

---

7. James, *Church Planting*, 228.

8. James, *Church Planting*, 227–28.

9. James, *Church Planting*, 228. I am not implying here that James suggests friendship as a relational recruitment strategy; in fact, his emphasis on mutuality would suggest otherwise.

10. From a Christian perspective, as depicted by Stanley Grenz within *The Social God and the Relational Self*, the biblical narrative begins with the creation of humans as *imago Dei*, moves to Christ as "the fullness of" the *imago Dei* and concludes with the "glorified new humanity sharing in the divine image" (Grenz, *The Social God*, 240).

11. This definition of friendship is borrowed from Cicero, *Amic.* 6.20.

12. Marsha Dutton, "The Sacramentality of Community in Aelred," in *A Companion to Aelred of Rievaulx*, 250.

Reflecting on the first biblical couple as the first friends, Aelred asserts that "nature might teach that all are equal or, as it were, collateral, and that among human beings—and this is a property of friendship—there exists neither superior nor inferior."[13] Aelred clearly recognizes that human beings need love, friendship, and companionship.[14]

I advocate for community gardeners to recognize the mutuality and interrelatedness of creation evident within their experience, within the biblical creation narratives, and within indigenous creation accounts. As depicted within Genesis 2, human beings are created for relationship with God, others, and creation.[15] This relationship, or right-relatedness, may be described as friendship. Indigenous creation stories and cultures also speak of right-relatedness between God, people, and land. Within these contexts also, right-relatedness implies a certain degree of mutuality, such as the mutuality inherent within friendship.

Yet these various forms of relationality are under pressure within contemporary Western contexts, including Cascadia. Within Cascadia, as within many colonized contexts, we currently experience alienation between God, people, and land.[16] Speaking specifically to the issue of person-to-person relationships within metro Vancouver, surveys have pointed to a growing sense of social isolation among its residents, with those in their mid-twenties to mid-thirties feeling most alone.[17] Within Vancouver, as within other contemporary fragmented, consumerist cultures, friendship is typically viewed as a private concern and as a recreational relationship. Yet despite friendship being sidelined and sentimentalized, the desire for friendship clearly remains.[18] Friendship remains integral to creation and to God. Friendship is not only God's intention *for* humankind, but also God's image *in* humankind.

Yet intriguingly, when it comes to the interrelationship between God and friendship, there is some ambiguity in Aelred's writing, quite possibly

---

9. Aelred, *De spiritali amicitia*, 1.57.

14. John R. Sommerfeldt, "Anthropology and Cosmology: The Foundational Principles of Aelred's Spirituality," in Dutton, *A Companion to Aelred of Rievaulx*, 105.

15. See, for example, Hoekema, *Created in God's Image*, 75–82, 102. Also Ellithorpe, "Towards a Practical Theology of Friendship," 65–66.

16. Many of us fail to recognize that we are treaty people, and to learn from those whose ancestors lived here for centuries before us.

17. This research has been carried out by the Vancouver Foundation. See Kassam, "Is Vancouver Lonelier."

18. See Ellithorpe, "Towards a Practical Theology of Friendship," 2.

intentionally. Within the dialogue of *De spiritali amicitia*, Ivo asks Aelred if he can say of friendship what John says of love: "God is friendship."[19] Aelred simply notes that this is a novel idea, he neither affirms nor explicitly denies this possibility. Yet Aelred does continue on to assert that the remainder of that verse about *charity* (1 John 4:16) the author does "not hesitate to attribute to friendship, because the one who remains in friendship remains in God, and God in him."[20] In her introduction to his work, Marsha Dutton states categorically that Aelred's response is a rejection of this idea.[21] Yet elsewhere she describes "Aelred's tacitly Trinitarian understanding of the universe, designed to join all God's creatures in peace and fellowship in a mirroring of God's own unity and society."[22] Others have interpreted Aelred's response as affirming that "God is friendship." Whatever Aelred's intention, he did not continue on to explore the possibility of friendship within the Trinity.[23]

Understandably, given contemporary theological controversy regarding the concept of the social Trinity, there is a lack of consensus amongst theologians as to whether we can speak of the relations within the Trinity in terms of friendship. Janice Soskice, for example, is concerned that saying the three persons of the Trinity are friends of each other would be dangerously near to tritheism.[24] Nevertheless, she allows for the possibility of saying that "the Trinity is friendship."[25] Yet regardless of whether we can appropriately say "God is friendship," or "the Trinity is friendship," I suggest that the mutual relations within the Trinity do provide a motif for friendship with implications for the nurturing of new faith communities.[26] The writings of Jürgen Moltmann, with his focus on the mutuality and perichoresis of the Trinity, point towards this possibility, as they speak of the invitation to human beings to participate in the communion, or "friendship," of the Trinity.

19. Aelred, *De spiritali amicitia*, 1.69.
20. Aelred, *De spiritali amicitia*, 1.70.
21. Dutton, *Spiritual Friendship*, 44.
22. Dutton, *Spiritual Friendship*, 250.
23. See also Carmichael, *Friendship*, 85.
24. Soskice considers friendship to be essentially a *human* good. See Soskice, *Kindness of God*, 161.
25. Soskice, *Kindness of God*, 161.
26. The essence of the Trinity is "relationship, a relationship characterized by communion and intimacy, love and friendship, joy and peace." Ellithorpe, "Towards a Practical Theology of Friendship," 101.

The analogy of friendship when it comes to God does have limitations. As I have noted elsewhere, much greater distance inevitably exists between human friends than between the trinitarian persons, and human friends (unlike the trinitarian persons) may experience times of separation and possibly even alienation.[27] Further, as Sarah Coakley emphasizes, without Christ's help we cannot imitate the life of the Trinity.[28] Nevertheless, the analogy of Trinitarian friendship has implications for the social practices to be fostered within new communities of faith, just as the social practices of new churches call for "missional reflection on the relational, social Trinity."[29]

As James notes, "For missional churches to be truly Trinitarian, they must not only attend to mission but also learn to reflect the perichoretic dance in their social practices."[30] Given that the Trinitarian dance is one of openness and mutual participation, social practices within new faith communities are to likewise reflect such qualities. To paraphrase James, the trinitarian friendship, into which we are invited, "provides an eschatological horizon for the church's practice of [friendship and] community."[31]

Further, as community gardeners seek to plant and nurture new faith communities, it is appropriate that they develop a spirituality of friendship, in response to the divine invitation to participate within the mutuality of the Trinity. The image of friendship with God is suggestive of intimacy along with respect for otherness, and of closeness as well as detachment.[32] Further, it is appropriate for community gardeners to develop collaborative leadership structures, to practice shared discernment and decision-making, to exhibit the willingness to be guest as well as host, and to foster unity amid diversity. All of these practices are in keeping with this friendship analogy.

Having identified the importance of friendship as inherent to creation and to God, I turn now to acknowledge friendship as a sacramental relationship. There is potential for repairs to the divine–human relationship to be fostered through human friendships. Through friendship one

---

27. Ellithorpe, "Towards a Practical Theology of Friendship," 102.
28. Coakley, *God, Sexuality and the Self*, 309.
29. James, *Church Planting*, 223.
30. James, *Church Planting*, 223–24.
31. James, *Church Planting*, 223.
32. Moltmann-Wendel, *Rediscovering Friendship*, 6.

becomes a "friend of God."[33] Indeed, both friendship and community have the potential to be sacramental, that is, "channels of grace, created by God, drawing humans to God and joining them together in [God's] presence."[34] As sacraments, friendship and community are a "foretaste of beatitude."[35] Friendship and community also foster the experience of beatitude in the present, even if such divine blessedness is brief and incomplete.[36]

Friendship involves the whole person. The holistic nature of friendship is implied in the "compelling imagery of food and drink" that Aelred threads throughout his work.[37] Yet this language of tasting, eating, and drinking is also metaphorical, pointing as it does to a divine reality. Through the love of friendship, men and women may "embrace Christ in this life and enjoy eternal friendship with God in time to come."[38] Hospitality then has a sacramental as well as a missional dimension.[39]

As community gardeners seek to plant and nurture new faith communities, they are encouraged to foster inclusive, holistic friendships, with the potential to be sacramental, thus bearing fruit not only now, but in eternity.[40] Aelred speaks of a time "when the friendship to which on earth we admit but few will pour out over all and flow back to God from all, for God will be all in all."[41] The joyful implication here seems to be that God ultimately "excludes no one from friendship and the community it creates."[42] May we extend the same eschatological inclusivity in our friendships and communities.

---

33. Dutton, "Introduction," 33. After all, as Aelred asserts as he innovates on 1 John 4:16, not only does the one who remains in friendship remain in God, but God also remains in him or her" (Aelred, *De spiritali amicitia*, 1.70).

34. Dutton, "Sacramentality of Community in Aelred," 246.

35. Dutton, "Sacramentality of Community in Aelred," 246.

36. Dutton, "Sacramentality of Community in Aelred," 258.

37. Dutton, "Introduction," 47.

38. Dutton, "Introduction," 22–23.

39. James emphasizes that hospitality is "the most elemental missional task of ecclesial practice in places like Seattle" and desribes this hospitality as forging new friendships and creating spaces and communities of conversation and belonging (James, *Church Planting*, 227).

40. Aelred, *De spiritali amicitia*, 2.9.

41. Aelred, *De spiritali amicitia*, 3.134.

42. Dutton, "Sacramentality of Community in Aelred," 266.

The Shape of Friendship

I am aware that the shape of friendships that foster transformative gardens of friends may exhibit both similarities to, and differences from, contemporary cultural norms of friendship. How then are we to describe such friendships? In dialogue once again with Aelred, I suggest that we understand friendships contributing towards the nurturing of "transformative gardens" as being Spirit-shaped and Christic.

Whereas Aelred speaks of spiritual friendships, I suggest that we speak of *Spirit-shaped friendship*.[43] This terminology acknowledges the Spirit's role in the gifting and shaping of friendships and in drawing human beings into the triune friendship. The terminology of Spirit-shaped friendship is also in keeping with the recognition that God's gifting and shaping of friendship may well come prior to the discovery of friendship in Christ. God the Spirit is identified by Jürgen Moltmann as "the go-between God" and "the deity who is sociality."[44] Life that is empowered and shaped by the Spirit seeks the well-being of others. Life in the Spirit, as depicted by the words and actions of Jesus, is characterized by compassion communicated through care, by liberation, and by affection expressed in action. "This hints at the connection between life in the Spirit and a pervasive culture of mutuality and friendship, that seeks the well-being of others."[45] As we collaboratively seek, through the guidance and empowerment of the Spirit, to plant new communities, we can expect to nurture a culture of friendship. What then are the characteristics of Spirit-shaped friendships?

Spirit-shaped friendships promote care, compassion, and mutuality. Within the book of Acts, we find a description of the Spirit-empowered early church that echoes the tradition of friendship.[46] Rather than emphasizing friends having all things in common, this description emphasizes *believers* having all things in common. This description of the Spirit-empowered early church also echoes the civic friendship implicit

---

43. Aelred's use of the term *spiritual friendship* is broader than some contemporary uses of this term; his work implies that while spiritual friendship may begin with two friends, "as in Eden," it then expands to include many. Dutton, "Introduction," in *Spiritual Friendship*, 38.

44. Moltmann, *Broad Place*, 347.

45. Ellithorpe, "Towards a Practical Theology of Friendship," 127.

46. Acts 4:44–46.

within Deuteronomy, with its emphasis on common care, ensuring that there were no needy among them.[47]

Further, Spirit-shaped friendships are open, reflecting the radically open and inclusive nature of the Spirit and of the triune God. As teams seeking to plant new faith communities live experientially within the friendship of God, the openness of their friendship has the potential to echo that of the triune God. I suggest that their open friendship not only mirror, albeit very dimly, God's hospitable welcome, but also become foundational to the community's perception of itself.

Open friendships both foster unity and acknowledge diversity within the community. Given that the Spirit is concerned with all aspects of life, Spirit-shaped friendships vary in their focus. Those who seek to plant new faith communities will certainly benefit from "spiritual friendships," that is, friendships that proactively encourage greater attentiveness to the triune God, as well as to one another. Yet community gardeners, as we may call those who seek to nurture new (and renewed) faith communities, will also benefit from recognizing "every day" friendships as being shaped by the Spirit.

The shape of friendships that foster transformative gardens of friends is also Christic. Aelred describes friendship as beginning in Christ, continuing with Christ, and being perfected by Christ (1.10). The Gospels present the friendships of Jesus as being open and inclusive and implicitly call his followers to a similar life of friendship.[48] Within the Fourth Gospel, Jesus not only models but also encourages the laying down of one's life through the accompaniment in everyday life that is typical of friendship. Empowered by Jesus' love, friendship, and accompaniment, we are also called to lay down our lives as we love, befriend, and accompany others within the communities of worship that we seek to foster.[49] "Befriending love begets ever more love" as the loving action of Jesus is "shared with human community more broadly."[50]

---

47. See Deut 15:4, for example.
48. John 15:9–17.
49. Ringe, *Wisdom's Friends*, 67.
50. Kimbriel, *Friendship as Sacred Knowing*, 172.

Suggestions for Community Gardeners

Considering the relevance and shape of friendship acknowledged above, what suggestions can be provided for local community gardeners, that is, for those who seek to nurture new faith communities within Cascadian soil? I encourage such gardeners to consider the ways in which they characterize their relationships with God, self, community, and creation, and the nature of the vision that informs their work and relationships. What metaphors shape their theological imagination and their relational practices? How do they perceive the nature of the community that they seek to foster, and what terminology do they use to frame these perceptions?

I used the image of "gardens of friends" within my introductory paragraph to speak of new faith communities characterized by relationships of mutuality and interdependence. However, new faith communities may also be conceived of as "friendship-shaped communities," with friendship serving as an analogy for both the worshiping and missional dimensions of such communities. The vision inherent within many of the biblical texts is of communities "characterized by a culture of positive reciprocity, based on recognition of the dignity of all, and on positive regard for each person within the community."[51] Practices that contribute to friendship-shaped community include practices of worship, hospitality, compassion, and justice. Communities that nurture such practices have the potential to become characterized by love, trust, reciprocal care, and the celebration of *difference*. New faith communities may also foster the friendship inherent to "beloved community."

"Beloved community" is a phrase that has been used to speak of the Triune community.[52] Beloved community has also been used to speak of new social spaces of reconciliation that reveal God as being "on the side of truth and love and justice."[53] Such spaces of reconciliation are a gift of the kingdom and of the inbreaking of God's reign. While beloved community is to be nurtured by the church, and through the fostering of new communities of faith, such community ultimately overflows the church's

---

51. Ellithorpe, "Towards a Practical Theology of Friendship, 148.
52. See Hinlicky, *Beloved Community*.
53. Marsh, *Beloved Community*, 50.

boundaries.[54] As Charles Marsh asserts, its pursuit is grounded, framed, and surrounded by the kingdom.[55]

Community gardeners are encouraged to be proactive in their cultivation of friendships and community. They may need to challenge cultural and ecclesial norms when it comes to friendship, and to wrestle with ways in which they can most appropriately attend to their own friendship needs. Within conventional pastoral contexts, mentors and supervisors have discouraged long-term friendships with parishioners.[56] This is typically based on a narrow perception of friend as confidante. Community gardeners, as with other pastoral roles, may well benefit from the gift of a confidante or "dustbin" friend outside of the new faith community, who has the wisdom to collect outpoured words and emotions without taking on an inappropriate problem-solving role, getting worked up, or judging.[57] Yet this does not prohibit the nurturing of other types of friendships within the new community.

I advocate for friendship to be reclaimed as an ethical relationship, integral to the life of new faith communities as well as the broader community. Restricted cultural concepts about friendship have resulted in friendship being understood too narrowly by pastors, and thus being rejected. Tim Brown, for example, in his blog post entitled "Why Your Pastor Is Actually Not Your Friend," portrays friendship as an enmeshed co-dependent relationship, where distance cannot be tolerated.[58] Yet friendship rather needs to be understood more broadly and more multidimensionally by pastor-gardeners rather than avoided. As community gardeners seek to plant and to nurture new faith communities, it is important that they are aware of both their own needs and desires for relationships of mutuality and friendship, and the needs and desires of others within the broader community.

Those who tend to gardens within Cascadian soil, as elsewhere, do of course need to be discerning. Even with a commitment to open friendship, pastor-gardeners cannot maintain close friendships with all. Rather,

54. Marsh, *Beloved Community*, 211.

55. "When the church defaults on its mission in the world, the Spirit places the beloved community in the embracing arms of the kingdom of God" (Marsh, *Beloved Community*, 208).

56. See, for example, Proeschold-Bell and Byassee, *Faithful and Fractured*, 69. Proeschold-Bell and Byassee both acknowledge and critique this discouragement of pastor–parishioner friendship.

57. Vanier, *Community and Growth*, 184.

58. Brown, "Why Your Pastor."

to paraphrase Simone Weil, each gardener must love specific human beings in ways that she would ultimately desire to be able to love each and every person.[59]

Nevertheless, those who seek to nurture new faith communities within Cascadia have the opportunity to foster friendship-shaped communities, characterized by compassion and justice, through the fostering of Spirit-shaped friendships. They are encouraged to collaboratively study various aspects of the prophetic tradition in ways that nurture an alternative imagination within their communities, thus fostering friendship, compassion, justice, and social transformation.[60] They are encouraged to bring this tradition into conversation with writings that explore the concept of civic friendship. Community gardeners are further encouraged to remember that discipleship, formation, mission, and worship are social rather than solitary endeavors.[61] As James notes, "Jesus's own pedagogy with his disciples was via an extended, relationally intimate cohort of apprentices."[62] These apprentices he later called friends.

Therefore, friendship is relevant to the calling and work of church planting. Friendship is to be celebrated and fostered as integral to new faith communities, as we are invited into the friendship of the Trinity, acknowledge the human need and desire for relationality and friendship, and through the empowering of the Spirit follow Jesus in living a life of open friendship. The life of reconciliation, community, and friendship to which we are called may be cultivated through new faith communities. As such communities are shaped by friendship, they may be described as gardens of friends and foster "beloved community." The friendship celebrated within this chapter is Spirit-shaped and Christic, drawing human beings into triune friendship and promoting care, compassion, mutuality, and open friendship. Its importance should not be overlooked. Rather, gardeners who seek to plant and tend new communities within Cascadian soil are encouraged to explore ways in which a theological vision of friendship may inform their work and relationships. Pastor-gardeners are further encouraged to cultivate a range of friendships, to reject narrow conceptions of friendship, to explore notions of civic friendship, and to collaboratively explore aspects of the prophetic tradition in ways that nurture an alternative imagination.

59. As in Weil, "Friendship," 135–36.
60. Brueggemann, *Practice of Prophetic Imagination*, 2–3.
61. James, *Church Planting*, 225.
62. James, *Church Planting*, 226.

In closing, I note that friendship in its various forms has contributed towards various reform movements throughout the centuries. Throughout the history of the church, friendship has contributed to the alternative and often more radical expressions of church that have existed alongside what we may call mainline Christianity or the institutional church. Friendship has contributed to the new monasticism of Augustine, the new apostolic order of Ignatius of Loyola, the Carmelite reform of Teresa of Avila, and the social reform of the Clapham community. As friendship is nurtured within and through new faith communities, they likewise have potential to contribute towards reform and transformation.

Bibliography

Brown, Tim. "Why Your Pastor Is Actually Not Your Friend." *Reluctant Xtian*, September 18, 2017.

Brueggemann, Walter. *The Practice of Prophetic Imagination: Preaching an Emancipating Word*. Minneapolis: Fortress, 2012.

Carmichael, Liz. *Friendship: Interpreting Christian Love*. London: T. & T. Clark, 2004.

Coakley, Sarah. *God, Sexuality and the Self: An Essay "on the Trinity."* Cambridge: Cambridge University Press, 2013.

Dutton, Marsha L., ed. *Aelred of Rievaulx: Spiritual Friendship*. Collegeville, MN: Cistercian, 2010.

———, ed. *A Companion to Aelred of Rievaulx (1110–1167)*. Leiden: Brill, 2017.

———. "Introduction." In *Aelred of Rievaulx: Spiritual Friendship*, edited by Marsha L. Dutton, 13–52. Collegeville, MN: Cistercian, 2010.

———. "The Sacramentality of Community in Aelred." In *A Companion to Aelred of Rievaulx (1110–1167)*, edited by Marsha L. Dutton, 246–67. Leiden: Brill, 2017.

Ellithorpe, Anne-Marie. "Towards a Practical Theology of Friendship." PhD diss., University of Queensland, 2018.

Grenz, Stanley J. *The Social God and the Relational Self: A Trinitarian Theology of the Imago Dei*. Louisville: Westminster John Knox, 2001.

Hinlicky, Paul R. *Beloved Community: Critical Dogmatics after Christendom*. Grand Rapids: Eerdmans, 2015.

Hoekema, Anthony A. *Created in God's Image*. Grand Rapids: Eerdmans, 1986.

James, Christopher B. *Church Planting in Post-Christian Soil: Theology and Practice*. New York: Oxford University Press, 2018.

Kassam, Ashifa. "Is Vancouver Lonelier Than Most Cities or Just Better about Addressing It?" *The Guardian*, April 4, 2017. https://www.theguardian.com/world/2017/apr/04/vancouver-loneliness-engaged-city-taskforce-canada.

Kimbriel, Samuel. *Friendship as Sacred Knowing: Overcoming Isolation*. New York: Oxford University Press, 2014.

Marsh, Charles. *The Beloved Community: How Faith Shapes Social Justice, from the Civil Rights Movement to Today*. New York: Basic Books, 2005.

McGuire, Brian Patrick. *Friendship and Community: The Monastic Experience, 350–1250*. 2nd ed. Ithaca: Cornell University Press, 2010.

Moltmann, Jürgen. *A Broad Place: An Autobiography*. Minneapolis: Fortress, 2008.

Moltmann-Wendel, Elisabeth. *Rediscovering Friendship: Awakening to the Power and Promise of Women's Friendships*. Translated by John Bowden. Minneapolis: Fortress, 2001.

Proeschold-Bell, Rae Jean, and Jason Byassee. *Faithful and Fractured: Responding to the Clergy Health Crisis*. Grand Rapids: Baker, 2018.

Ringe, Sharon H. *Wisdom's Friends: Community and Christology in the Fourth Gospel*. Louisville: Westminster John Knox, 1999.

Schwarzenbach, Sibyl A. "Fraternity, Solidarity and Civic Friendship." *AMITY: The Journal of Friendship Studies* 3.1 (2015) 3–18.

Sommerfeldt, John R. "Anthropology and Cosmology: The Foundational Principles of Aelred's Spirituality." In *A Companion to Aelred of Rievaulx (1110–1167)*, edited by Marsha L. Dutton, 98–112. Leiden: Brill, 2017.

Soskice, Janet Martin. *The Kindness of God: Metaphor, Gender and Religious Language*. Oxford: Oxford University Press, 2007.

Vanier, Jean. *Community and Growth*. New York: Paulist, 1989.

Weil, Simone. "Friendship." In *Waiting for God*, translated by Emma Craufurd, 131–42. New York: HarperCollins, 1951.

9

Soldiers to Midwives

An Exploration of Belief and Practice around Evangelism

JENN RICHARDS

"THE WORD BECAME FLESH and made his dwelling among us."[1] This statement holds incredible implications for the church's theology and praxis of evangelism and the theological significance words embody. Yet so often those who follow the Word are afraid to use words to bear witness to the Word. We may be open to dwelling among our Cascadian neighbors, colleagues, and friends, but the thought of bearing witness to the God-Made-Flesh through speech is so daunting that it becomes simpler to hope that niceties, politeness, and the occasional generous deed will be enough—that God will see it as being enough.

In his book *Evangelism after Christendom*, Bryan Stone argues that those who regularly think about theology rarely think about evangelism, and those who frequently think about evangelism seldom take the discipline of theology seriously.[2] He goes on to observe that a crucial implication of this divide is that little attention has been given to the relationship

---

1. John 1:14. All Scripture references are NIV unless otherwise indicated.
2. Stone, *Evangelism after Christendom*, 18.

between the practice of evangelism and its proper telos or end.[3] How we think about evangelism and how we judge its effectiveness depends on our theology. Stone contends that problematic theology has led to problematic practice. The aim of this chapter is to integrate the theology and praxis of evangelism, specifically within the context of considering the metaphorical framework we use in the evangelism conversation. Overall, I contend for a shift in the primary metaphor used around evangelism from military-focused to birth-focused. The work of evangelism involves accepting the invitation God is lavishly offering God's people to be spiritual midwives in the redemptive work God is birthing and to bear witness to this work through our everyday actions and words.

Military imagery is a common metaphor used within the context of Western evangelism. If one were to simply scan the table of contents of evangelism books in a theological library they would find chapter and section titles such as "Out Beyond the Walls,"[4] "Mission Impossible,"[5] "Mobilizing Inactive Congregations,"[6] and "Penetrate Subcultures: Don't Become One."[7] And yet even though military imagery can be found in both the Old and New Testaments, if we look carefully at these passages in context, especially those in the New Testament, we find that military imagery is rarely directed to how Christians should view or act towards nonbelievers.[8] For example, in Ephesians 6:12 Paul reminds the church in Ephesus that "our struggle is not against flesh and blood, but against the rulers, against the authorities, against the powers of this dark world and against the spiritual forces of evil in the heavenly realms."

Furthermore, integrating this metaphorical framework into our evangelistic imagination can be exceedingly dangerous. Rick Love observes that the two major ways military imagery is used in the New Testament are for comparison and contrast: to compare the Christian life to the disciplined, single-minded life of a solider and to contrast spiritual warfare with physical warfare.[9] There are significant lessons we can learn from the discipline of soldiers, including the important reminder to always know who the

---

3. Stone, *Evangelism after Christendom*, 18.
4. Sweazey, *Effective Evangelism*, 257–63.
5. Willis, *Won by One*, 1–13.
6. Stebbins, *Evangelism by the Book*, 77–102.
7. Morris, *The High Impact Church*, 151–53.
8. Love, "Muslims and Military Metaphors."
9. Love, "Muslims and Military Metaphors."

enemy is and who it is not, and yet broadening our scope of the metaphor past its biblical range is exceedingly dangerous.

When we use military language in the human sphere of evangelism, it subtly shapes how we view the people to whom we are sent.[10] We begin to see them as "targets," we look to "mobilize the missionaries," and we aim to "penetrate the land."[11] Moreover, even if we never explicitly use this language, to have it as an undercurrent within our mindset leads to depersonalization and a skewed vision of success.[12] When a means of communication does not accurately communicate theological or biblical truths, the means itself should be questioned.

Furthermore, military imagery brings theological misguidance to whose fight we are fighting. "Evangelism is ultimately an activity of the Holy Spirit and is not subject to our own calculus of effectiveness and 'return on investment.'"[13] This does not deny that Christian practice requires faithful obedience and hard work, but rather we must always remember that, in a strange sort of way, Christian practices always involve both a "doing" and a "be it done unto me."[14] "The invitation of God is to incarnate in the way of Jesus, living wholeheartedly in the world as we are transformed by the presence of the Holy Spirit in the places where we live, work, serve, and play. It is the Spirit within us that impacts and alters the environments we inhabit. It is the same Spirit in us and all around us that impacts and alters us."[15] Military imagery suppresses the dance of initiation and invitation involved in evangelism that occurs between oneself, others, and the Holy Spirit. This does not mean that strategic thinking is to be discarded or that the military metaphor is not appropriate for other theological concepts, but rather that a "new rhetorical vision must be developed . . . that is more fully biblically informed, anthropologically sound and worthy to guide the whole church in God's mission in the 21st century."[16] My suggestion for this new rhetorical vision is the topic I will turn to next.

---

10. Love, "Muslims and Military Metaphors."
11. Rynkiewich, "Corporate Metaphors," 221.
12. Love, "Muslims and Military Metaphors."
13. Stone, *Evangelism after Christendom*, 21.
14. Stone, *Evangelism after Christendom*, 228.
15. Frost and Rice, *To Alter Your World*, 49.
16. Rynkiewich, "Corporate Metaphors," 234.

I am proposing that the church shift from a military metaphor to a birth metaphor in our discussion and praxis around evangelism.[17] Birth imagery is not only generously developed across the Scriptures, but it is also used both explicitly and implicitly in texts involving missional instruction.[18] For example, in Isaiah 66:9 God is revealed as the one who gives birth to the newborn nation of Israel; in Romans 8 Paul uses the birthing metaphor to describe the groans and pains of creation waiting for the realization of God's full reign and rule, and a coherence between the birth metaphor and conversion is evident in Jesus' conversation with Nicodemus in John 3. Furthermore, one could connect Paul's discussion of the fruit of the Spirit in Galatians 5 to a "birthing" that occurs within believers. In the way that fruit is birthed beyond the strength and effort of the branch, so does the Spirit birth fruit within disciples.[19]

If a birth metaphor lends itself as an accurate scriptural framework, what are the implications for how we think, act, and live evangelistically among our "affable agnostic"[20] Cascadian colleagues, friends, and neighbors? I believe the overarching implication is that our role in evangelism is to be midwives with the Spirit.[21] I will now consider three implications of being midwives with the Spirit within the framework of evangelism.

The first implication around spiritual midwifery is the idea of intentional partnership. "The literal meaning of the word [midwife] is 'with-woman' that is, the person who is with the birth-giver."[22] Just as a midwife comes alongside a laboring mother, so we are invited to come alongside the powerful force of the Spirit who is working in each human to birth the miracle of divine new life.[23] This partnership is anything but passive, rather our call is to intentionality—to listen attentively to every murmur and groan and look beyond surface behavior to observe what a casual onlooker

---

17. I use the term "birth" to include the physical act of childbirth, but also other types of birth such as vegetation in nature, the birthing of creativity in the artistic process, and the birth of mutuality and connection that happens within relationships.

18. I was first introduced to this metaphor in Michael Frost and Christiana Rice's book *To Alter Your World*.

19. Frost and Rice, *To Alter Your World*.

20. I have borrowed this term from Rev. Dr. Ross Lockhart.

21. Valuable insight for this research came from interviewing two women, Rachelle Fulford and Tracy Kemp, who both currently practice midwifery in Vancouver, BC.

22. Guenther, *Holy Listening*, 86.

23. Frost and Rice, *To Alter Your World*, 65.

would miss completely.[24] Intentionality involves prioritizing practices such as asking good questions and listening well, in the desire to come alongside the Spirit's active work. Furthermore, spiritual practices such as prayer find their place in evangelism in a way that involves not prodding God to act, but rather connecting, debriefing, and seeking direction with the One who's actively championing it all.

A crucial part of this intentional partnership is what Margaret Guenther calls "mutual presence."[25] This is where the birther feels solidarity with the midwife due to their emotional involvement.[26] Guenther points out that, until recently, the only factor that made someone qualified to be a midwife was that they themselves had given birth.[27] The implications of this for spiritual midwifery is that value is placed not on being an expert or having a formal role, but rather simply being fully present and freely sharing personal experiences of one's own faith-birthing process. In contrast, military imagery places the believer in an oppositional stance against unbelievers. The goal is to "win over." Rather, if we view the unbelievers around us as being on the same journey we are on and our desire is to simply point to the One we follow and find rest and security in (knowing that the Lord of Mutual Presence is involved more than we ever could be), suddenly we can simply share and offer to walk with fellow travelers, rather than striving to win over or convince.

Second, midwives honor and value time and waiting. There is a deep understanding in midwifery that in the process of waiting, important things are happening that are unseen by the human eye.[28] "We mustn't forget that there are almost ten months of gestation before new life emerges into the world. And those months of waiting and growth are often filled with a blend of excitement, fear and uncertainty."[29] In the times when it is easy to believe God's work is falling on deaf ears and cold hearts, let us continually remember that some of the most important periods in the birthing process transpire while hidden from the human eye.[30] Rather than worrying or

---

24. Frost and Rice, *To Alter Your World*, 71.
25. Guenther, *Holy Listening*, 97.
26. Guenther, *Holy Listening*, 97.
27. Guenther, *Holy Listening*, 97.
28. Guenther, *Holy Listening*, 92.
29. Frost and Rice, *To Alter Your World*, 54.
30. Frost and Rice, *To Alter Your World*, 54.

pushing, we are called to respond to God's work during these times with receptivity, patience, and prayer.

Finally, midwifery welcomes both the universal and the specific nature of the birthing process. There are almost always certain elements that are present in all births and yet no two births in all of history have ever been identical. When applied to evangelism, the mixture of universality and specificity found in a birth framework gives room for the process of coming to faith to be far more unscripted than traditional frameworks allow. Reverently holding both the universal and the unique elements of the birthing of faith in holy tension involves viewing the process as person-centered rather than content-centered.[31] A birth framework allows us to hold the wider God-centered perspective in view, to be intentionally present with the person with whom we are interacting, and to not attempt to simply cover specific content in a one-size-fits-all way or feel overwhelmed and therefore doing nothing at all.

There are two specific implications of being person-centered in the ethos of midwifery. First of all, valuing both the experience and the outcome of the birth process allows midwifery to flourish in vastly diverse settings. There are certain standard tenets that are present in all midwifery practices, and yet the practice itself translates just as beautifully to rural farmhouses as it does to large urban hospitals.[32] This idea has interesting implications for evangelism. It speaks into the conversation around how core tenets in our faith need to always be held, but stemming from those tenets can be a freedom to participate in the spiritual particularities God is birthing in each person, in each culture, and in each time.[33] We see Jesus following this principle when, for example in Mark 1, he instructs and inspires his first disciples by telling them that if they choose to follow him then their lives will no longer be about fishing for fish, but rather fishing for men. Jesus took a general Christian tenant regarding mission and applied it specifically to the context that his disciples were familiar with. In other contexts, such as in Matthew 10, Jesus instruction involves warning these same disciples that they're going out like sheep among wolves. Why the different metaphor? Different contexts require it. Where apologetics training within a military framework may involve memorizing a set of scriptural

---

31. Frost and Rice, *To Alter Your World*, 207.
32. Hawkins and Knox, *The Midwifery Option*, 1.
33. This does not mean that cultural translation of content is not important, but rather where this idea lies within its importance in the larger conversation is critical.

laws or given responses for specific arguments against the Christian faith, a birth metaphor looks to communicate broad Christian concepts using the wealth of connections one can make to the human person and experience that would be applicable to specific individuals in specific contexts. This requires creativity, imagination, and the ever-present help of the Spirit. It is far less safe than memorizing a set of answers, but I dare say it is also a lot more fun.

Second, midwifery's ability to value both the birther's experience as well as the outcome makes this birth option especially attractive and effective among marginalized populations of women who do not fit into mainstream societal practices.[34] This implication extends powerfully to evangelism in our day. When we view the church's involvement in spreading the Christian faith as participating in God's work of cherishing people and their experiences, we will be able to participate in the faith God is birthing in those whom we do not typically see sitting in our church pews, and who may have been historically marginalized from viewing themselves as having a place within the kingdom of God.

I will now consider what specific praxis looks like in light of the theological implications of the birth and midwifery metaphor in evangelism. It would be easy to fall into the trap of seeing the practices of spiritual midwifery as solely involving witness through action, and yet this would be a tragic mistake. We see in Scripture the portrait of Creator God who speaks through burning bushes, donkeys, angels, and ultimately through Jesus Christ. And yet through all these various means, there is a clear pattern in the biblical narrative that God desires to birth redemption through the spoken word of his people.[35] If this is true, then bearing witness to God's rule and reign must include the act of speaking. Fortunately, we do not need to stumble in the dark in figuring out what this means; rather we have strong examples in the Scriptures to mold our speech. We can look to the words of the prophets, to the powerful speeches of the apostles in Acts, and to the most powerful example of witness-bearing dialogue of all: the ministry of Christ. "Jesus' authority for prophetic vocation came from the same Spirit that breathed life into creation in the beginning. His authority was expressed through voice. The integrity of his life lay in the congruity between his actions and speech in relation to God's action and speech."[36]

---

34. Tracy Kemp (practicing midwife), interview with the author, March 6, 2019.
35. Turner and Hudson, *Saved from Silence*, 20.
36. Turner and Hudson, *Saved from Silence*, 51.

We follow and serve a God who was embodied for our salvation, which includes the embodiment of human speech, and part of the invitation to bear witness to his goodness comes through the embodied expression of speaking words. It is not a coincidence that creation was birthed through breath and that the act of speaking also begins with this most basic act of life itself.[37] Bearing witness to God's rule and reign must include the act of speaking.

And yet when we think about verbal practices in relation to evangelism, exercises such as door-to-door evangelism or street preaching may be what comes to mind. Even though these practices are valuable in certain situations, I would like to propose two simple practices that all Christians are called to in their daily spiritual midwifery work.

The first spiritual midwifery practice is the use of liturgy that focuses on God's initiation and action. In his book *You Are What You Love,* James K. A. Smith proposes that the recalibration of our heart's desire happens when we start from the assumption that human beings are not first and foremost thinking things, but rather lovers who are defined by what we desire.[38] Smith proposes that we need "to immerse ourselves in liturgies that are indexed to the kingdom of God precisely so that even our unconscious desires and longings . . . are indexed to God and what God wants for his world."[39] Practice birth habits which in turn birth the good of what these practices have to offer.[40] Smith encourages Christians to be intentional with the liturgies we allow in our lives because they undeniably shape us. If we are desiring to participate in God's birth of redemption in the world, I believe the rhythm of speaking liturgies that proclaim this truth is a crucial practice.

Rather than our liturgies prompting God to do something, they should verbalize our desire for Creator God to give us eyes to see what God is already doing and asking for grace, bravery, and vision to join in. If we're not intentional, our liturgies can sound more like the frantic pleading of the prophets of Baal and Asherah on Mount Carmel in 1 Kings 18, seeking the right formula of action and word to get their god's attention, rather than the words of Elijah, who confidently proclaimed who God is and the simple

---

37. Turner and Hudson, *Saved from Silence,* 8.
38. Turner and Hudson, *Saved from Silence,* 7.
39. Smith, *Desiring the Kingdom,* 24.
40. Smith, *You Are What You Love,* 24.

request for God to reveal God's self to God's people.[41] When we recite and sing liturgies that emphasize what God is birthing in the world, our hearts will be formed toward this very mindset. Both together as worshiping communities and alone in personal times of prayer, if we intentionally are proclaiming God's birthing action, our hearts, minds, and hands will be slowly trained to see in the world what our words are testifying.

Second, a practice that I believe will equip and encourage our role as midwives with the Spirit is storytelling. There is extensive discussion in Christian literature currently around embodying the story of God,[42] and while I do not want to downplay the importance of this, I believe embodied storytelling cannot replace verbal storytelling. I am not referring here to formal, crafted stories, but simply small stories in conversation that bear witness to God's goodness in everyday life. "Not only are word pictures and stories essential to good speech communication, they are inherent to the revelation of God in Scripture. Ours is a historical faith . . . the experiences of ordinary people made extraordinary by [God's] special involvement in [our] lives."[43]

The practice of conversational storytelling is highly relevant in our Cascadian context. Postmodern culture has developed a high degree of skepticism toward the notion of metanarratives and accuses such frameworks as homogenizing all individual narratives for the sake of oppression.[44] "But what if Christianity can offer a metanarrative that is . . . relational yet not collectivist, personal yet not atomistic, one that can absorb all the personal stories into one grand story without obliterating the identity of each story in doing so?"[45] I believe that natural storytelling in our daily conversations is one of the most effective ways of doing this. Sam Chan points out that "a postmodern person is likely to accept our testimony as a valid source of knowledge. Moreover, our testimony demonstrates that the gospel works. And even better, while our non-Christian friend can argue against a truth claim, there is no argument against our personal story."[46] This does not

---

41. I first heard this application to the 1 Kgs 18 story in a lecture by Andrea Tischer in "Preaching and Worship" class on March 17, 2018, Regent College.

42. For example, James K. A. Smith discusses the embodied practice of telling the Christian story in his book *Introducing Radical Orthodoxy*, 181.

43. McDill, *The 12 Essential Skills for Great Preaching*, 223.

44. Hastings, *Missional God, Missional Church*, 89.

45. Hastings, *Missional God, Missional Church*, 89.

46. Chan, *Evangelism in a Skeptical World*, 118.

mean that our full testimony needs to be shared in every story, but rather that in sharing small pieces of our faith through organic stories that bear witness to God's work in the world, we are planting and cultivating seeds in people's lives, even invisible to us at the time, that God uses to birth faith.

The type of environment in which I primarily envision these types of storytelling conversations occurring is what David Fitch refers to as "half-circle environments."[47] This type of situation is when our Christian identity is a guest and a minority within a group.[48] Examples of such environments include the staffroom at work, a parent–child play group at a community center, or a dinner party at a neighbor's house. In contrast, what Fitch refers to as a "close circle environment" would be a Sunday morning church service where Christ is the host and we are the recipients, or Fitch's "dotted circle" represented by our homes where our Christian identity is the host to others who do not follow Christ. Fitch argues that in half-circle environments, just as in the close and dotted circles, we are to always humbly tend to Christ's presence, even when that presence is difficult to see.[49] In this situation, when we feel an invitation by the Spirit, we are called to proclaim the good news of Christ through our own stories.[50] We cannot control what happens in these types of situations, nor should we strive for control; rather it is through our actions and in humbly sharing our stories that we have the privilege of participating in the redemption of the world by bearing witness to God's faithful presence.[51]

In conclusion, I desire for the church to reimagine a framework for evangelism that is scripturally and theologically sound and also reveals a vision for the proclamation of the gospel that is good news in both process and content. In order to see this vision become reality in our time, I believe a shift is required in the primary metaphor used around evangelism, moving from military-focused to birth-focused. God is calling his people to understand evangelism as life-giving, unique, and exciting. As we seek to have eyes to see our role in sharing the gospel as participating in God's work of birthing redemption and restoration for all of creation, we will find our place and our voice as midwives in this work to be life-giving for both ourselves and the people with whom we have the privilege of journeying.

---

47. Fitch, *Faithful Presence*, 108.
48. Fitch, *Faithful Presence*, 108.
49. Fitch, *Faithful Presence*, 108.
50. Fitch, *Faithful Presence*, 108.
51. Fitch, *Faithful Presence*, 108.

Bibliography

Chan, Sam. *Evangelism in a Skeptical World: How to Make the Unbelievable News about Jesus More Believable.* Grand Rapids: Zondervan, 2018.

Fitch, David E. *Faithful Presence: Seven Disciplines That Shape the Church for Mission.* Downers Grove: InterVarsity, 2016.

Frost, Michael, and Christiana Rice. *To Alter Your World: Partnering with God to Rebirth Our Communities.* Downers Grove: InterVarsity, 2017.

Guenther, Margaret. *Holy Listening: The Art of Spiritual Direction.* Cambridge: Cowley, 1992.

Hastings, Ross. *Missional God, Missional Church: Hope for Re-evangelizing the West.* Downers Grove: InterVarsity, 2012.

Hawkins, Miranda, and Sarah Knox. *The Midwifery Option: A Canadian Guide to the Birth Experience.* Toronto: HarperCollins, 2003.

Love, Rick. "Muslims and Military Metaphors." *Evangelical Missions Quarterly* 37 (2001) 65–68.

McDill, Wayne. *The 12 Essential Skills for Great Preaching.* Nashville: Broadman & Holman, 1994.

Mollenkott, Virginia Ramey. *The Divine Feminine: The Biblical Imagery of God as Female.* New York: Crossroad, 1984.

Morris, Linus John. *The High Impact Church: A Fresh Approach to Reaching the Unchurched.* Houston: Touch Publications, 1993.

Rynkiewich, Michael A. "Corporate Metaphors and Strategic Thinking: 'The 10/40 Window' in the American Evangelical Worldview." *Missiology* 35 (2007) 217–41.

Smith, James K. A. *Introducing Radical Orthodoxy: Mapping a Post-Secular Theology.* Grand Rapids: Baker Academic, 2004.

———. *You Are What You Love: The Spiritual Power of Habit.* Grand Rapids: Brazos, 2016.

Stebbins, Tom. *Evangelism by the Book: 13 Biblical Methods.* Camp Hill, PA: Christian Publications, 1991.

Stone, Bryan P. *Evangelism after Christendom: The Theology and Practice of Christian Witness.* Grand Rapids: Brazos, 2007.

Sweazey, George E. *Effective Evangelism: The Greatest Work in the World.* New York: Harper & Row, 1976.

Turner, Mary Donovan, and Hudson, Mary Lin. *Saved from Silence: Finding Women's Voice in Preaching.* St. Louis: Chalice, 1999.

Willis, Geoffrey. *Won by One: How to Help Your Friends Find Faith.* Basingstoke: Marshall Pickering, 1994.

10

New Witnessing Communities in an Age of Decline

Andrew Stephens-Rennie

We were introduced after the service by a member of the greeting team at St. Brigid's. Worship had just come to a conclusion and we were headed downstairs to continue in the hospitality of Christ's table over coffee, tea, and whatever snacks had been brought that evening. I showed him over to the coffee station, and we each helped ourselves and found a place to sit. Before too long, he shared his name and revealed, "I think that I would like to become a Christian. Could you tell me more?" I stood stunned for a moment before regaining composure. The seeds of new faith were seeking to take root, and I was momentarily unprepared to receive them.

Over the course of the next hour, he told me more of his story, of how he found himself walking by the church a few days after Christmas. He heard the bells ring and was drawn to attention. He looked up, from the street corner at Burrard and West Georgia streets, to see the sign reading *Open Doors, Open Hearts, Open Minds*, and it resonated. After these two signs—one audible, the second visual—he responded by doing the only thing he could do. He walked up the stairs, crossed the threshold, and came in. He walked from the back of the church, past the greeters, past the rows of mostly empty chairs (it was noon on a Friday) and up to the chancel where Eucharist was about to start. He took a booklet, looking at the unfamiliar words, following along with his part in the bold. When it came to Eucharist, he received the bread and the wine, answers to questions he was still forming. Afterwards he spoke to the priest (visiting from another parish), asking about the ritual he had just participated in. What did it all mean? At the end of that conversation, she invited him to return to one of the Sunday services, where he could connect with the community, a member of the Cathedral's clergy, and enroll in classes where he might learn more about the Christian faith. And that, he told me, was how we had now come to be drinking coffee and eating chocolate chip cookies together that night.

In the six years since the Rev. Marnie Peterson and I co-planted St. Brigid's, the evening congregation at Vancouver's Christ Church Cathedral, conversations like these have only increased. Even so, each one catches me ever-so-slightly off guard.[1] For much of my life, conversations about Jesus have either been with those who consider themselves to be a part of the Christian household or with those whose religious trauma and negative experiences of church require a lot more unpacking.

For a period in my late twenties, living in Ottawa, nearly every party I attended would end with me sitting in a corner listening to someone's life story as they tried to unpack a hurtful experience with church. When people found out I worked for the church, they wanted to talk. One of the many upsides of this period was the way in which I was saved from needing to make small talk—a fate worse than death. Another, of course, was the sacred gift of hearing and bearing witness to someone's story, their questions, and first steps towards resolution. In these moments I often received the gift of sharing my story of faith lost and rediscovered, and of praying with people seeking to navigate a way forward in their complicated relationship to Jesus and his church.

For years, these conversations have carried a common theme: a deep curiosity about Jesus intertwined with suspicion of the institutional church. More recently, different conversations are coming my way. It has been an unexpected—if disorienting—change to talk about Jesus without first having to help unpack years of disappointment with the church. My evangelical upbringing prepared me to speak to people about Jesus. In Sunday school and youth group I learned how to make winsome arguments for God's sovereignty, to be a defender of right belief. I could be combative at times, and other times—as my faith evolved and my own questions arose—I learned to extend more grace to those who had walked away or were considering some sort of return. Reflecting on the teaching, mission trips, and evangelistic events in which I participated, I had not been adequately prepared for

---

1. For more on the St. Brigid's congregation, visit www.stbrigid.ca.

this particular moment when a person of another faith walked in off the street, announcing their desire to follow Jesus.

For weeks in a row, my new friend and I would meet after the service to talk about Jesus. We'd often start with reflections on the liturgy in which we'd just participated, moving on from there. He would wonder at the Christian story woven throughout: the Scriptures read, the sermon preached, the prayers prayed, the songs sung. And then he would bring questions. Is there one God, or are there three? Who is this Jesus? Why is he so important? What did he do? Why is he to be worshiped? Why do you think that he is God? Why do you follow after him? Why should I? How should I do so? What is baptism? And then (perhaps most pressing): how would you support me, a Hindu, if I chose to follow Jesus instead?

I grew up a Christian, the child of Christian parents, a member of a tightly knit group of Christian friends to whom I did not have to explain myself or my beliefs. This has been true from birth. It was this same Christian community that prayerfully and financially supported me when I travelled to Kolkata, India, to serve alongside Mother Teresa's Missionaries of Charity in the summer of 2005. My time there was humbling, challenging, transformative. Looking back on my searching journal entries and emotionally confused emails to folks back home, I'm surprised that my family and friends didn't worry more. My world was being turned upside down. God was fundamentally rewiring my faith. Partway through my time in Kolkata, needing a retreat, I left the scorching plains behind for several weeks of relief in the Eastern Himalayas.

My new friend's question about what support he should be prepared to receive from this congregation brought me suddenly back to the daily Bible study I attended while staying in Darjeeling. The study group gathered in the home of a local pastor I had befriended after attending his church. Each morning I would trudge half-asleep up and down misty streets from my hostel to his modest flat across town. I would enter. We would sit. Chai was waiting. Together we would read the Scriptures aloud and pray that God would teach us how to faithfully live.

Our contexts were different. I was a traveler in town for a short period of time. Eventually I would head back down the mountain to meet up with another group coming from Canada. He was a pastor with a young family who had grown up in the region. He shared with me his hopes of one day visiting the United States or Canada. We were warmed by tea, fire, and a sense of connection. We fought off the early-morning mountain chill in shared hospitality and nourishing conversation. Even though I had come to this place as a means of retreat, it was in that room, steaming mug in hand, that I came face-to-face with the more divisive implications of the gospel.

Joining us at several of these gatherings was a young man in his thirties, a new convert to Christianity. He came to the gathering with the look of one struggling with the weight of a great decision. And the decision was weighty. What would it mean to become a part of this congregation? What would it cost to publicly embrace this faith in Jesus? What relationships would be lost? How would his business be impacted by his faith in Jesus? His fears were real and present: social isolation, poverty, loss. Those hazy mountain mornings called into question the givenness and relative ease of following Jesus with which I had grown up. I had a family and a community that would support me in that relationship. But if I walked away? What would that look like? If I didn't have those supports, what would happen to my life? Discipleship is costly. My life back home was not. Thousands of miles away from the Himalayan foothills I wonder: how prepared are our churches, accustomed as we are to a place of privilege, to receive those Jesus is calling to himself on this Cascadian soil?

In February 2018, a one-hundred-year-old Anglican church was put up for sale in Vancouver's beachside Kitsilano neighborhood. Asking price: $12 million. The remaining congregation had moved out a number of years earlier, merging with a parish across town and meeting in a small building near Vancouver General Hospital. Even though the people of St. Mark's moved out in 2015, ministry did not cease in that neighborhood—in fact it continued to flourish. Tenth Church, a multi-site evangelical church in need of a home for its multigenerational west side congregation, started to rent. Tenth became involved in the neighborhood, even taking on some of the ministries (including a holiday meal for those suffering loneliness at Christmas) that had been organized by the previous congregation. They followed Jesus' call and ended up partnering with other congregations of a variety of denominations to respond to the neighborhood's needs. This exploration led to the development of the "Kits Cares Café," a Thursday-evening community meal hosted by a group of local churches at Kitsilano Neighbourhood House every week.

When St. Mark's was put up for sale, several news outlets picked up the story.[2] They gave the specs of the property: its large frontage and square footage. It read in part like an ad for redevelopment. After some time, a

---

2. Lazatin, "You Can Own St. Mark's."

developer bought the property, rezoning it with plans to construct five storeys of rental housing.[3] The site is now under construction. The city is, of course, in need of rental housing. All anybody talks about in Vancouver is the cost of housing (and the lack of supply). The sale of this building is addressing this challenge in some small way. And yet there is a significant part of me that sees the sale of this building as a failure of imagination and a significant loss to the community in Kitsilano.

There are several ways to tell this story. We might tell the story from the perspective of a shrinking congregation no longer able to pay the bills and keep the lights on. We might tell the story from the perspective of denominational leadership who have a responsibility to engage in and to fund ministry across an entire diocese. We might tell the story from the perspective of the vibrant Tenth Church congregation as they are forced to move from this space into an elementary school auditorium. We might hear this story through the voices of those who live in the neighborhood, the people for whom that building and community offered a place of shelter and connection on Sundays and beyond.

There are many ways to tell this story. Some are more troubling than others. In an interview about the closure, a diocesan representative is quoted as saying, "Housing prices in Vancouver have grown so rapidly and so high that the grandchildren of the grandparents who built the church are no longer living nearby." There is much that is true of this statement. Housing prices have grown rapidly. A January 2020 report by the Real Estate Board of Greater Vancouver demonstrates the rapid rise of sale prices for apartments and houses, with major spikes following the 2010 Vancouver Olympics and again in 2016 and 2018.[4] The market has seen increased volatility in the last two years.

Not a day goes by without someone new writing a blog post or magazine article about why they have been forced out of the city. Bob Kronbauer, founder and editor of the popular city-focused blog *Vancouver Is Awesome*, moved from the city at the end of 2019.[5] His departure—along with that of many others—leaves those of us who remain to wonder how awesome Vancouver actually is. How awesome is Vancouver, and for whom? If the people who make a living from celebrating its awesomeness are leaving, what do we have left? What of those who struggle to keep work? Personally,

---

3. O'Connor, "Vancouver Council Approves Rental Project."
4. Real Estate Board of Greater Vancouver, "Statistics Package," 9.
5. Lawrence, "Vancouver Is Awesome," 20.

the outmigration of friends for small-town BC—Comox Valley, Prince Rupert, Salt Spring Island, or Rossland—has taken its toll. As friend after friend packs up to leave, I'm left wondering with increasing regularity if I should join them. And yet, this city has been my home since the fall of 2011. I've put down roots. I cofounded a new congregation with a dear friend. That place feels like home. Over the course of several years, I worked with neighbors to develop Vancouver's first cohousing community.[6] I have invested so much in making this city home. And yet it is hard. When I think about leaving, however, my stubbornness kicks in. I feel as though I have something to contribute to this city and to a church in this region that is entrenched in particular ways of seeing and hearing the signs of the times.

What the church—and especially the mainline church—in Cascadia needs is a liberated imagination. When we say that the reason a church has to close is that the congregation's founders' grandchildren have left for Maple Ridge or Port Moody, we display the captivity of our imaginations for all to see. Our analysis needs to be more robust. Are the Anglican churches in those suburban communities growing? A few are, most aren't. What about congregations in other denominations? How can we fill in this picture? It would be incredibly convenient to blame millennials for the decline of the church. Rather than attending church, they're probably at brunch eating avocado toast. And yet, the leaders of the Anglican Church have known about this downward trajectory since 1960s or 1970s—twenty years before the first millennial was conceived. We Anglicans have relied on birthrates and migration to sustain our numbers. This plan has not borne the expected fruit. Birthrates amongst Anglicans are in apparent decline. Successive waves of migrants have come from places other than England and Europe, no longer bolstering our already declining number. With this as background, ought we not to wonder about the role of evangelism, discipleship, and community formation in the unfolding mission of the church? How much longer can we rely on Christendom's contention that the way in which new Christians are made is by virtue of their birth into a Christian household? Doesn't this somehow lose the messy, complicated, ragamuffin way of Jesus and his earliest followers, none of whom were born into it? Our analysis may lead us to ask questions of and about young people. And yet, if these questions do not lead to self-examination, towards individual and corporate repentance for the ways in which we have fallen short, what do we expect will happen?

6. de Boer, "In Vancouver."

As we listen to the voices of people who are no longer a part of the church, many of whom are our neighbors, what might we learn about the integrity of Christian witness? What might we learn about the places in which we as individuals, congregations, and denominations have fallen short of God's dream for the neighborhoods, networks, and relationships in which we find ourselves? As we peel back layer after layer, what are the structures and practices that serve the proclamation and embodiment of the gospel in our communities? And what are the Christendom-era structures that serve us no longer? If we identify these things, what will it take to cast them into the fire so that their energy might be released in a different way?

In their exquisite book *Tree: A Life Story*, David Suzuki and Wayne Grady take us on a sweeping journey of life through the eyes of the Coast Douglas Fir, a species native to Cascadia. The story does not begin, as you might expect, with a group of children, faces smeared with dirt, patting the soil around a fragile seedling in the back corner of the school's grounds. It does not start with a single seed in a well-manicured backyard. It all begins with a raging forest fire laying waste to a landscape that had—for centuries—seemed so permanent. In an instant, all that was solid, all that had carried life, all that had served as home to creatures of the land and air is wiped out as the "lightning bolt illuminates the sky, striking the highest point of the forested ridge."[7] Moment by moment the fire grows as brush, then branches, then entire trees and groves catch fire. The fire does not take hold, the authors write, "where the trees are young and strong, but slightly lower down, where over the years snags and fallen branches have accumulated to form a stack of dried kindling."[8] Over the years, these strong trees have shed branches and needles. Some have fallen as a result of disease. Others have fallen in the usual way, over the course of a life stretching ever-upward through the canopy towards the sun. Detritus falls to the forest floor where it slowly decays. Nutrients are returned to the earth from which they came. This process can be slow. And yet with fire, a sudden release.

This image causes me to wonder. What are the snags and fallen branches of Christendom in this soil? What are the assumptions and practices that served the church in this place for some time but are now collecting on the forest floor around us? Are we waiting for lightning to strike, or has the

---

7. Suzuki and Grady, *Tree*, 9.
8. Suzuki and Grady, *Tree*, 9.

spark already caught flame? And how might we respond should the fire of Holy Spirit descend upon the church in this time? Suzuki and Grady write,

> Fire is whimsical. It can sweep through thousands of hectares of timber in a few days, seemingly bent on destroying everything in its path, yet leave a sapling here, a mature tree there, an entire stand of trees somewhere else. After this particular fire, a hasty glance across the blackened, burned-out valley might take in nothing but charred spires leaning above mounds of gray ash.[9]

Is this the future we have in store? Will charred spires remain as the only visual evidence of the teeming Sunday schools of the 1950s? Perhaps. And yet I wonder if, in this time and place, the Holy Spirit is already preparing the ground to receive the seeds of the gospel untethered from structures that have reduced it to something comfortable, palatable, relevant, or safe. We have built so many of our expectations around waves of immigration and the birth and baptism of the next generation of Christians. But what if we are being called out from under the canopies that have served us for so long to find life in ways we did not previously expect? I have mixed feelings about church buildings. I love the beautiful old architecture of so many of these spaces, constructed with love and care, to draw our attention to the magnificence and mystery of God. At the same time, I know that these buildings are tools. God's mission has a church. Sometimes churches have buildings. Sometimes they do not. A building is a tool for ministry. Sometimes that tool can lose its utility. There's part of me that wishes we treated church buildings as crabs treat shells. Outgrow it or die, and another church moves in. I would prefer that these buildings be made available to congregations who have a vision for ministry in neighborhoods where our vision has been lost. Is that evidence of my own captivity? Sometimes I'm not sure. Even so I wonder: how might God be present in this moment, preparing us for whatever comes next?

The headline reads, "Gone by 2040?" The article that follows explores the data collected in a statistical report by the Rev. Dr. Neil Elliot in light of which he suggests that "there will be no members, attenders or givers in the Anglican Church of Canada by 2040."[10] The information is not new, of course. The church has been in decline since at least 1961, when the Anglican Church of Canada had 1,358,459 members on parish rolls. Archbishop Linda Nicholls admits as much when she says, "Anybody who's been in the

9. Suzuki and Grady, *Tree*, 14.
10. Folkins, "Gone by 2040?" 6.

church in the pews, or as a priest, or as a deacon or a bishop has known that this decline has been happening."[11] As of 2017, the number of members on parish rolls across the country was down to 282,412. Persistent, steady decline is evident. The primate calls this statistical reality a wake-up call. After hitting the snooze button for decades—the world changing around it—is the Anglican Church of Canada finally ready to roll out of bed?

I often reflect on my own experience co-planting the St. Brigid's congregation with Marnie. I think about how hard we had to fight to free up the resources (people and funds) we needed to plant this congregation, our first service taking place on May 4, 2014. I am so grateful that we were able to do this work together. Had we not been able to do this work together, I'm certain this wouldn't have happened. In addition to growing a new community, we spent a disproportionate amount of time educating our denomination on what was helpful and necessary to plant a church. There is much more work yet to be done.

The Anglican Diocese of New Westminster had no recent experience of planting a congregation. Depending who you ask, it had been somewhere between thirty and fifty years since the creation of the next most recent congregation. While people were notionally and verbally supportive, the processes we were forced to go through communicated differently. The hoops we had to jump through included funding applications with constantly changing goal posts, and the perpetual threat of unemployment. These applications took days upon days to fill in and were always met with a half dozen further questions requiring immediate answers. If we wanted to proceed to the next round of interviews, we would turn them around right away. We went through this process every year. It was gruelling. It was more than just the paperwork that drained me—it was the prevalent sense of suspicion. There was no offer of coaching or support. No community of practice. We had to reach out to people on the other side of the country—whose contexts were very different—to find solidarity in the work. When our original core team left us within six months of starting, I met with another local church planter, who said, "I've never heard of that happening before." I felt dreadfully alone except that I had Marnie. Without this team approach, the congregation that started with five people meeting in the cathedral basement may never have grown to the more than fifty people we see on an average Sunday evening.

11. Folkins, "Gone by 2040?" 1.

I often wonder how our experience would have been different had it been oriented around greater partnership amongst the planters, parish, and the diocese. Didn't we all have a stake in the growth, sustenance, and witness of this emerging expression of Christian community in Vancouver's downtown core? Weren't we partners in this mission, together? The denominational assumptions, structures, resources and patterns of authority that made sense in Christendom, supporting established parishes, no longer made sense in this contex. What we needed were structures that made space for, empowered, and supported experimentation and innovation. What we needed were outwardly focused communities of Christian witness seeking to embody their faith in the neighborhoods around them. To get there, however, will require further challenge to and change in the habits that guide our work. We have been dependent upon doing things in a particular way, with particular assumptions for so long. What's needed next is adaptive change on all levels—within and amongst individuals, existing parishes, new witnessing communities, and diocesan structures alike.

In response to the statistics of decline, Brendon Neilson observes that competition, slow change, and (misaligned) incentives are significant "barriers to our free and faithful response to the realities presented by Dr. Elliot's report."[12] Neilson is the Diocese of British Columbia's vision animator, tasked with helping the Anglican congregations of the islands and inlets to live into God's vision for the future. In doing so, he has found it useful and important to dialogue with Charles Taylor's understanding of the "Secular Age," alongside other scholars paying attention to shifting attitudes towards and participation in religion in North America.

What interests me most in Neilson's reflection—from the perspective of a church planter in a system not yet ready to support church plants—are his thoughts around incentives. At this point in time, the Diocese of New Westminster incentivizes parish development. Its emphases both in granting programs and educational opportunities are skewed towards the revitalization of existing congregations. This is, of course, an important part of the overall ecclesial puzzle. And yet, a single-minded focus on revitalizing what already exists does not create favorable conditions for the emergence and growth of new witnessing communities. Reforestation requires the planting of seeds. If there are to be ecclesial homes for the breadth of people seeking God, and whom God is calling into relationship with God's self, then we need to respond to the needs of our neighbors in a diversity of

---

12. Neilson, "Transforming Futures," 4.

ways. For such communities to reach maturity and to flourish will require the investment of time, energy, money, attention, and public support from those in the highest echelons of leadership.

I dream of a day when we can unreservedly support new expressions of faith that are not attached to preexistent parishes. I dream of a day when we no longer find ourselves holding our breath, hoping that these fledgling church plants grow up to become "real parishes" someday. This is far from the point. What we need are diverse, resilient, and adaptable communities of faith that are responding to the needs of God's people—the whole of God's good creation—in their particular place. When intentional communities, watershed discipleship groups, wild churches, dinner churches, and other ministries begin to be seen as full-fledged expressions of Christ's body, we'll know we have begun to incentivize the right things. In his paper, Neilson writes:

> If we are wanting to free up the space in the lives of our people to live into the new possibilities that are emerging for faithful expressions of Anglicanism . . . we need to understand and then begin to shift the implicit and explicit rewards and incentives in our diocese. We need to ensure our polity reflects our convictions and shifts along with us as we journey.[13]

Since the planting of St. Brigid's, several new witnessing communities have emerged in the diocese of New Westminster. These fledgling plants are growing beautiful expressions of faith. And yet, they don't fit neatly into the parish box. Salal + Cedar, St. Hildegard's Sanctuary, and Hineni House are all hopeful expressions of faithful Christian witness on Cascadian soil. That they don't neatly fit worries me—not because they ought to, but because our structures have yet to adapt to support their emerging expressions. This structural adaptation will take time and will require layers of change. All of these will take time. Some will come more easily than others:

- The provision of low-barrier pilot-project grants for groups to take on missional experiments.
- Resourcing new ministry leaders with evaluation frameworks that are developmental in nature—focused on ongoing learning rather than the end result.

---

13. Neilson, *Transforming Futures*, 4.

- Next-level grants supporting successful missional experiments as they seek to scale.
- Clear, easy-to-navigate funding streams to support partnership between the diocesan office and new witnessing communities.
- Funding streams that account for the additional time and money associated with the risks and failures of starting new things.
- Resource sharing, staff sharing, and the sharing of best practices between multiple denominations to support leaders of new witnessing communities with best practices that emerge from on-the-ground experience.
- Coaching and pastoral care for leaders of new witnessing communities clearly separated from denominational accountabilities and funding streams.
- Communities of practice where leaders of new witnessing communities are able to gather to focus on common challenges and to offer mutual support.
- Clear and consistent support from the bishop's office for new missional experiments, and for the formation of diverse teams to engage in these experiments.
- Education for key members of staff, councils, and committees about the costs, needs, time, and training required to establish new witnessing communities.
- Restructuring of funding to create specific pockets of money solely for the development of new witnessing communities.
- Creating different classifications for ministries that allow emergent ministries to develop organically without forcing them into the dominant parish framework.
- Not restricting the development of new witnessing communities to ordained clergy. Considering diverse teams who have the giftings and vocational calling to enter this ministry together.
- Engaging in the work of decolonization and anti-racism in all diocesan structures to make it more possible for leaders of new witnessing communities to be Black, Indigenous, People of Color.
- Dismantling structures that create barriers for LGBTQIA/2S+ people from exercising leadership in the church.

I do not know what will come of my new friend's journey towards Christianity. I do not know what will come of new witnessing communities like St. Brigid's and others in my church. We are entering a world without maps, and we are seeking to be faithful to the call that is within us. As we do so, we may find ourselves confronting individuals, systems, and structures that stand in the way. And yet as we do, as we step out in faith, we can pray that the Holy Spirit is preparing the way before us. There is a cost to discipleship, and sometimes that means entering uncharted territory. At other times it means pointing to and doing something about systems that stand in the way of human and creational flourishing.

Perpetual growth is a myth divorced from earthly reality. As in the world of God's beloved forests, so in God's beloved church. There will always be seasons of decline and reorganization. Whatever befalls the forest of Christendom and whatever happens to the Anglican Church of Canada in Cascadia, we know that even as the church sheds branches that no longer serve life, it does so releasing nutrients into the soil. Even in the midst of loss, there are glimmers of hope. As Suzuki and Grady remind us, "A closer look, especially after a rain, would reveal an occasional slash of green, a glint of sunlight from streaks of running resin, and in a sheltered spot on the downwind side of a low ridge, a small oasis of spared forest."[14]

In the midst of all of this unknowing, I know one thing. I know how to get into my car, head into the forest, and listen for the Spirit's voice on the wind. Freed from the distractions of our mechanistic world, a world that demands technical solutions to the problems that face us, I'm awed by the forest's ability to grow back after seemingly complete destruction. From breakdown to breakthrough, from reorganization to growth to conservation, each of these are integral stages in the lifecycle. As the church goes through these stages before our very eyes, we may come face-to-face with fear. And yet, there are glimmers of hope—yes, even here—and more than we could ask or imagine.

Bibliography

de Boer, Alex. "In Vancouver, Thinking New Ways of Housing." *The Tyee*, July 5, 2016. https://thetyee.ca/News/2016/07/05/Vancouver-New-Ways-of-Housing/.
Folkins, Tali. "Gone by 2040? Statistics Report a 'Wake-Up Call' to Church, Says Primate." *Anglican Journal*, January 6, 2020. https://www.anglicanjournal.com/gone-by-2040/.

---

14. Suzuki and Grady, *Tree*, 14.

Lawrence, Grant. "Why Vancouver Is Awesome Founder Thinks Moving Out of the City Is More Awesome." *Vancouver Courier*, December 19, 2019. https://www.vancourier.com/community/why-vancouver-is-awesome-founder-thinks-moving-out-of-the-city-is-more-awesome-1.24036259.

Lazatin, Emily. "For $12M, You Can Own St. Mark's Anglican Church in Vancouver's Kitsilano Area." *Global News*, February 20, 2018. https://globalnews.ca/news/4035015/st-marks-anglican-church-sale-vancouver/.

Neilson, Brendon. "Transforming Futures and the 'Elliot Report.'" Anglican Diocese of British Columbia. https://bc.anglican.ca/news/transforming-futures-and-the-elliot-report.

O'Connor, Naiobh. "Vancouver Council Approves Controversial Kitsilano Five-Storey Rental Project." *Vancouver Courier*, December 18, 2019. https://www.vancourier.com/real-estate/vancouver-council-approves-controversial-kitsilano-five-storey-rental-project-1.24037893.

Real Estate Board of Greater Vancouver. "January 2020 Statistics Package." http://members.rebgv.org/news/REBGV-Stats-Pkg-January-2020.pdf.

Suzuki, David, and Wayne Grady. *Tree: A Life Story*. Vancouver: Greystone, 2004.

11

IKEA Christians in the School of Jesus
Catechesis in Post-Christendom

Ross Lockhart

I was on the treadmill of my North Shore gym early in the morning, watching the news while experiencing a pseudo-religious moment. The morning anchor on one of our local television channels was speaking to a couple of gentlemen back east in Hamilton, Ontario, about a new program designed to encourage children to *give their lives to football*. The news anchor noted the alarming decrease across North America in the number of children enrolling in football programs. "Why the decline?" she asked with a furrowed brow. Her guests helped with both the diagnosis and the cure. Two former Canadian Football League players turned television analysts confessed that the challenge wasn't necessarily with the children *but with their parents*. "They don't trust football anymore because of concussions," offered one analyst in a pastoral tone. "We need to regain their trust—to tell them it's safe." Looking straight into the camera, the former football player said, "There are three ways for children to play depending on their parents' comfort level—tackle, flag, or touch football," offering angst-ridden helicopter parents a virtual trinity of sporting delight. Then, in a mystical moment, he continued, "We just want the children to . . . hold a football, you know, to have that transformative feeling when you throw your first spiral." He made it sound like First Communion for a Catholic. "We believe that football can change a child's life forever, and for good," the other analyst confessed in a soteriologically infused moment, live on air. "Yes," nodded the news anchor approvingly, before inviting their testimony. "As we close and go to commercial, can you tell our viewers your own story of how football changed your life?" What followed was thirty seconds of the sports equivalent of 1 Peter 3:15. He was indeed ready to give an account of the "hundred and ten yard, three down" hope that was within him. "This touchdown is for you, Jesus," I said a little too loudly in the crowded gym, removing my earbuds and slowing the treadmill down to a walking pace.

It was a beautiful example of what happens when the culture stops shaping and making people via a set of practices and beliefs that we take for granted—when the habit falls out of the habitus, if you will. Once upon a time, I used to go up to the playground at Strathmillan School in St. James with my childhood friends—football in hand with dreams of playing for the Winnipeg Blue Bombers (which one of my buddies actually did years later). We pounded the living daylights out of each other throwing, catching, tackling—all with our parents' tacit approval. Today, the culture has shifted. And so too with Christian identity, practice, and witness.

Early church leader Tertullian once declared that "Christians are made, not born."[1] And yet since the Emperor Constantine's fourth-century embrace (or perhaps domestication?) of the Christian movement, Christians were actually *born, not made*. But it was not always so. Our Christian ancestors in the early church took catechesis seriously. In fact, the "seeker-sensitive" services of the 1990s appear polar opposite to the practice of the early Christians, who didn't worry about getting the coffee just right, the dry ice and lasers functioning, or the PowerPoint slides to perfect sequence. No, as Alan Kreider reminds us in *The Patient Ferment of the Early Church: The Improbable Rise of Christianity in the Roman Empire*, the church was careful about who it let into its worship time and limited participation depending on one's commitment level. Deacons were essentially bouncers at the door, pagans were not welcome. So much for bring your neighbor to church day or Rally Sunday in September. Those who were sponsored into the church and began catechesis, known as catechumens, were only allowed to be present for the opening part of worship. Once the service of the Word was complete with readings and sermons, they were dismissed, and only baptized Christians (and those with letters of recommendation from

---

1. Tertullian, *Apol.* 18.4.

other churches) remained for the sharing of the Eucharistic meal.[2] If you were an extroverted pagan and suffered from FOMO[3] in second- or third-century Rome, Alexandria, or Ephesus, this Christian movement would have driven you crazy. Of course, we live in post-Christendom times, not in pre-Christendom. Our Christian witness has passed through and has been indelibly marked by the fifteen-hundred-plus-year experiment of Christendom, where Christianity went from being a sporadically persecuted religious tradition across the Roman Empire (estimated by some scholars to be around 10 percent of the population) to the official state religion by the year AD 381. While relieved by the end of persecution, and even wooed by the possibilities of access to state power and resources, church leaders may not have realized how much was lost in this transition from persecuted minority to religious arm of the state. As Christendom developed over several centuries, it eventually became taken for granted that one was born, lived, and died within a so called "Christian society."

Missiologist Stefan Paas suggests that the average person in the West "would be baptized as a child, and he or she would grow up in a society where everything expressed and confirmed religious belief. A certain number of these Christians would be active in their local parish, study the Scriptures, and maintain a life of prayer and good works. Many others would be fairly inactive, but they would be counted as Christians nonetheless."[4] This Christendom parish lifestyle embraced everyone within earshot of the church tower's bells regulating daily activities and rites of passage, from birth to death. In that society, the habitus of the people was one that placed the church in the center of society and people's daily activities. Assumed, even unquestioned as an essential part of human existence, catechesis meant simply teaching people once baptized as infants how to act "Christianly" within a Christian society, whereby the gospel made peace with the state and supported its agenda. Canadian philosopher and retired McGill University professor Charles Taylor notes that in a premodern social imaginary or worldview, the "porous" person accepted Christian faith as a given, and that in an enchanted world, spiritual issues could easily affect physical reality. In other words, the good standing of your neighbors' spiritual and moral life (or lack thereof!) could actually impact the health and well-being of the community. For the last five hundred years, however,

---

2. Kreider, *Patient Ferment of the Early Church*, 11.
3. The fear of missing out.
4. Paas, *Church Planting in the Secular West*, 90.

we have been undergoing dramatic shifts in understanding. Taylor calls this a move from the porous self to the buffered self, something I practice daily while jammed in cheek and jowl on the crowded bus coming to the UBC campus, pretending that the person a breath away from me (sometimes with bad breath) is totally other than my own social reality. I'm in my own little world, and what happens in others around me does not impact my thoughts or personhood. As a result, Charles Taylor notes that in the West today "the shift to secularity . . . consists . . . of a move from a society where belief in God is unchallenged and indeed, unproblematic, to one in which it is understood to be one option among others, and frequently not the easiest to embrace."[5]

As people leading Christian communities well into the twenty-first century's so-called secular West, there is a growing awareness that catechesis, the early church's insistence on "making Christians," is desperately in need of revival. Some of our graduates are still called to serve communities across Canada where Christendom's memory lingers and where people pine for the "good old days." It might sound a little like this: "Reverend, I remember when we had a thousand children in our Sunday school and had to use the janitor's closet and Mrs. Jones's Oldsmobile in the parking lot as classrooms. We're glad you're here now and can't wait for you to revive the Sunday school." You know the story. But even in those corners of Canada where Christendom lingers, the broader secular forces are taking hold.

The context of Christian leadership today in post-Christendom Canada requires a new approach to the calling and formation of Christian disciples. No longer will the broader cultural context make even half-baked cultural Christians; rather, today the Christian community must revisit our assumptions that a quick membership class will help someone follow the crucified Jew who rules the cosmos. That would be more like simply pulling a new bedside table out of a box and removing the packaging. Voila! A finished product without any effort. No, today we have "IKEA Christians" who require a whole lot more assembly than in the past. We call that making, that assembling, *catechesis*—and it takes place within the school of Jesus we call the church.

From the Greek word κατηχέω (*katecheo*)—meaning to sound the echo—"catechesis" is used, in part, to refer to the process adults went through in the early church prior to baptism, being asked several questions based on the baptismal creed and their response or echo of the teaching,

---

5. Taylor, *Secular Age*, 3.

affirming what they learned and practiced in catechesis.[6] This active and urgent shaping of "human beings being human" with a desire to be more like Jesus is picked up in Rick Osmer's definition of catechesis being "an interpretative activity undertaken by congregations and their individual members who see themselves as participants in the Theo-drama of the triune God and are seeking to better understand their roles in this drama by deepening their understanding of Scripture and Christian tradition."[7]

Osmer's emphasis on the participatory nature of catechesis has impacted the mainline churches[8] and those who long for a thicker description of community and formation. Jessica Duckworth, a graduate of Princeton Theological Seminary where Osmer taught, offers an example of a way forward in her book *Wide Welcome: How the Unsettling Presence of Newcomers Is Changing the Church*. In it, she charges Protestant congregations with the crime of simply accepting newcomers off the street into full membership. She writes, "This happens because there is not a distinction between the cultural practices of Christianity established in North America per se and Christianity practiced within a particular congregation."[9] Essentially, she is asking a question important to all of us as church leaders today: how do you make a Christian when the culture no longer forms even a basic "cultural Christian" through Sunday school, a vague knowledge of Jesus' atoning death, or a sense of obligation to attend church maybe at Christmas or Easter? In this sense her work echoes the research of others who are taking seriously the barriers and challenges of what it means to take steps towards faith in Jesus in a more secular context. Some have even suggested specific steps such as "The Five Thresholds" that people must choose to cross over, with support from a Christian community, such as trust, curiosity, change, seeking, and following Jesus.[10] All of this is crucial for an effective catechetical ministry in post-Christendom. If the culture no longer assists in a basic Christian identity, what are the specific steps required to help an adult move from a pre-baptismal to a post-baptismal identity in Jesus Christ?

---

6. Osmer, *Teaching Ministry*, 27.

7. Osmer, *Teaching Ministry*, 237.

8. I am increasingly experimenting with the language of "formerly mainline church" as a corrective to the perception that "mainline" suggests mainstream or presumed to still be at the center of Western society and power.

9. Duckworth, *Wide Welcome*, 24.

10. Everts et al., *Breaking the Huddle*.

Duckworth researches and profiles congregations creating low-barrier, high-expectation churches instead of the opposite we so often find in too many mainline Protestant churches. Duckworth notes four critical steps in creating a space that over time will help people take steps towards faith in Jesus with integrity and lasting effect. She calls these four distinct periods *inquiry, catechumenate, baptism,* and *baptismal living.* Inquiry is a time when a newcomer is matched with a sponsor—a baptized Christian who walks alongside the inquirer answering basic questions and supporting them as a mentor in their exploration of the faith. A catechist comes alongside these two and invites the inquirer over time into a small group where they move to the second phase: the catechumenate. This time lasts as long as necessary to help the person as they participate in Bible study, worship, prayer, service, and fellowship of the church. The third period is when they feel called to baptism and includes engaging more deeply the doctrine, creeds, and confessions of the church. Following baptism, they enter into the final period shared with church members, known as "baptismal living"—"a lifelong period during which the newly baptized grow more deeply into the practice of faith and Christian life."[11]

According to Duckworth, the catechumenate provides a distinguishing mark in an otherwise indistinguishable posture of Christianity within Christendom; it is countercultural, by which she means it is "the posture of the people under the cross . . . to be a movement that engages the world with suffering love."[12] Darrell Guder picks up on this call for churches to be countercultural when he notes in *The Continuing Conversion of the Church* that the challenge for churches today is a missiological one: "Can they perceive the nature and task of these new secular cultures and address them missionally? Can they find out how to translate the gospel? Can they learn the language, the interior shape of these cultures and become, within them, culturally bilingual? Can they become, again, light, salt, and leaven in their contexts?"[13] In the model explored by Duckworth there is no longer a Christendom outsourcing of baptismal vows to paid clergy, but rather a rigorous engagement between clergy, lay people, and those newcomers that, when done effectively and by the Spirit's power, has a transformative effect on all.

---

11. Duckworth, *Wide Welcome,* 26.
12. Duckworth, *Wide Welcome,* 26.
13. Guder, *Continuing Conversion,* 95.

Duckworth's revisioning of the role of the laity and clergy in catechetical leadership, as well as the extended period of time that it takes to form mature disciples, all feature prominently in the revised Christian Education course I teach at the Vancouver School of Theology, entitled "Catechesis and Community in Post-Christendom." No longer having the luxury of assuming that our graduates will be called to serve Christian communities with professional Christian educators on staff, the reality today is that the majority of our graduates will either be serving Christian communities in need of revitalization or planting new witnessing communities altogether. To that end, we explore traditional catechesis as you might expect—what does discipleship formation look like for children, teens, unchurched adults, new converts, and longtime members? We also explore where people are glimpsing signs of the Holy Spirit building new communities of Christian faith and wondering what catechesis looks like for the online church, church plants, house churches, and new monastic or intentional Christian communities.

One of the books that has helped me understand this shift in Christian leadership and formation is Tod Bolsinger's *Canoeing the Mountains: Christian Leadership in Uncharted Territory*. Drawing on the story of explorers Lewis and Clark, he explores their unconventional leadership style in the quest to reach the West Coast of America. When they encountered the Rocky Mountains, they were overwhelmed and unprepared for the journey. Ditching their canoes (because, after all, who can canoe the mountains?) they needed to adapt their strategy, employing Indigenous guides and riding horses instead to reach their goal. Bolsinger draws on this imagery in order to challenge Christian leaders in North America today to consider that

> leadership is a way of being in an organization, family, team, company, church, business, nation or any other system that, in the words of Ronald Heifetz, "mobilizes people to tackle tough challenges and thrive." Therefore, leadership is always about personal and corporate transformation. But because we are hard-wired to resist change, every living system requires someone in it to live into and lead the transformation necessary to take us into the future we are resisting.[14]

Bolsinger aims squarely at his own people, writing, "We Presbyterians are so good at talking about problems that after a while we think that we have

14. Bolsinger, *Canoeing the Mountains*, 21.

actually done something. . . . Conceptually stuck systems cannot be unstuck simply by trying harder."[15] He reminds us that Christian leaders today require a balance of technical and adaptive leadership. Indeed, often the church is critiqued for remaining in technical leadership that is no longer working, like Canadian missiologist Lee Beach, who, in *The Church in Exile*, bluntly states,

> In some sectors of the church, congregations define themselves by their buildings. They spend large amounts of money to manage them and to restore them as they get old. The building is not only a source of ecclesiastical pride but also the only place for real ministry to take place. In many of these cases, congregations have lost all influence in their communities and are barely managing to hang on in terms of members, yet the building is maintained at all costs. Exile will kill these churches. They will die within a generation (or less), and the buildings will be sold, probably at a bargain price.[16]

Whether in ecclesiology tied to heritage buildings, worship and preaching that no longer translate the gospel effectively in the culture at hand, or catechetical programs that fail to help people take steps towards faith in Jesus, the critique of "what is no longer working" is valid, but that does not mean that theological colleges should no longer teach, nor ministry leaders practice, technical leadership.

After all, technical leadership is the kind of work we do already that is fairly comfortable and within our own skill set—for example in preaching, leading Bible studies, Sunday school, youth group, and so forth. It is the default job description we have been using in pastoral searches for the last several decades. Bolsinger notes, "What makes a problem technical is not that it is trivial, but simply that its solution already lies within the organization's repertoire."[17] Therefore, preparing Christian leaders today (including to be catechetical instructors) requires a curious mix of technical and adaptive leadership. This means that if Christians are made, not born—if we have IKEA Christians in the school of Jesus today—people require assembly, and technical leadership will only take us so far. I worry that too much of Christendom catechesis relied on the broader cultural support of our faith to help form Christian identity. Take teenage confirmation classes, for example, where many teens in recent decades were pushed by the

---

15. Bolsinger, *Canoeing the Mountains*, 32.
16. Beach, *Church in Exile*, 149.
17. Bolsinger, *Canoeing the Mountains*, 41.

expectations of parents or grandparents to attend a few classes and make a half-hearted confession of the faith, before receiving gifts and attending a fancy family luncheon. This thin description of catechesis did not do much for helping young disciples encounter the risen Christ, equip them to participate in God's saving mission, and empower them to live out the "character and content of mission [that] is the shalom of the gospel."[18] But what do we do now that the broader cultural norms have stopped making even a half-hearted cultural Christian? Surely, if the traditional "confirmation as graduation" approach to catechesis has stalled, we are in the realm of adaptive leadership.

Therefore, alongside technical leadership Bolsinger advocates for adaptive leadership that he defines as requiring "us to understand that adaptive challenges require learning, facing loss and negotiating the gaps of our values and actions."[19] Before we go off track, however, and imagine this is setting us up for a lone-ranger style of ministry leadership, we should note that adaptive ministry requires deep trust between Christian leaders and the community of faith. "In uncharted territory, trust is as essential as the air we breathe. If trust is lost, the journey is over," according to Bolsinger.[20] That's why technical leadership is so important—as Bolsinger notes, if people don't trust you on the map, they are not going to follow you off the map. If you don't love your people and prove yourself as a caring, competent pastor, it will be a difficult road leading change. Many of us can think of examples of ministries gone wrong, where a leader had a great idea but failed to get the kind of support from the people to bring about that change. In fact, in many ways, adaptive leadership requires learning, creating a space for experimentation, expecting failure, and taking the opportunity to grow as a result.

It also requires something else: attending more carefully to the presence of the triune God in our midst. Technical leadership can lean heavily on human agency—we know how to do this! Adaptive leadership in post-Christendom, including the catechetical focus on making disciples, requires a posture of humility, one attuned to what God is doing in the world. Missiologist David Fitch calls this renewed attention on God's activity *presence*. He writes, "In the simplest of terms, a group of people gather and become present to God. In our life together, we recognize God in the

---

18. Hastings, *Missional God, Missional Church*, 26.
19. Bolsinger, *Canoeing the Mountains*, 15.
20. Bolsinger, *Canoeing the Mountains*, 65.

presence of Jesus Christ through disciplines in which he has promised, 'I am with you in your midst.'"[21] From Fitch's stripped-down definition of ecclesiology, we can see how important catechesis in post-Christendom has become. Who is equipping people, whether those taking initial steps towards Jesus, new Christians, or long-time disciples, to discern the presence of the living Lord in their everyday, ordinary lives? As Andrew Purves reminds us, there is nothing redemptive about our ministries; only the ministry of Jesus is redemptive: "Our people don't need us; they need Jesus. Our job is to bear witness to him, trusting that he continues to be the One who forgives, blesses, heals, renews, instructs and brings life out of death."[22] For too long now I fear we have placed an undue expectation that Sunday morning worship alone can equip us for this kind of vital attentiveness to God's activity in the world. By asking too much of Sunday morning (or by preachers assuming the sermon covers all the bases), we have often left Christians with a malnourished discipleship and shaky sanctification. As Fitch reminds us,

> God's presence is not always obvious. He requires witnesses. God comes humbly in Christ. He so loves us, he never imposes himself on us. Instead he comes to us, to be with us, and in that presence he reveals himself. In his presence there is forgiveness, reconciliation, healing, transformation, patience, and, best of all, love. In his presence he renews all things. Presence is how God works. But he requires a people tending to his presence to make his presence visible for all to see.[23]

This attending to the presence of God through adaptive leadership will engender what Bolsinger calls "reframing," noting that there must be a shift in values, expectations, attitudes, or habits of behavior necessary to face the difficult challenges of Christian witness today requiring a different lens in order to see new possibilities for ways of being and leading.[24] Duckworth's research, for example, is a reframing of catechesis within a formerly mainline tradition. Bolsinger describes reframing this way: "For church leaders facing this missional moment, the reframing of church strategy from a sanctuary-centered, membership-based, religious and life service provider to a local mission outpost for furthering the Kingdom of God enables our

---

21. Fitch, *Faithful Presence*, 26.
22. Purves, *Crucifixion of Ministry*, iii.
23. Fitch, *Faithful Presence*, 26.
24. Bolsinger, *Canoeing the Mountains*, 96.

congregations to discover a faithful expression of our corporate identity in a changing world."[25]

If we are to return to our IKEA Christian metaphor for a moment, this means that catechetically not only are Christians made (not born) but also that the often-confusing instruction booklet provided in Swedish requires improvisation and interpretation. For any of us who have assembled IKEA furniture, usually somewhere around page eight, we find ourselves saying out loud with mild frustration, "But that doesn't make sense," and instead having to improvise with the tools and hardware in front of us. What else could explain all those extra pieces left over at the end of assembling something from IKEA? But there is an excitement to that as well, never having the full (or perhaps false) assurance of completing a task by one's own skill and ability. No cookie-cutter, one-size-fits-all approach to making disciples through catechesis in post-Christendom is possible. Yes, disciples are made, not born, but *how* they are made will look different depending on the context and gifts of those present. Adaptive leadership in a changing landscape is not undertaken from some distant, neutral position, but rather it is a fully immersive activity between Christ and his people in the world. As Bolsinger challenges the church, "At the heart of adaptive leadership is learning. To put it bluntly, if you are not learning anything new, it is not adaptive work."[26]

My fellow missiologist Christopher James acknowledges the formation aspect of catechesis that requires a mix of technical and adaptive practices but calls us to a deeper transformation. He notes that Christian religious education is the pluriform activity of the faith community that seeks to train Christians in the way of Jesus—life lived in the kingdom of God. Acquiring this way of life includes: cultivating a personal, interactive relationship with God, characterized by renewed identity, attentiveness, and cooperation; undergoing spiritual formation in Christlikeness, such that the inner life bears the fruit of the Spirit; and reorientation of action toward the blessing and liberation of others and the redemption of cosmos.[27]

Within the highly secular context of Vancouver where I live, teach, and minister there is an urgency to this question of formation and catechesis. Missional catechesis, echoing those early church ancestors of ours, involves trying to figure out what Christian witness looks like in a culture

---

25. Bolsinger, *Canoeing the Mountains*, 96.
26. Bolsinger, *Canoeing the Mountains*, 97.
27. James, "Education That Is Missional," 141–58.

where we are not always welcome or appreciated. We still live with the memory of our recent past, where the broader Canadian culture offered not only tacit support of Christianity, but often enlisted support of the churches in the work of the state, including with devastating consequences of the Residential Schools program in Canada.[28] Today, however, Christianity finds itself on the margins of mainstream culture and the expressions of Christian faith that are growing in Canada are rarely the formerly so-called "mainline" churches. This is particularly so as highlighted by recent historical work, including by Lynn Marks in her book *Infidels and the Damn Churches: Irreligion and Religion in Settler British Columbia* and that of her former graduate student Tina Block in *The Secular Northwest: Religion and Irreligion in Everyday Post-War Life*. Marks pushes hard even against the classic secularization theory being applied to British Columbia, noting, "To become secularized, a culture must first be religious. Was this ever true of settler British Columbia?"[29] Whether living on the secular West Coast or sniffing a scent of the fumes of Christendom in eastern Canada, the landscape of Christian witness has changed for formerly mainline Protestant churches; as one scholar remarked, "Canadian culture holds a hermeneutics of suspicion regarding the church."[30]

In *Leaving Christianity* Canadian church historians Stuart Macdonald and Brian Clarke note the decline in church attendance with the baby boomers who opted for the church's alumni association beginning in the 1960s, leaving and never coming back. Therefore, for church leaders today, "the distinction between being de-churched and non-churched is a crucial one. The de-churched are those who at some point in their lives attended church but now no longer do so. The non-churched have never attended except perhaps for a funeral or wedding of a friend or relation."[31] Macdonald and Clarke offer by way of conclusion the rather glum assessment that

---

28. In the nineteenth and twentieth centuries, the Roman Catholic and Mainline Protestant churches in Canada partnered with the federal government to forcibly remove Indigenous children from their homes and send them to church-run residential schools with the intention of replacing their culture with a Western identity and skill set. Not only did these schools attempt to destroy Indigenous culture, but there was much physical and sexual violence inflicted on children that is now well (and painfully) documented. For an example of a mainline church's apology, see the Presbyterian Church in Canada's statement here: https://presbyterian.ca/healing/.

29. Marks, *Infidels and the Damn Churches*, 11.

30. Donald Goetrz, "Toward a Missional Theology of Worship," in Rob and Ngien, *Between the Lectern and Pulpit*, 167.

31. Clarke and Macdonald, *Leaving Christianity*, 171.

"first, people are not only leaving churches; they are leaving Christianity. And many of them have no interest in returning. Second, an increasing and significant proportion of the population has never had any firsthand experience of organized religion."[32]

Therefore, how Christian witnessing communities today in Cascadia engage in the practice of catechesis is critical for the ongoing flourishing of the gospel and the planting of the church in rocky, secular soil. Tertullian's argument that Christians are made, not born, does not come as a shock in this place or many others across Canada. Rather, it is both a challenge and a promise to those who would engage in gospel work and witness, with an appreciation that much of the old technical leadership is no longer relevant and adaptive leadership challenges have now become the norm. While some within the church are showing signs of suffering under what Charles Taylor calls the "malaise of Modernity," there are also beautiful signs of Christian witness taking place all around us as the Holy Spirit remakes the face of Christianity across North America.

A recent example of this was an invitation from a member of Richmond Presbyterian Church to attend a barbeque in her backyard. A real estate agent, originally from the Philippines, our hostess for the party sells homes primarily to people moving to the Vancouver area from mainland China. The majority of her clients arrive in the Vancouver area as what Statistics Canada would simply classify as "atheist," but this modern-day Lydia supports her congregation by sharing the gospel with clients through her work and inviting them to church. The day I arrived for the barbeque she had seventy people in her backyard, a local church choir singing, and enough food to feed an army. After a half an hour of gospel songs she invited me to preach. "Just tell them about Jesus, he's new to them," she had urged me in an earlier email.

Fascinated by this challenge of cross-cultural witness, I began by saying, "We're all here tonight at this wonderful party at the invitation of our friend Eleanor. Eleanor and I have another friend in common whom I'd like to introduce you to." Remembering James B. Torrance's line that "even more important than our experience of Christ, is the Christ of our experience,"[33] I spoke first for several minutes on the significance of the life, death, and resurrection of our Lord Jesus Christ for the whole world and then, more personally, on how Jesus even saved me—an angry, fatherless, bitter teenage

---

32. Clarke and Macdonald, *Leaving Christianity*, 210.
33. Torrance, *Worship*, 34.

boy who grew up to be a preacher. The choir sang, the buffet line filled, and people chatted over dinner while others prayed quietly in the garden. My testimony was not as impressive as that "football player turned analyst" that I had heard on the treadmill at the gym earlier in the week. But it didn't need to be. After all, our fragile, fallible human words are offered up like a sacrifice, that the Holy Spirit might use them for the glory of the triune God. As the dinner party ended that night, I left more hopeful about the possibility of Christian witness in a so-called secular society. I also left curious about what kind of Christian community, what kind of school of Jesus, had formed our hostess over the years such that she felt free, unashamed in fact, to invite friends, coworkers, and clients to such a party—a party to which she may have invited friends, neighbors, and coworkers to attend but by the end of the night it was clear Jesus himself was the host. Jesus' faithful presence was evident in the midst of the gathering, for those who had eyes to see and ears to hear. If Christians today are once again made, not born, then who knows what God can do in the rocky soil of the Pacific Northwest, with the humble, adaptive, and missionally minded assemblies of believers busily equipping people for Christian witness in Cascadian soil. God knows—and I can't wait to find out.

Bibliography

Beech, Lee. *The Church in Exile: Living in Hope after Christendom*. Downers Grove: InterVarsity, 2015.
Bolsinger, Ted. *Canoeing the Mountains: Christian Leadership in Uncharted Territory*. Downers Grove: InterVarsity, 2017.
Clarke, Brian, and Stuart Macdonald. *Leaving Christianity: Changing Allegiances in Canada since 1945*. Montreal: McGill-Queen's University Press, 2017.
Clements, Rob, and Dennis Ngien, eds. *Between the Lectern and Pulpit: Essays in Honour of Victor A. Shepherd*. Vancouver: Regent College Publishing, 2014.
Duckworth, Jessica. *Wide Welcome: How the Unsettling Presence of Newcomers Can Save the Church*. Minneapolis: Fortress, 2013.
Everts, Don, et al. *Breaking the Huddle: How Your Community Can Grow Its Witness*. Downers Grove: InterVarsity, 2016.
Fitch, David. *Faithful Presence: Seven Disciplines That Shape the Church for Mission*. Downers Grove: InterVarsity, 2016.
Guder, Darrell. *The Continuing Conversion of the Church*. Grand Rapids: Eerdmans, 2000.
Hastings, Ross. *Missional God, Missional Church: Hope for Re-evangelizing the West*. Downers Grove: InterVarsity, 2012.
James, Christopher B. "Education That Is Missional: Toward a Pedagogy for the Missional Church." In *Social Engagement: The Challenge of the Social in Missiological Education*;

The 2013 Proceedings of the Association of Professors of Mission, 141–62. Wilmore, KY: First Fruits, 2013.

Kreider, Alan. *The Patient Ferment of the Early Church: The Improbable Rise of Christianity in the Roman Empire*. Grand Rapids: Baker, 2016.

Marks, Lynn. *Infidels and the Damn Churches: Irreligion and Religion in Settler British Columbia*. Vancouver: University of British Columbia Press, 2017.

Osmer, Richard. *The Teaching Ministry of Congregations*. Louisville: Westminster John Knox, 2005.

Paas, Stefan. *Church Planting in the Secular West: Learning from our European Experience*. Grand Rapids: Eerdmans, 2016.

Purves, Andrew. *The Crucifixion of Ministry: Surrendering Our Ambitions to the Service of Christ*. Downers Grove: InterVarsity, 2007.

Taylor, Charles. *A Secular Age*. Cambridge: Harvard University Press, 2007.

Tertullian. *Apology of Tertullian*. Translated by W. M. Reeve. http://www.tertullian.org/articles/reeve_apology.htm.

Torrance, James B. *Worship, Community and the Triune God of Grace*. Downers Grove: InterVarsity, 1996.

AWAITING THE HARVEST

"Ask the Lord of the harvest, therefore,
to send out workers into his harvest field."

—MATTHEW 9:38 (NIV)

"What a huge harvest!" he said to his disciples. "How few workers!
On your knees and pray for harvest hands!"

—MATTHEW 9:38 (MSG)

12

Dying and Rising for Mission

Richard Topping

Introduction

In this essay I want to address the need for Christian imaginative formation for mission. In the first part of the essay, I address what I think are two formidable barriers to developing a theological vision for mission. Secularity is a powerful reality in the West, and while it doesn't have complete hegemony, it does render theological language and notions of God's agency in the world suspect. It creates an awkward moment when God is introduced into the sense-making repertoire of the speaker at a dinner party still. Postmodernity has proven no more friendly than modernity to divine agency. And, of course, a divine agent, the triune God, is the one who sponsors—calls and commissions—the church to be a witness in the world. I wonder whether reticence about mission is rooted in the church's conformity to the secular world, when God is not a legitimate actor or factor in sense-making. A second barrier to formation for mission, I believe, is critical/suspicious hermeneutics. In the academy the two are conflated. This approach to texts, including scriptural texts, invites a posture of estrangement, distance, and power analysis that is not always amenable to formation. Missional interest is lit up by the God who is missional, and we gain that insight and motivation in the power of the Spirit as we are porous to Scripture, not laying out the "barbed wire of criticism" to protect ourselves from it. I want to make a case for imaginative engagement with the Bible through a hermeneutic for the baptized that is enamored with the missional God revealed in Scripture. In short, I want to question two ways we can be conformed to the world, and then offer a case for imaginative transformation in the service of God's reconciling mission.

> Do not be conformed to this world [this age], but be transformed by the renewing of your minds, so that you may discern what is the will of God—what is good and acceptable and perfect. (Rom 12:2 NRSV)

We jump into the middle of a cumulative argument that St. Paul has been making in Romans with this verse. To put the matter baldly, he's documented God's great acts of mercy toward the world with hardly an imperative. And now he turns the corner. It is God's great acts of mercy toward the world that invite a response. God is so extraordinarily gracious that all that's left to be done is "living sacrifice." Because God has moved so decisively toward the world in Jesus Christ, our only fitting response is to present ourselves, everything we are and have, to God.

The gospel of reconciliation through Christ does not engender half measures. Hear this news, this glorious good news, where God does what only God can do; see it made visible in bread and wine and water, hear it proclaimed in word, and as a person pushes her chips to the center of the table, she goes all in with God. And what's more: this isn't extraordinary, it isn't extremism or wild enthusiasm; it is just *reasonable*. What does that sort of commitment look like? What are the practical implications of going all in with God? There are two parts: "don't be conformed to this world" but "be transformed by the renewal of your minds." What we get here is a "pull weeds and then plant seeds" approach. In the light of the gospel of God's reconciliation with the world through Jesus Christ, offer yourselves to God. That means don't offer yourself to this world (not the planet but the system) but be transformed by the renewal of your minds.

God has worked God's moves on the world for the renewal of the world. A regime change is underway—there is a world that is coming and there is an arrangement that is passing away; let's go with the world on the way instead. Don't start calling the current arrangements on the ground "our context"—as though they were fate and there's nothing to do but fit in, adjust, accommodate. Christian life is now more tensive than that; we've got options.

"Don't be conformed"—don't fit into what is fashionable, the customs and manners of what is already served up, don't be house-broken by what everyone calls necessity; don't fit in chameleon-like with what's served up at the moment and call "fitting in" radical. Don't be captured by what G. K. Chesterton called "the small and arrogant oligarchy of those who merely happen to be walking about at the moment." Don't get pressed into the shape of the current dog-eat-dog carnivorous arrangements. "Don't let yourself be conformed," passively and through time, by going with the flow until you speak in slogans that simply show you've caved to common sense. Next thing you know you are saying things like: "You've got to think outside the box"—who doesn't do that now? There's no one left in the box. Don't allow yourself to bless the arrangements that we know harm people, make you settle for too little too soon. "Be not conformed to this world."

I want to take up two obstacles that formation for mission encounters in our culture. One is really a tacit dimension of our lives in the West—secularism. There are regions of public life, like the university,[1] where talk about God is regarded as special pleading or rhetorical excess and it is policed out of the explanatory repertoire. The other is related to the first but it has to do with the preponderant practices and mood of biblical and theological interpretation—critical and suspicious. The mode of engagement with Scripture in many cases effectively alienates the reader from the subject matter of the Bible. I want to make the case that both factors inhibit mission where they take root in the life of the church and its adjunct institutions. Both make speech about God and deep theological and spiritual engagement with Scripture problematic.

First, I think we often conform to naturalism. We live in a world in which agnosticism is the default position and references to God sound like special pleading or rhetorical excess. Let me give you an example. A young person in your congregation makes an appointment to speak with you. That is great news! This young person wants to talk with you about an experience of God. They ask, "Do you think God may be leading me?" What do we say? I don't know about you, but I am tempted to ask, "Did you have a fight with your parents? Everything ok at school? What did you eat for dinner? How is your partner doing?" Only when absolutely reduced to it, do I say, "Well go figure, it must have been God." Maybe you all do better than that. But this response is the result of what Charles Taylor calls

---

1. Taylor, *Secular Age*, 549–50.

the "immanent frame."[2] That is to say that in our world just now, references to God as an agent in the world are not a part of government-sponsored, state-sanctioned explanations.

Secularity has been rather successful in its catechesis. Talk about God is special pleading and is ruled out of order in the ways we make sense. We feel the sanctions against theological talk in our work as pastors and ministers, church leaders. Taylor writes, "As we function within the various spheres of activity—economic, political, cultural, educational, professional, recreational—the norms and principals we follow, the deliberations we engage in, don't generally refer us to God or to any religious beliefs."[3]

And so, we reason, feel, and make sense without reference to God—Father, Son, and Holy Spirit. I think that the fact that so many clergy look for adjunct vocations with more cultural cachet may be a sign of this. You have more cultural currency if you're a teacher, a counselor, or a social worker since you can do all these things without reference to God. Try theologian—I'm kind of stuck. Without God I lose my subject matter!

Various surrogates function in the place of God these days—like culture, feeling, context as destiny, and community, among others. The fact that we get caught up in reductive accounts of life almost as a matter of comfortable habit, and that our hearts race and palms sweat when God gets introduced as crucial to sense-making, indicates the marginalization of faith. As Terry Eagleton says in his book *Culture and the Death of God*, "Societies become secular not when they dispense with religion but when they are no longer especially agitated by it."[4] God often doesn't matter much to sense-making—life-making—in secularity. That's a problem for those who yearn to participate in the reconciling mission. It is, after all, God's mission, not ours. God is the sponsoring agent for mission through Jesus Christ in the power of the Spirit.

Second, I think there's also a temptation to conform to the world where it comes to what we imagine a well-formed and educated Christian person to be. Call this the temptation to be a troubler of ideas, a "problematizer." We live in a culture that imagines that an intelligent, well-educated person is a "critical" thinker. And along with the word "critical' comes the word "suspicious." Some have made the case that these two words are

---

2. Taylor, *Secular Age*, 542–57.
3. Taylor, *Secular Age*, 2.
4. Eagleton, *Culture and the Death of God*, 1.

almost synonymous. Michael Roth, president of Wesleyan University, helps identify some of the liabilities here.

> In a humanities culture in which being smart often means being a critical unmasker, our students may become too good at showing how things *don't* make sense. That very skill may diminish their capacity to find or create meaning and direction in the books they read and the world in which they live. Once outside the university, our students continue to score points by displaying the critical prowess for which they were rewarded in school. They wind up contributing to a cultural climate that has little tolerance for finding or making meaning, whose intellectual and cultural commentators delight in being able to show that someone else *is not to be believed*.[5]

Don't get me wrong. This isn't a pitch for naïveté and fundamentalism. And yet, why do we think one must be either critical or naïve, as though these were the only options? I wonder what the result is for spiritual formation for mission when the approach we take to Scripture study and liturgical participation is almost exclusively suspicious and critical. This is a barrier to formation since the critical-suspicious move almost always involves distance, detachment, estrangement, and severing affective connection. A greater and greater number of scholars in English literature, for example, are noticing this disengagement and the lack of love for literature it engenders in their students. We can wonder at what this distancing and estrangement does to a sense of call, to a sense of formation by the Spirit speaking through Scripture.

Some, like the late Eve Sedgewick, have written rather masterful accounts of the devastating consequences of what she calls "paranoid" reading of texts. Her article entitled "Paranoid and Reparative Reading, or You're So Paranoid, You Probably Think This Essay Is about You"[6] is especially pertinent. She makes the case that a person can come to a text with such an arsenal of high-power theory that every text just becomes another instance

---

5. Roth, *Beyond the University*, 183, emphasis in original.

6. Sedgewick, *Touching Feeling*, 133–36. Lisa Ruddick, a professor of English at the University of Chicago, also notices how literary scholars use "theory—or simply attitude—to burn through whatever is small, tender, and worthy of protection and cultivation. Academic cool is a cast of mind that disdains interpersonal kindness, I-thou connection, and the line separating the self from the outer world and engulfing the collective" (Ruddick, "When Nothing Is Cool," in Bammer and Joeres, *Future of Scholarly Writing*, 72).

of it. Haunted by a fear of authority or a paranoia about power, suspicious readers tend to demean submissive readers as pietistic. Such reading does not speak truth to power, rather it speaks power to dissolve truth. And as Rowan Williams notes, "The cost of giving up talking of truth is high: it means admitting that power has the last word. . . . Without a notion of truth that is more than simply the things people prefer to believe, no such account can be given."[7]

Rita Felski, a feminist literary scholar, also alerts us to the limitations of suspicious hermeneutics. She asks a very hard question about the affective mode of critical-suspicious engagement: "Why are we so hyperarticulate about our adversaries and so excruciatingly tongue-tied about our loves?"[8] She speaks of the "barbed wire of suspicion" and how we use it to avoid "contamination by the texts we read."[9] That raises questions around Christian formation for mission: don't the baptized want to be contaminated (sanctified) and commissioned by the texts they contemplate in the power of the Spirit? When this style of suspicious reading becomes the preferred method in seminaries and pulpits, then sacramental, Spirit-dependent, and community-connected modes of engagement are thought of as low-brow. It arrests engagement with Scripture for formation—to read to discern the Word in the words, to receive Scripture on the *pallatum cordis* (the palate of the heart)—where critical theory and suspicion police Scripture study for formation. St. Bernard said that Scripture is "the wine cellar of the Holy Spirit."[10] That's an invitation to engagement if ever I heard one. Who would want to be at a distance from that?

I wonder if both of these acts of conformity, living in the immanent frame and critical-suspicious reading, are instances of what I want to call revenge of the Egyptians. In Augustine's *On Christian Doctrine*,[11] he speaks of using ideas and practices from the wider world to assist the church in its task of interpreting and articulating the Christian message for its own time. Augustine recollects that Israel requisitioned property from the Egyptians—that is, liberated loot like precious metal and clothing, as a kind of back pay for years in slavery. What had been Egyptian became repurposed in the service of God and God's people—recycled, if you will. The metaphor

---

7. Williams, *Faith in the Public Square*, Kindle locs. 5380–86.
8. Felski, *Limits of Critique*, 12.
9. Felski, *Limits of Critique*, 13.
10. Cited in Griffiths, *Religious Reading*, 42.
11. Augustine, *On Christian Doctrine*, 75–77.

is apt—Christians have always made use of the tools at hand in their own cultural time and place to give expression to the gospel of reconciliation. So, grab every golden idea you can get and recontextualize it to serve the gospel, or so Augustine encourages.

However, he also cautions against revenge of the Egyptians. Remember when God's people were in the wilderness and the pressure was on? Pretty soon the gold they had lifted when they left became serviceable to a golden calf—and the plunderers became the plundered. You know how this goes, you borrow a few postcolonial ideas to serve the gospel and pretty soon you've been colonized by postcolonial thought and your only lens is power. You think a few organization insights from *Harvard Business Review* will help and the next thing you know you're talking about ROI (return on investment) on customers, not formation for mission by disciples.

Karl Barth warned against the alienation of the church from its identity, and its mission, when it does not engage in theologically rooted critical appropriation of interpretative practices and tools. Alienation takes place when the community allows itself to be radically determined, established, engaged, committed, and imprisoned in this respect: in its knowledge by the adoption of a particular philosophy or outlook as the norm of its understanding of the word of God. It will usually be argued that it is a question of mediation, of bridging the gap between those outside and those inside. Some will say that it is a question of the translation of the Christian into the secular, of a kind of baptism of non-Christian ideas and customs and enterprises by new Christian interpretations and the giving of a new Christian content, or of minting Christian gold on behalf of poor non-Christians.

And it is all very fine and good so long as there is no secret respect for the fashion of the world, no secret listening to its basic theme, no secret hankering after its glory, and conversely, no secret fear that the community cannot live solely by Jesus Christ and the grace of God. The Christian community must be on guard that there is no secret unwillingness to venture to allow itself to live and grow simply from its own and not a worldly root as the *communio sanctorum* (communion of the saints).

Where there is this respect, this listening, this hankering, this fear and unwillingness, it always means the secularization of the community. "Secularization is the process by which the salt loses it savor. And when the church becomes secular, it is the greatest conceivable misfortune for both the church and the world. The church then loses its specific importance and meaning; the justification for its existence."[12]

Don't be conformed to this age. Metamorphosis through renewal of the mind is what the text urges on us. Renewing the church, a life, comes here through stoking the mind with the gospel to the end of living out God's will in the world. Since the life, death, and new life of Christ, this age can no longer regulate life for those who have died and now live with Christ. The old regime is ending, the new life is coming, renewal has begun in baptism, and it advances through the reformation of the mind.

One of my favorite authors, Northrop Frye, a Canadian literary scholar and United Church of Canada minister, gave the Massey Lectures on CBC in 1963. *The Educated Imagination*[13] is now in its twenty-fifth printing. In this book Frye asks a simple question: Why study literature? His answer is rich with possibility. He says that the study of literature, what he calls "man's revelation to man," is for the sake of funding imagination. Literary studies are hard work. They require critical finesse and directed attention, but the goal is to beef-up imagination with pictures of the way the world could be but isn't yet.

Frye claims that if imagination is stoked (educated) with ideas from other times and places, you quickly realize that what's served up by your culture right now is only one way of doing things. There are better worlds than the one around us right now; there are worlds we want to live in. And the lure of a life-giving possible world could lead to action. When you compare what is with what might be, it could make us so restless with the dead-ends and stale leftovers of the present that whole communities could start living toward a better arrangement, a more humane option, an utterly solicitous world!

But now we have discovered that the imaginative world and the world around us are different worlds and that the imaginative world is more important. The society around us looks like the real world, but we've seen that there's a great deal of illusion to it, the kind of illusion that propaganda and slanted news and prejudice and a great deal of advertising appeal to.

You soon realize that there's a difference between the world you're living in and the one you want to live in. The world we want to live in (not the world that is) is a vision that is inside our minds, born and fostered

---

12. Barth, *Church Dogmatics*, IV.2:668.
13. Frye, *Educated Imagination*.

by imagination, yet real enough for us to try to make the world we see conform to it.[14]

Now, I wonder if Frye's way of putting it might be jazzed into a theological frame, in the manner St. Augustine suggests—of borrowing an idea without becoming a hostage of it. Could we speak of God's revelation to people as the place a theological imagination, a missional imagination, is born? What about Christian formation as focused attention on "God's revelation to people" in Jesus Christ in the power of the Spirit? Here there is a critical moment to be sure; but it is critical of the way the world is in the light of the world God is bringing.

Could the community born of the gospel dare to envision what might be because the triune God has stoked their imaginations through prophets and poets, Scripture and saints, testifying to the kingdom coming on earth as it is in heaven? After all, isn't faith "the assurance of things hoped for, the conviction of things not seen"?[15] Could a theologically educated imagination envision a reconciled world, fired by visions of lions and lambs lying down together, with visions of swords beat into plowshares, of a detoxified heaven and earth through the Lamb that was slain? Could a people become so enamored with these solicitous visions that they grow discontent with what is, and start living toward more humane arrangements, where justice and peace embrace, get all caught up in the reconciling work of God? And they could do it, not because they *have to*, but because they *may*, because they have the freedom of the children of God and so live and lean toward the kingdom.

Subject yourself to Christian education and Scripture study and enter the world of worship, and priorities could get reversed, altered, changed. Fund an imagination with the gospel of reconciliation and the next thing you know someone says, "I have a dream . . ." and then audacious people—like Martin Luther King Jr.—move nonviolently toward a more humane arrangement, a kingdom that is coming. They just start to believe that history bends toward justice! Talk about being grasped by a vision!

Another interpreter that is really helpful around the formation of imagination is the late philosopher Paul Ricoeur. What he helps us see is that imagination is a human faculty that has more of a pull than a push about it. Maybe part of the appeal of imagination in our own time is precisely this. Talk about commanding obedience does not go over well in the

14. Frye, *Educated Imagination*, 65–66.
15. Heb 11:1 (NRSV).

world in which we live. Not too much preaching these days specializes in the imperative mood. We're not fond of authoritative demand; we are more likely to use the carrot than the stick. What good preachers do these days is get all solicitous in the pulpit; we woo people with the world of worship. We're trying to put the imaginative moves on our congregations. We're inviting people into living in a way that corresponds to a whole new world. And we do it by appeal to imagination. "It could be different than it is. What might happen if... can you imagine?"

Paul Ricoeur says that's the way we could think about the word "revelation."[16] It's God's appeal through Scripture and the preacher inviting you into a world other than the one you live in right now. "How would you like to occupy a space where lions and lambs lie down together? In our world lambs are a lion's lunch; but what would it be like to live in freedom from fear? Could there be a way of living together that isn't carnivorous? Is competition the only way to relate to each other?" Well, listen to the prophet, we preachers say; the prophet dares to imagine that the way things are isn't the way things have to be. And thus, we might begin by the enticing vision of the prophet and grace of God, to live and act toward a world that is not yet but could be.... Lambs and lions together... who would have thought.

I have been positively enthusiastic for imagination these days. I think the emphasis on imagination in theological education, preaching, and in church life is salutary. What might be—could be—that is not yet? I'm tired of the laissez faire, unimaginative, "that's just the way it is" attitude, which hunkers down and fits in to worn out ways of being and doing, and, in its progressive form, sometimes champions conformity to secularity as edgy. I see the relevance of imagination in the current life and times of the church. I think imaginative preaching also keeps the good-news good because it is more solicitous and invitational than threatening and punitive and legislative (whether the legislation of the left or the right) pronouncement. Imaginative vision of the world God wants, offered in biblical pictures, moves us to witness to what has yet to come in the here and now.

Leaders of communities of faith witness to the world on the way, the kingdom of God, with words. In this postmodern time, we are trying to narrate a world in Jesus' name that is habitable and already on the horizon. In an introduction to theology class I teach, I have students read an essay

---

16. See Ricoeur, *Figuring the Sacred*. Ricoeur's seminal essay on revelation is "Toward a Hermeneutic of the Idea of Revelation," *Harvard Theological Review* 70 (1977).

by Serene Jones titled "Inhabiting Scripture, Dreaming Bible."[17] She talks about how the stories of the Bible have formed her imagination since the time she was a child, not inhibiting but opening up new vistas for engagement with the world God loves. Listen to what she writes:

> Shaped by the world of churchly, scriptural speech, it is impossible for me to imagine a world without God . . . and in the ongoing play of my imagination there is also a strong tendency for me to impose on everything I experience some sort of story about sin and redemption. . . . I cannot look at another person without seeing Jesus loving him or her . . . it is impossible for me to frame humanity in any other way than as Jesus-loved. . . . I see Jesus looking up at Zacchaeus in the tree or toward the lepers living in caves outside the city walls [and it] moves me toward the edge of what we normally see in search of what we do not. . . . It is an impulse that drove me toward feminism, liberation theology, a deep commitment to radical justice and a suspicion of the exclusions and repressions that religion itself is constantly enacting.[18]

I think I'd call that sanctified imagination: a person so stoked in the scriptural witness to the gospel, so formed by the church gathered to worship, that a frame of reference for how to move and act and see the world is born. Imaginative formation births a frame of reference for mission. Transformation by the story Scripture tells, especially of the life, death, and resurrection of Jesus, directs those baptized into that story toward the world God loves.

Again, we return to Scripture's prompting, "Don't be conformed to the present age, but be transformed by the renewing of your mind that you might prove what is the will of God." I drove my son to Castlegar, some years ago, where he enrolled in wildlife and fisheries management. He loves animals. He loves the outdoors. His bent in life was to do this from the time he could move. I'd say it was his calling. On the way to the school, we noticed things like mountains, trees, flowers, and wildlife. We observed the world, as far as we could.

Two years later, I went to pick him up and bring him home. I had to take a truck now. He had accumulated all kinds of stuff—snowshoes, skis, a large backpack, heaps of outdoor camping equipment, and books, tons of books. The drive home was different than the drive there. It wasn't just the

---

17. Serene Jones, "Inhabiting Scripture, Dreaming Bible," in Brown, *Engaging Biblical Authority*, 73–80.

18. Serene Jones, "Inhabiting Scripture, Dreaming Bible," in Brown, *Engaging Biblical Authority*, 78–79.

load of stuff we carried in the car. He brought home a load of learning. The conversation went something like this:

"Dad, will you look at that: the angiosperms are blooming."

"What?"

"And did you see that path through the woods, ungulates' love corridors?"

"Uh?"

"And Dad, did you know that the pinus ponderosa has tout needles growing in scopulate (bushy, tuft-like) fascicles of two to three with flame retardant bark?"

"Well no, I didn't know that."

I have to say he had great teachers. I couldn't even get him to do the dishes, and these strangers, these educators, altered his world! Coming home, this son of mine had a new take on reality because of his training. They did not just educate him—populate his brain with new ideas—they formed him. He saw a different world coming home than he was able to see when he left. He got called.

My son lives and acts in the world differently now—he cares, he knows watersheds, does live releases of sturgeon early in the morning, rides on a bike to the Fraser River just to watch sea lions, gets up at 5:30 a.m. to go whale watching and, enthusiast that he is, he drags me with him. He tries to get me to see what he sees. His joy just pulls other people into the wake of his love for the delights of the created world; he's even latched on to other people who love what he loves.

We can't eat fish in a restaurant unless he sees the Ocean Wise endorsement on the menu. I don't think it's an exaggeration to say that his imaginative repertoire was enlarged by his education. He's now got more purchase on the world. In fact, I think he sees a different world now, and seeing that different world means he engages the world in new ways, humane ways, even more loving ways, at least most of the time. What an achievement! Talk about renewal of the mind for mission. May it be so for us.

Bibliography

Augustine. *On Christian Doctrine*. Translated by J. F. Shaw. Mineola, NY: Dover, 2009.

Bammer, Angelika, and Ruth-Ellen Boetcher Joeres, eds. *The Future of Scholarly Writing: Critical Interventions*. New York: Palgrave Macmillan, 2015.

Barth, Karl. *Church Dogmatics*. Translated and edited by G. W. Bromiley and T. F. Torrance et al. Edinburgh: T. & T. Clark, 1958.

Brown, William, ed. *Engaging Biblical Authority: Perspectives on the Bible as Scripture.* Louisville: Westminster John Knox, 2007.

Eagleton, Terry. *Culture and the Death of God.* New Haven: Yale University Press, 2014.

Felski, Rita. *The Limits of Critique.* Chicago: University of Chicago Press, 2015.

Frye, Northrop. *The Educated Imagination.* Toronto: Canadian Broadcasting Corporation, 1963.

Griffiths, Paul. *Religious Reading.* New York: Oxford University Press, 1999.

Ricoeur, Paul. *Figuring the Sacred: Religion, Narrative and Imagination.* Translated by David Pellauer, edited by Mark I. Wallace. Minneapolis: Fortress, 1995.

Roth, Michael. *Beyond the University: Why Liberal Education Matters.* New Haven: Yale University Press, 2014.

Sedgewick, Eve Kosofsky. *Touching Feeling: Affect, Pedagogy, Performativity.* Durham: Duke University Press, 2002.

Taylor, Charles. *A Secular Age.* Harvard: Harvard University Press, 2007.

Williams, Rowan. *Faith in the Public Square.* Kindle ed. Toronto: Random House, 2012.

13

The Church God Is Planting in Cascadian Soil

Christopher James

WHEN I BEGAN RESEARCHING the new churches in Seattle, Washington, I knew that the city had a reputation as a church planting graveyard and hostile soil for the gospel. I also knew that this reputation was backed up by a host of statistics about the low levels of church attendance and the high percentages of unaffiliated "Nones." While I was not in denial about these statistics, I went to Seattle to tell an alternative story about that strikingly post-Christian place. I wanted to tell a story rooted in hope rather than fear, a narrative more shaped by imagination than grief. As a practical theologian and missiologist, I did my research in order to be able to speak faithfully—as well as factually—about a place that is famously short on the faithful.

The first thing any good missiologist will say about a place is "God is here," and that's precisely the witness I sought to bear through my research. I knew there had to be good news to be shared from the None Zone since the sower of Jesus' parable is recklessly extravagant—tossing seeds every which way without regard for the quality of the soil. My research into 105 church plants offered some data to texture what is fundamentally a confession of faith: the triune God is present and actively planting new life in Cascadia's post-Christian soil. This ought to be a word of encouragement to missional practitioners across the evolving West: if it can happen there, it can happen anywhere.

What clues do these promising signs of life in the midst of one of the most post-Christian settings in North America offer to us as we seek to discern what kind of church God is planning and planting for the future? In the following pages I highlight three clues that emerged as I explored the priorities and practices of these new churches in Cascadia's post-Christian soil.

Church, Re-placed

Many of the churches I encountered in Seattle demonstrated a deep commitment to their immediate context. Two-thirds of those surveyed indicated that "identifying with our neighborhood" was "very" or "extremely" important. Nearly a quarter of all new churches' names included the name of their neighborhood. By God's Spirit, the church is being re-placed.

While an obsession with "successful" megachurches has led many church leaders in recent decades to opt for approaches that attract large numbers of commuters, the clues from Seattle suggest that missional practitioners seeking to join God in the Cascadian harvest will increasingly need to be responsive to how place matters in urban, post-Christian soil.

This reflects a widespread and increasingly felt displacement that is part of the human experience in the West. Perhaps especially in cities plagued by gridlock and lacking a robust public transit system, people are becoming increasingly disillusioned with the commuter lifestyle. Indeed, the flood of young people opting for downtown lofts over suburban plots attests to a revival of interest in the walking village.

Among new churches in Seattle, I observed the embrace of place playing out in three primary ways. *Many churches are being re-placed by placing a new priority on their members living in the neighborhood in which the church gathers.* When I showed up at Valley and Mountain, a United Methodist mission started in the Hillman City neighborhood, I was greeted with a friendly but pointed question: "Are you living in the neighborhood?" More than one pastor told me that they actively discourage commuters from coming to their church from other neighborhoods. They don't just want to be a church in this neighborhood, they want to be a church of neighbors. This was also and often especially true in neighborhoods facing significant challenges. As Eugene Peterson memorably paraphrased John

1:14, "The Word became flesh and moved into the neighborhood." By moving into the neighborhood, these churches are living out a commitment to practicing the incarnation.

The church is also being re-placed by entering into partnerships with local organizations committed to serving the common good. This reflects a growing awareness of the holistic character of the gospel, an understanding that places—not just souls—are to be the beneficiaries of Christ's reconciling work. In many cases this was enacted through partnerships with local elementary schools in which pastors established relationships with the principal and offered to help in any way they could. Sometimes these relationships developed into churches assisting identified families in need, providing school supplies to teachers, and recruiting volunteers or even taking responsibility for running school events. Other churches lived out their commitment to love of neighbor through partnerships with art collectives or other nonprofits.

The third way I witnessed churches being re-placed related to the way they used their space. For many churches, this is about where they gather for worship. Forty-four percent met for worship in spaces other than church buildings, and most of these spaces had multiple purposes throughout the week. Many gathered for worship in already existing public spaces like schools, community centers, and theaters. Gathering for worship in such spaces was not only a practical solution, but also demonstrates that even ordinary, secular spaces can be holy ground—a vision that projects from these worship gatherings out into the wider community.

Others are taking a fresh approach to use of space by choosing to purchase and design buildings with a primary purpose of creating "third places" in the neighborhood—locations where neighbors could gather and get to know one another. These third places included coffee shops, coworking spaces, a community living room, and an event venue. Whether through gathering in non-traditional spaces or creating their own third places, these churches were living out a commitment that their use of space would be a benefit to the neighborhood—that their practices of gathering would contribute to the common good in that place.

These non-typical ways of churches inhabiting space are not driven by a longing to be hip or trendy, even though starting a coffee shop might seem pretty cool. Going local for these churches was not merely about catching the localism wave; it was about reenacting Christ's incarnational mission. Echoing his solidarity with humanity, these disciples are living out a commitment to be a church in, of, and for their place. They're seeking to be God's people for the life of the world. These followers of Jesus are waking up to their places. They're recognizing that it is not enough to say, "God is everywhere." We have to also be able to say, "God is *here*" and to inhabit spaces in a way that reflects the conviction that "this neighborhood, this community, is a place where God dwells."

Church, in Conversation

Churches rooted in post-Christian soil cannot assume that those whom they seek to reach—or even their own members—have a durable vision of transcendent reality. As Charles Taylor observed in *A Secular Age*, the peculiar feature of this historical moment in the West is the fragility of all positions of belief. Those who believe are haunted by doubts. Those who doubt are haunted by "rumors of angels," longings for something more. This dynamic reality is particularly felt in Cascadia's urban centers in which "Nones" typically account for the largest religious grouping.

In such contexts, churches have to take seriously the challenge of cultivating among their members a vision of the world in which God is a real and present actor. Sociologist Nancy Ammerman has studied what contributes to a person having what she calls "sacred consciousness"—the sense that there is more to life than meets the eye.[1] Sacred consciousness is not just a *belief* in the existence of God, it is the *lived experience* of God as present and active in daily life. A person with sacred consciousness sees spiritual significance in everyday experiences, encounters, and places.

The reason sacred consciousness matters is that it is a fundamental element of a missional church. Being a missional church is not about a church having lots of mission programs. A church can have a soup kitchen, a tutoring program, and mission trips all without the members being able to speak like God is a real actor in the life of the church. A missional church is a community of faith in which the ordinary people of the church believe and live out a sense that they are cooperative partners with the triune God in the renewal of all things.

This is why so much of the emphasis on Matthew 25 in many progressive churches misses the point by simply stressing the importance of helping the "least of these." Of course, we should serve. But that glorious passage is not just an admonition to benevolent service; it is a revelation of

---

1. Ammerman, *Sacred Stories, Spiritual Tribes*.

the mysterious action and presence of God in the persons who are unable to offer us anything but their presence. My own denomination is currently in the midst of a campaign around Matthew 25. I wish I could get excited about it because it really is a passage with an incredibly rich theological vision, but I fear that for the most part the campaign is merely another effort of well-meaning, privileged, white liberals to save their churches by showing everyone that they value serving the needy. That is all well and good, but where is God in that equation? Serving is valuable in itself, but sacred consciousness marks the difference between a church and other nonprofits.

What Ammerman found is that those who show signs of sacred consciousness typically participate in conversations with fellow believers about everyday life in the context of a shared spiritual vision. Sociologist Peter Berger identified these as "sustaining conversations,"[2] and Ammerman makes it clear that having a *spiritual* outlook is usually linked with having *religious* conversation partners.[3] As a result, the popular concept of being "spiritual but not religious" is not what it sounds like. Rather than being an accurate description of either belief or practice, it is usually only an indicator of the identity a person wants to project. Again, what the research shows is that those who are genuinely "spiritual"—that is, those who have a spiritual outlook on life, who see spiritual significance in daily life, who evidence sacred consciousness—are mostly those who also participate in sustaining conversations facilitated by religious communities.

Having the *eyes of faith* requires a *fluency with faith-talk*.[4] We come to see God in daily life only as we get comfortable naming and narrating the activity of God in life. This is, of course, how all languages work. They not only convey meaning, they make meaning possible. Learning to name and to narrate the presence and activity of God is an act of discernment, and this kind of faithful activity is the bread and butter of a missional church. New churches in post-Christian places tend to be somewhat more aware of the need to cultivate this fluency, but in our secular age it is equally essential for every church. It doesn't come easy. It doesn't come any more naturally than learning a new language as an adult. But it is worth every ounce of effort and every minute because nothing else can connect the people of God to their true identity and to the source of their life and power.

2. Berger, *Sacred Canopy*, 21–22.
3. Ammerman, *Sacred Stories*, 292–304.
4. I have written further about what is involved in having the eyes of faith in James, "Missional Acuity."

My research among new churches confirmed the vital role of sustaining conversations. Many of the most vibrant churches had built-in settings in which they talked their way into a sense of missional identity and vocation. It was through these regular, holy conversations that they learned to narrate their lives as stories in which God was active, and thus, they were able to see that God was, indeed, active.

The most central practices of holy conversation I observed were happening outside of worship in informal, conversation-centered small groups or prayer groups or missional communities. Smaller, conversational settings like these are of primary importance—and I'll describe these in the following section—but worship gatherings can also play a role. More than half (52 percent) of the new churches in the Seattle study reported that they "often" or "always" make space in worship for people to "share personal thoughts or experiences of God." Frequently this looked like having a regular slot for testimonies in worship. Testimonies are, of course, a prime opportunity for the one sharing to narrate how God has been active in their life, but it is also an opportunity for the rest of the congregation to see that kind of narration modeled. In other churches, opportunities to share in worship were often in the form of invitations to name aloud prayer requests.

Some churches make conversation even more central to their liturgy. For example, Wits' End Church would sit around round tables during worship, and the sermon would always be followed by ten minutes of table talk. Once a month conversation was the main event; they would have what they called a Midrash service, which meant that the word would be read, the pastor would give a brief five-minute homily, and the congregation would then have extended conversation at tables and as a whole group in an attempt to discern what God was saying to them from that text. The pastor described this practice to me as their "monthly pneumatological wager," their bet on the Holy Spirit to speak to them as they wrestled together with Scripture.

Though most Christian leaders instinctively understand the importance of sacred consciousness, they often overlook the role of sustaining conversations in forming and maintaining it. This, I suspect, is in part due to misplaced confidence that they can create sacred consciousness in others through their preaching. The preacher may feel like it is working because it is, in fact, working for them. The regular practices of prepping for and preaching a sermon gives the preacher the formative experience of narrating their world and life through the gospel, the result of which is a deepened sacred consciousness. But no amount of passively listening to sermons will do that for those in the pews. With all due respect to Paul, faith in a post-Christian age comes not merely by hearing; it comes by talking. This is one reason I am a big fan of sharing the pulpit with the ordinary people in our churches. They ought to be given the opportunity to talk themselves into faith rather than for clergy to hoard these formational opportunities.

While conversation has always been important for discipleship, in a cultural environment that largely regards faith as fantasy, having faithful conversation partners is simply indispensable. As churches in an increasingly post-Christian place, Christian communities in Cascadia and elsewhere will need to increasingly center faithful conversation and storytelling. Practicing holy conversation means learning to narrate our lives as stories in which God is a real, active agent, in which the key plot line for us, individually and as a community, is our collaborative friendship with the triune God who is always up to something out ahead of us.

Liturgy, as is well known, means the work of the people. One of the most important types of the work among God's people is holy conversation, and in major swaths of the North American church it has been largely lost. In order to sustain faith in a post-Christian society, we must consistently bear witness to one another. We need to tell each other, to hear each other, and to hear ourselves tell each other our stories about encountering the risen Christ, our brushes with the unpredictable Spirit, and how we've beheld the glory of our sovereign Creator. In order to do so, we need to continue to experiment with ways of making such conversation central in our worship gatherings as well as in the other key gatherings which make up our shared life.

Church, as Rhythm

As the preceding discussion suggests, the typical Sunday worship service is not sufficient for forming a Christian community in sacred consciousness. Sunday worship is even less adequate as a stand-alone approach for discipleship. Recently, I was sharing my research with a group of Lutheran pastors:

> I bet many of you could quote all five solas to me. You know, faith alone, grace alone, Scripture alone, Christ alone, to God alone be the glory. But you might not know that five hundred years after Luther nailed the Ninety-Five Theses to the Wittenburg door,

there is a groundswell of support for a sixth sola: worship alone. You see, for many Americans doing church and being church simply means going to worship. It's as if they show up on Sundays and say: "Here I stand, I can do no other. So help me, God."[5]

The laughter in the room indicated how closely this picture was to the truth of the matter. Of course, this isn't just a Lutheran phenomenon. It's true in churches of all types. I don't blame them; this is the church that we, the leaders, the theologians, and the pastors, have given them. It's an ecclesiology that is basically subsumed in worship—with all the other stuff—discipleship, mission, and the rest represented as extra credit. One of the important voices in the missional church conversation, Craig Van Gelder, has been known to quip succinctly that in North America the Sunday worship hour has become a substitute for church.[6]

While so many of the recent attempts to fix, revive, and renew church in the West have focused on improving "the worship experience," it seems that such a myopic effort at boosting attendance for that one hour on Sunday will do nothing to address the deeper crisis. The true crisis is that many churchgoers don't experience God as an active agent in the world. Even fewer have shaped their lives around discerning and joining God's activity. Simply put, an hour or two on Sunday morning—no matter how "transformational"—is not going to be sufficient for forming mature followers of Jesus.

New churches in the None Zone, by contrast, are forging their church life not only around the shared practice of worship, but just as importantly around shared practices of discipleship and witness outside of Sunday gatherings. These pioneering churches in post-Christian soil take their understanding of all that it means to be a follower of Jesus and they build that into the common life of the church. This means imagining church beyond Sunday worship, recognizing that there are essential dimensions of what it means to be Christ's church in the world that simply cannot happen in a Sunday morning worship service.

Of course, we all know that being a Christian isn't just a Sunday thing. But in practice, most pastors and most churches only address this by naming all that other stuff in the sermon application points or in the charge:

---

5. Keynote by the author, "Good News from the None Zone," at Annual Congregational Vitality Training Conference for Evangelical Lutheran Church in America Mission Developers and Re-developers, Seattle, August 24, 2018.

6. Barrett, *Treasure in Clay Jars*, 110.

"Go serve the needy! Go build friendships with your neighbors!" Who knows if anyone actually does it, right? But pastors *tell them to* every week and we probably have a couple programs or events each year in which we serve the less fortunate or maybe throw a community event.

Again, by contrast, many of these church plants in Cascadia build core practices of discipleship and witness into the shared life of the church itself. They include them in the rhythms that the whole church participates in. They don't leave disciple formation and witness as bonus add-ons; they structure how they are going to do church in order to explicitly include discipleship and witness for everyone.

One example of this comes from Westminster Community Church. It was a ninety-year-old Assembly of God church that began a slow decline which drove them to ask what was going on and what they ought to do. As they read the Gospels, they saw Jesus doing two things all the time: hanging out with the poor and eating meals. "So," they said, "if that's what Jesus did, and we want to be Jesus followers, then we need to do that—not as extra-curricular stuff but as the way we do church." They began asking themselves, "What would it look like to be a church in which these were central to our common life?" When they discovered the agape meal tradition, they said, "That's it! That's how we do it." So, they rented out their church building, renamed and replanted the church as "Community Dinners," and began doing church by hosting a weekly feast in a community center with music, live art, and a brief word of hope from the Gospels. A few months later they started another two community dinners in different neighborhoods. I saw this week that they are currently hosting ten of these dinner church gatherings every week across the city. What is important to note is that if you want to do church with them, you are going to hang out with the poor over a meal. You're going to engage in discipleship and witness. They built their understanding of following Jesus into their way of doing church.

Another example of how these pioneers go about integrating practices of discipleship and witness into their shared rhythms of their common life is the prevalence of the missional communities planting model. This approach to planting has become pretty popular, especially among evangelicals, and involves starting with one or two mid-sized groups that gather following a monthly pattern, with a different focus each week. The specific rhythms vary by church but typically include a week focused on Bible study, a week where the gathering is all about fellowship, and another week where the focus is on serving others. Churches being planted in this model wait to launch regular corporate worship until a few of these missional communities are well established. As a result, when they begin holding weekly worship, strong majorities of the Sunday worshipers are already active participants in the rhythms of their missional communities.

The genius of this approach is how having a pattern of monthly group activities provides the leadership with an opportunity to establish a shared life of church practices reflecting their understanding of what it looks like to be followers of Jesus, rather than mere churchgoers. The Hallows Church uses a monthly rhythm of study-serve-study-play in their missional communities. "Study," for them, is a Bible study connected to the key sermon texts for the week. On "serve" weeks they do projects like stuffing shoe boxes for mission agencies. In their rhythm, "play" meant that group members would simply have a good time fellowshiping together over a meal. Another church, Lux Communities, had a similar monthly rhythm, but instead of a second study week, they had a week focused on the practice of hospitality. One of their missional communities was hosting a monthly barbeque block party. Another had started a monthly margarita night with the friends they had made at Trader Joe's. Hospitality, as they saw it, was a central part of being a Jesus follower, so they built it into the shared rhythms of their church life. Note how for both of these churches, some form of mission (service, hospitality) is elevated from its typical extra-credit status to a central, regular practice of large majorities of those who are actively engaged in the church. The same is true of holy conversation, which is typically prominent in study and fellowship gatherings, especially as they pray for and with one another.

The future church God is planting in Cascadian soil is a church embodied in a rhythm of shared practices—a way of life in community—rather than one encapsulated by a Sunday morning event.

The Church God Is Planning

God's Spirit is on the move in Cascadia. The new churches now taking root in Cascadia's urban soil offer clues about the kind of churches God has in store for the post-Christian era we are waking up to in the West. In these places, God is previewing churches that are awakened to, and deeply embedded in, their places—living out a holistic gospel, incarnationally. They are churches whose life and identity flow from a heartbeat of holy conversation. They are churches in which practices of discipleship and witness are integral parts of the common life of the community. It is churches like these—that have been re-placed, engage in holy conversation, and shape their common life around a shared rhythm—that promise to thrive in Cascadia's increasingly post-Christian soil.

Bibliography

Ammerman, Nancy. *Sacred Stories, Spiritual Tribes: Finding Religion in Everyday Life.* Oxford: Oxford University Press, 2014.

Barrett, Lois. *Treasure in Clay Jars: Patterns in Missional Faithfulness.* Grand Rapids: Eerdmans, 2004.

Berger, Peter. *The Sacred Canopy: Elements of a Sociological Theory of Religion.* Anchor, 1967.

James, Christopher B. "Missional Acuity: 20th Century Insights toward a Redemptive Way of Seeing." *Witness: The Journal of the Academy for Evangelism in Theological Education* 26 (2012) 29–43.

14

Beloved Community as Missional Witness

Jonathan Wilson

There doesn't seem to be much love in the world right now. So where might we find this "beloved community" that is "missional witness"?

The Beloved Community, Part One

The term "beloved community" is introduced and developed by Josiah Royce, most notably in *The Problem of Christianity* (1913) and *The Hope of the Great Community* (1916).[1] Royce's idea of "beloved (or 'great') community" influenced a range of thinkers through the 1920s and 1930s.[2] Among those were the "Boston personalists" who taught Martin Luther King Jr.[3] The vision of the beloved community pervades King's work and gives it life. As a result, the beloved community is most often associated with King.[4]

Here's a summary of King's vision for the beloved community:

> Dr. King's Beloved Community is a global vision, in which all people can share in the wealth of the earth. In the Beloved Community, poverty, hunger and homelessness will not be tolerated

---

1. Royce, *The Problem of Christianity*; *The Hope of the Great Community*.

2. See the brief exposition in Jensen and King, "Beloved Community," esp. note 1.

3. See the exposition of Dorrien, *Social Ethics in the Making*, 391–96. For King's own exposition, see Martin Luther King Jr., *Where Do We Go from Here*.

4. See Marsh, *Beloved Community*.

because international standards of human decency will not allow it. Racism and all forms of discrimination, bigotry and prejudice will be replaced by an all-inclusive spirit of sisterhood and brotherhood. In the Beloved Community, international disputes will be resolved by peaceful conflict-resolution and reconciliation of adversaries, instead of military power. Love and trust will triumph over fear and hatred. Peace with justice will prevail over war and military conflict.[5]

This vision is rooted in the conviction that all human beings are made in the image of God. The work of justice and reconciliation brings social relations into proper alignment with that conviction and creates the beloved community.

But might there be more to "the image of God"?

Missional Witness, Part One

The word "missional" has become something of a logo or brand. The history of the term and the literature around it is prodigious. In spite of the dissipation of its power, I still find the term useful as a pointer to the precedence of the mission of God over the church's mission; as well, it signals the dissolution of Christendom in the West and the impact of that dissolution inside and outside the West; and finally, it indicates an ecclesiology of mission and the concomitant call to move from an "attractional church" to a "missional church." In my own exposition of *Missional God, Missional Church*, I have always begun biblically with a reading of Matthew 28:18–20 that grounds our mission in the triune God and extends discipleship to all of life.[6]

Here's how I used to put this biblical teaching in a theological summary:

> God's redemption of all creation in Jesus Christ and the calling of a people formed, equipped, and guided by the Holy Spirit to participate in and bear witness to that redemptive work.

Here's how I put it missionally (and familiarly):

> The whole gospel for the whole world by the whole church.

---

5. "The King Philosophy," https://thekingcenter.org/king-philosophy/#sub4.

6. But see Hastings, *Missional God, Missional Church*, who bases his exposition in the "Greatest Commission" of John 20:18–23. See especially pages 26–28 for a summary.

But now I invite you to explore with me a recasting of this understanding of "missional witness," before we return to the beloved community.[7]

Missional Witness, Part Two

Where does God first give us a "mission"? If we recast the question not in terms of "church" but in terms of "the people of God," then we are driven to Genesis 1:

> Then God said, "Let us make humankind in our image, in our likeness, so that they may rule over the fish in the sea and the birds in the sky, over the livestock and all the wild animals, and over all the creatures that move along the ground."
> So God created humankind in his own image,
> in the image of God he created them;
> male and female he created them.
> God blessed them and said to them, "Be fruitful and increase in number; fill the earth and subdue it. Rule over the fish in the sea and the birds in the sky and over every living creature that moves on the ground."
> Then God said, "I give you every seed-bearing plant on the face of the whole earth and every tree that has fruit with seed in it. They will be yours for food. And to all the beasts of the earth and all the birds in the sky and all the creatures that move along the ground—everything that has the breath of life in it—I give every green plant for food." And it was so.
> God saw all that he had made, and it was very good. And there was evening, and there was morning—the sixth day. (Gen 1:26–31)

This is, of course, a jam-packed passage. Here, to develop my new account of missional witness, I will focus on "the image of God" and unpack that relationally.[8]

Consider that this passage commissions the first humans for their relationships and responsibilities in creation. If we are seeking to understand the "mission of God's people," this is where we begin. This beginning point changes the missional narrative. Although some accounts of the mission of

---

[7]. Much of my thinking in this chapter is the consequence of my continued reflections on the work that I did in Wilson, *God's Good World*.

[8]. See my narrative account of the image of God as relational, "Grace Incarnate: Jesus Christ," in Jones et al., *Grace upon Grace*, 141–52.

God and of God's people include the work of "creation care," that work is placed within the narrative of fall and redemption.

Consider, as an example, the work of Christopher Wright. In *The Mission of God*, Wright asserts that the mission of God begins with "the God of purpose in creation."[9] But then the narrative moves almost immediately away from that beginning and does not return to creation until chapters 12 and 13. Moreover, Wright's exposition in those chapters grafts the meaning of creation and human care for creation onto the narrative of fall and redemption. This becomes quite clear in Wright's later book *The Mission of God's People*.[10] There he states, "God's mission is what spans the gap between the curse on the earth in Genesis 3 and the end of the curse in the new creation of Revelation 22."[11] Wright's suppression of the beginning of the story when it comes to mission is particularly striking because he is so committed to care for creation.[12]

So, let's go back to the beginning of the story and a relational account of the image of God as the root of missional witness.

The Image of God

Consider that "the image of God" plots four relationships for which God makes humankind: God, other humans, the rest of creation, and self. Three of these relationships are evident in Genesis 1: God blesses the first humans by giving them a mission in creation. That mission depends first on their relationship to God, but the mission also depends upon their relationship to one another and the rest of creation. Because the relationship to self is "whole" in Genesis 1 and 2, that relationship does not become evident until these humans sin and become divided selves: "They realized they were naked" (Gen 3:7). To understand what has happened we must recall Genesis 2:25: "Adam and his wife were both naked, and they felt no shame." The narrative of Genesis 3 confirms this relational account of the image of God. There we learn of our broken relationship with God (3:8), with one another

---

9. Wright, *Mission of God*, 63.

10. Wright, *Mission of God's People*. See also his exposition of "the image of God" in *Mission of God*. The exposition occurs quite late in the book (421–53). For Wright, the missional narrative really begins in Genesis 12.

11. Wright, *Mission of God's People*, 46.

12. Wright, *Mission of God's People*, 48–62; *Mission of God*, 397–420.

(3:12, 16), with the rest of creation (3:17–19), and with self (as we have anticipated, 3:7).

Now, consider how this relational, narrative account of the image of God shapes missional witness: God's mission in the world is the realization of the telos for which God created the world by restoring the relationships for which God created humankind. In this is God's glory: God is not defeated by our sin or by the death that comes as the wages of sin. In this also is God's glory: God the Son becomes incarnate in order to restore the relationships that are broken by our sin. The mission—the going out of the Father, Son, and Spirit—in creation is realized in the redemptive mission of the Father, Son, and Spirit.

The next step is to recognize that the passages we identify as the calling of a people to join God's mission cohere beautifully with the reclaiming of the four relationships for which we are made. In the interest of space and active reading, I invite you to consider how:

- Torah establishes the covenant between God and people and prescribes the right alignment of our lives with other humans and the rest of creation.

- Prophets recall God's people to life according to the covenant that God has made.[13]

- Writings form a people who can see and live according to God's purpose for all creation.

In the Old Testament, we begin to understand the story of creation and redemption as one story—what I have elsewhere exposited as "the dialectic of the kingdom."[14] In the New Testament, we see this story and purpose of God reach its fulfillment in the coming of Jesus Christ. In him, we see the four relationships fully restored and the "image of God" sharpened and deepened. We see the image of God more sharply and more deeply as we disciple ourselves to Jesus. We may say, "Ah, now I am beginning to see more clearly what it means to be in right relationship to God, to other humans, to the rest of creation, and to myself." And we understand why Paul, at the end of an exposition of the contrast between "life" (really death) in *sarx* and Life in *pneuma* and a consideration of the groaning of creation,

---

13. In this regard, Isaiah 55–66 is the high point of prophetic vision of the holistic mission of God and God's people.

14. Wilson, *God's Good World*, 49–71.

assures us that "those God foreknew he also predestined to be conformed to the image of his Son, that he might be the firstborn among many brothers and sisters" (Rom 8:29).

Growing from this root, the mission of God's people becomes our participation in the restoration of the image of God in all its dimensions: reconciliation to God, to other humans, to the rest of creation, and to ourselves. And as we participate in this reconciliation through Jesus Christ by the power of the Spirit, we also become witnesses of Jesus Christ in our practices that reconcile us to God, one another, the rest of creation, and ourselves.[15] This account provides us with the most holistic and integrated account of God's mission and the call of God's people to join with God. In this we participate in the realization of God's purpose for all creation.[16]

Missional Witness, Part Three

With this narrative of "the image of God" as relational and holistic, my previous account of missional witness must be recast.

Biblically, missional witness begins with Genesis 1:26–30. We understand that the first humans in this passage are the original "people of God." God gives God's people their mission—bearing God's image in relationships that follow from God's own relationships. Beginning here means that "the mission of God's people" is fundamental to the reality of creation. This mission is not something added after the fall. But the fall does change the way that mission is carried out. "Mission" now acquires a tragic dimension. It entails suffering. It requires a different set of virtues and practices to form God's people for mission. But mission is also always pursued in faith, hope, and love because God is realizing the telos of creation and the mission of

---

15. I have used "reconciliation" in my account, but I am instructed by the study of Swartley, *Covenant of Peace*. Swartley notes that "*peace* in nominal, verbal, adjectival, and compounds forms occurs over 100 times in the NT, while reconciliation in its noun and verb forms occurs only seven or eight times!" (*Covenant of Peace*, 6; his italics). Swartley also notes that "the God of peace" is used several times by Paul as a title for God, while "God of reconciliation" is nowhere used as a title. We will return to "peace" below.

16. We could develop this further by turning to the narratives of God's work in Ephesians 1, where we are told that God's plan is "to bring unity to all things in heaven and on earth under Christ" (1:10). Or we could turn to Col 1:15–20, after declaring that "all things have been created through [the Son] and for him," he brings this Christ-hymn to its telos: "For God was pleased to have all his fullness dwell in him, and to reconcile to himself all things, whether things on earth or things in heaven, by making peace through his blood shed on the cross."

God's people. Matthew 28:18–20 becomes Jesus' commissioning of his disciples for this same mission.

Theologically, missional witness must be recast in something like the following: rooted in God's intention for all creation (by and for Jesus Christ—Colossians 1), the mission of God's people is to live in such a way that we participate in God's realizing of the telos of creation in new creation through Jesus Christ and bear witness to that telos as the Holy Spirit forms us, guides us, and equips us.

Missionally, missional witness rooted in Genesis 1 sees all of life integrated under one mandate. There is no "cultural" or "creation" mandate rooted in Genesis 1 that is separate from, alongside, or subordinate to the missional mandate. Rather, there is one mandate—missional—that draws us into and makes us witnesses to God's realization of the telos of all creation through and for Jesus Christ. And so, it turns out that rooting missional witness in Genesis 1 is, at its deepest, thickest, and clearest, *Christological*.

Beloved Community, Part Two

Now that I have recast missional witness, we must return to the "beloved community." It turns out that the "beloved community" created by God in Genesis 1 and being realized in Christ by the Spirit is the community of all creation. We must not only imagine a beloved community of just and peaceful social relationships. That may be one of the most pressing calls of God's people in the world today. God knows that our relationships with one another are broken at many levels, in many dimensions, and violently. But if we take seriously the blessing and mission that Creator gave the people that God had just created in Genesis 1, then the renewal—reconciliation—of *each* relationship is implicated in *every other* relationship. One name for this full reconciliation is *peace*—the wholeness of all life, the wholeness of all creation—embodied by the people of God engaged with whole mission of God. This is holistic mission. So, the beloved community is the peace of all creation witnessing to the glory of the one Creator God—Father, Son, and Spirit—who loves creation. The people of God are those image bearers whom God has called now to be participants in the beloved community and witnesses to it.

Missional Witness to the Beloved Community in Cascadia

Missional witness to the beloved community is always (scandalously) particular. Modernity was, and many today are, offended by the particularity of the gospel of Jesus Christ.[17] But even the most "modern" of thinkers has to communicate in a particular language that depends for its meaning on very particular grammar, syntax, and usage. For the people of God who witness to the beloved community, the particularity of our witness faithfully bodies forth our creatureliness and the reality that God's love for creation and the peace of Christ depend upon the incarnation.

To empower our witness to the beloved community in Cascadia, I will identify two elements that are in the air and two that are on the ground. By "in the air," I do not mean that these elements are ephemeral or insubstantial. Rather, I mean that they are simply a part of the air that we breathe in Cascadia. Most of the time, most people do not notice them. But as we breathe the "cultural" air of Cascadia, we absorb these elements and they become part of us.

"In the Air" of Cascadia: Fragmentation and Liquidity[18]

Although these two elements are imperceptible to most people of Cascadia, they may be familiar to many of my readers, though they still deserve our continuing attention in our quest to be missional witnesses to the beloved community. The best diagnosis of our fragmentation is still Alasdair MacIntyre's *After Virtue*.[19] There, MacIntyre shows that our moral fragmentation and incoherent lives and social realities follow from the Enlightenment denial of teleology—not any one claimed teleology, but the very conviction, previously shared by many traditions, that the cosmos and human life has a teleological structure. What MacIntyre does not show is the denial of

---

17. For some consideration of this, see Wilson, *God So Loved the World*. For a scholarly dismantling of the "scandal of particularity" as presented by Gotthold Ephraim Lessing, see Michalson, *Lessing's "Ugly Ditch."* Although references to his work are problematic, John Howard Yoder has an excellent consideration of these matters in "'But We Do See Jesus': The Particularity of Incarnation and the Universality of Truth," in Yoder, *Priestly Kingdom*, 46–62.

18. There are other ways to describe the "air" of Cascadia: secularism, spiritual(ism), and paganism come to mind. But I think that fragmentation and liquidity get to the underlying dynamics of the principalities and powers at work in Cascadia.

19. MacIntyre, *After Virtue*.

"creation" that makes possible and plausible this rejection of teleology.[20] In Modernity—the culture created by the Enlightenment—we humans become our own creators. Modernity is our freedom to create our own lives.

This element in the air of Cascadia makes witness to the beloved community very challenging. And just when the people of Cascadia need the people of God to witness to the peace of creation, they mostly hear and read and see how the "people of God" are enslaved to fragmentation. And in that enslavement, the people of God become unfaithful witnesses to the beloved community.

What then are we to do? The first act is to (re)learn the story of Jesus as the realization of the peace of all creation, which is also the beloved community in which the image of God in humans is conformed to the image of Christ.[21] The second act is to make peace—understood as the healing of all creation—the center and circumference of our life and witness. The third act is to recognize the a-teleological convictions that shape much of Cascadia.

The people of God have good news for the people of Cascadia—including ourselves. In Jesus Christ the purpose of the cosmos—all creation—has been revealed and realized and we are invited to participate in the formation of that beloved community. This news requires us to change our minds and our lives—to repent of the attempt to be our own creators.[22] Only then may our fragmentation begin to be healed as we participate in God's plan to "bring unity to all things in heaven and on earth under Christ" (Eph 1:10).

After using "fragmentation" to identify the air that we breathe and the particularities within which we are called to missional witness, I am now convinced that another element in the air we breathe is more determinative today than fragmentation. Following Zygmunt Bauman, I find great illumination from the term "liquidity."[23] Liquidity describes a social

20. See "Part One" of Wilson, *God's Good World*, for an analysis of the loss of creation in the church, academy, society.

21. Two authors that have taught me a lot about this are Michael Gorman and N. T. Wright. For Gorman, see his series of books on "cruciformity": *Becoming the Gospel* and *Abide and Go*. See Wright's books *Surprised by Hope* and *After You Believe*.

22. I am conscious that I have only pointed to a path that we have to walk but have not taken us down that path. To read a little bit of what this might look like in very different kinds of communities as the people of God, see Wilson, *Living Faithfully* and *Why Church Matters*.

23. All of Bauman's work is instructive for mission and ministry today. For liquidity, see the seminal work by Bauman, *Liquid Modernity*, and the many titles that follow from that work.

reality other than fragmentation. The latter assumes that something solid existed which has now become fragmented. It also implies that we may rebuild something solid from the rubble. But fluids do not "fragment." They "'flow', 'spill', 'run out', 'splash', 'pour over', 'leak', 'flood', 'spray', 'drip', 'seep', 'ooze'; unlike solids, they are not easily stopped—they pass around some obstacles, dissolve some others and bore or soak their way through others still."[24] Fluids cannot be "formed" into something on their own. Moreover, their liquidity means that they can take on the shape of any "container" without themselves being changed.

In one of Bauman's iconic sayings, he observes that "in a liquid modern life there are no permanent bonds, and any that we take up for a time must be tied loosely so that they can be untied again, as quickly and as effortlessly as possible, when circumstances change—as they surely will in our liquid modern society, over and over again."[25] When I first put together Bauman's analysis of liquidity and his observation about impermanent bonds, I felt despair. Is there any way for us to communicate to this culture—Cascadia— the good news of Jesus? How could reconciliation and peace be realized in such a time? I thought about this for quite a while—and it troubled me deeply. Then I remembered that the Holy Spirit is breath and water and fire. These are supposedly insubstantial and fluid images. But they are images of the power of the risen Christ in the world today. Transforming the Cascadian air that we breath is the "breath" of God. That same "breath" of God brings eternal life to a world ruled by death through water that quenches our thirst and flows forever. (See John 4:1–15; 7:37–38; consider the presence of "water" through the Gospel of John.) Uniting the first church in Jerusalem at Pentecost and throughout history are the tongues of fire that enable us to understand and commune with one another.

"On the Ground"

In this section I will be appropriately brief, because what is called for "on the ground" are practices that entail words but require so much more of us.

The first practice that missional witness to the beloved community must engage in is "convivence." This new word is a call to the healing of our lives with the rest of creation rooted in the conviction that creation is God's

---

24. Bauman, *Liquid Modernity*, 2.

25. Bauman, *Liquid Love*, vii. This quote occurs in almost every popular article about Bauman and represents his work well.

gift. If we line our lives up with the way God calls us to live as creatures in God's good world, then God may heal our land. We are in a place today where we humans cannot heal what is broken in creation—any more than we could heal our sins in social relationships. The missional witness of the church should embody publicly the practices of confession and repentance, wisdom and hope, lament and joy, fasting and feasting, that submit our lives and all creation to Creator.

Convivence calls us to repent—to confess that we cannot save ourselves or this planet and to change our thinking and living. Convivence calls us to reliance on the abundant grace of God for the healing of creation; but that reliance does not lessen the call to lives that are earth-careful—it deepens that call.[26] Convivence calls us to live before Creator in this good world by living wisely, joyfully, hopefully.

The second practice that missional witness to the beloved community must engage in is the healing of racist wounds. Increasingly, I am convinced that the language of "reconciliation" is used primarily to privilege the dominant culture. In Canada, the witness of God's people to the beloved community must have as its hope the "peace" of which Paul writes in Ephesians 2. We are only in the preliminary work of engaging in this practice as settlers and Indigenous peoples.

In closing, "the beloved community as missional witness" invites us to reread Scripture and to locate mission in the story of creation and the realization of the telos of the story of creation. "Creation" is not a stage set or container for the story of "redemption." Rather, redemption is the action of the triune God by which the purpose of creation is realized. Let us be faithful in our witness to "the beloved community" of God, human creatures, the rest of creation, and healed "selves" dwelling together in shalom for all eternity.

Bibliography

Bauman, Zygmunt. *Liquid Love: On the Frailty of Human Bonds.* Cambridge: Polity, 2003.
———. *Liquid Modernity.* Malden, MA: Polity, 2000.
Dorrien, Gary. *Social Ethics in the Making: Interpreting an American Tradition.* Oxford: Blackwell, 2008.
Gorman, Michael. *Abide and Go: Missional Theosis in the Gospel of John.* Eugene, OR: Cascade, 2018.

---

26. On this matter, I call to mind Rom 6:1–4.

———. *Becoming the Gospel: Paul, Participation, and Mission*. Grand Rapids: Eerdmans, 2015.

Hastings, Ross. *Missional God, Missional Church: Hope for Re-evangelizing the West*. Downers Grove: InterVarsity, 2012.

Jensen, Kipton, and Preston King. "Beloved Community: Martin Luther King, Howard Thurman, and Josiah Royce." *AMITY: The Journal of Friendship Studies* 4.1 (2017) 15–31. https://pdfs.semanticscholar.org/ad2a/74e0bc458d516a6febe0b6822eed3cf8de87.pdf.

Jones, L. Gregory, et al., eds. *Grace upon Grace: Essays in Honor of Thomas A. Langford Jr.* Nashville: Abingdon, 1999.

King, Martin Luther, Jr. *Where Do We Go from Here: Chaos or Community?* New York: Harper & Row, 1967.

MacIntyre, Alasdair. *After Virtue: A Study in Moral Theory*. 3rd ed. Notre Dame: University of Notre Dame Press, 2007.

Marsh, Charles. *The Beloved Community: How Faith Shapes Social Justice from the Civil Rights Movement to Today*. New York: Basic Books, 2005.

Michalson, Gordon, Jr. *Lessing's "Ugly Ditch": A Study of Theology and History*. University Park: Pennsylvania State University Press, 1985.

Royce, Josiah. *The Hope of the Great Community*. New York: Macmillan, 1916.

———. *The Problem of Christianity*. New York: Macmillan, 1913.

Swartley, William. *Covenant of Peace: The Missing Peace in New Testament Theology and Ethics*. Grand Rapids: Eerdmans, 2006.

Wilson, Jonathan R. *God So Loved the World: A Christology for Disciples*. Grand Rapids: Baker, 2001.

———. *God's Good World: Reclaiming the Doctrine of Creation*. Grand Rapids: Baker, 2013.

———. *Living Faithfully in a Fragmented World: From "After Virtue" to a New Monasticism*. 2nd ed. Eugene, OR: Cascade, 2010.

———. *Why Church Matters: Worship, Ministry, and Mission in Practice*. Grand Rapids: Brazos, 2006.

Wright, Christopher J. H. *The Mission of God: Unlocking the Bible's Grand Narrative*. Downers Grove: InterVarsity, 2006.

———. *The Mission of God's People: A Biblical Theology of the Church's Mission*. Grand Rapids: Zondervan, 2010.

Wright, N. T. *After You Believe: Why Christian Character Matters*. San Francisco: HarperOne, 2010.

———. *Surprised by Hope: Rethinking Heaven, the Resurrection, and the Mission of the Church*. San Francisco: HarperOne, 2008.

Yoder, John Howard. *The Priestly Kingdom: Social Ethics as Gospel*. Notre Dame: University of Notre Dame Press, 1984.

Contributors

Stephen Bell is a recent master of divinity graduate from St. Andrew's Hall and the Vancouver School of Theology living and ministering in Vancouver's Downtown Eastside.

Jason Byassee is a senior fellow for the Centre for Missional Leadership and holds the Butler Chair in Homiletics and Biblical Interpretation at the Vancouver School of Theology.

Young Tae Choi is assistant minister at Richmond Presbyterian Church and founder of Poieo Centre of Arts Ministry.

Tim Dickau is the Centre for Missional Leadership associate for missional certificate programs and director of City Gate Leadership Forum. For three decades he served as pastor of Grandview Church, a missional community in east Vancouver.

Anne-Marie Ellithorpe is a research associate at the Vancouver School of Theology and a board member of Sanctuary Mental Health Ministries. She is also director of children and youth ministries at Richmond Presbyterian Church.

Darrell Guder is emeritus professor of missional and ecumenical theology at Princeton Theological Seminary and senior fellow in residence at the Centre for Missional Leadership. Darrell now lives in Seattle, Washington.

Contributors

Christopher James is associate professor of evangelism and missional Christianity at Dubuque Theological Seminary. James has researched and published on church plants in Seattle, Washington.

Ross Lockhart is dean of St. Andrew's Hall, professor of mission studies at the Vancouver School of Theology, and founding director of the Centre for Missional Leadership.

Andrea Perrett is the Centre for Missional Leadership associate in new worshipping communities and director of Cyclical Vancouver church planting networks.

Jenn Richards is associate pastor at Life Church, a church plant in Vancouver's Olympic Village, as well as a Teacher in the Vancouver School District.

Andrew Stephens-Rennie is director of ministry innovation at Christ Church Cathedral in Vancouver. His past work in this role includes church planting (St. Brigid's) and transforming the food outreach program of the cathedral to a more holistic model of ministry.

Richard Topping is principal of the Vancouver School of Theology and professor of studies in the Reformed tradition at St. Andrew's Hall.

David Warkentin is general studies director at Columbia Bible College in Abbotsford, British Columbia.

Todd Wiebe is a pastor, podcaster, and avid cyclist. He lives in North Vancouver.

Jonathan Wilson is a senior fellow of the Centre for Missional Leadership at St. Andrew's Hall, Vancouver. He is also a teaching fellow for Regent College and a senior consultant for theological integration with Canadian Baptist Ministries.